Eight Principles for a Modern CBT

Eight Principles for a Modern CBT is a training guide for both new and experienced clinicians who want to understand and apply the newest developments in cognitive behavioral therapy. It's a hands-on manual that helps readers sort through competing models for addressing cognitive change, emotion processing, and behavior change. When is acceptance indicated, and how does one "do" acceptance in therapy? How can mindfulness be incorporated in ways that are brief, simple to teach, and effective? How should therapists use clients' values and hopes as guides for setting a course in therapy, rather than focusing exclusively on medicalized diagnoses? How does one tailor treatment for varying levels of severity of impairment? In these pages, readers will find answers to and insights on these questions and much more, including perspectives on evolutionary psychology and newer, process-based models that put human suffering in a less medicalized and stigmatizing frame.

Scott Temple, PhD, is a clinical psychologist and emeritus professor of psychiatry at the University of Iowa. He is a founding fellow and a certified trainer/consultant in the Academy of Cognitive and Behavioral Therapies. He is the author of two previous books.

R. Trent Codd, III, EdS, is a private practitioner and author. He is a fellow and certified trainer and consultant for the Academy of Cognitive and Behavioral Therapies. He is author or co-author of six books.

Modern Integrative Cognitive Behavioral Therapy
Scott H. Waltman and R. Trent Codd, III
Series Editors

The art and science of therapy continues to evolve. Clinical innovation, cultural awareness, and research findings continue improve the state of the art. Modern Integrative Cognitive Behavioral Therapy is a series dedicated to illustrating, in a practice-oriented manner, the latest developments in Cognitive Behavioral Therapy. Authors are welcome from all traditions within the big tent that is modern cognitive and behavioral therapy. With an emphasis on innovation and integration, this series focuses on shaping and sharing the future of therapy.

"*Eight Principles for a Modern CBT* provides clinicians with a humane, sophisticated, realistic, flexible, and practical guide to using a wide range of CBT approaches. Written in a user-friendly style, the years of clinical wisdom gained by treating patients and training therapists comes through in every chapter. Specific case examples illustrate the real room of therapy without a rigid fidelity to a therapeutic model. What I loved about this book was the openness to other approaches, the appreciation and validation of human suffering as an inevitable part of the human condition, and the practical insights and metaphors that the authors provide throughout."

Robert L. Leahy, PhD, *director, American Institute for Cognitive Therapy and clinical professor, Weill Cornell Medical College*

"Temple and Codd address a persistent challenge for training clinicians in cognitive-behavior therapy, namely, how do we give them the most effective tools in the most efficient timeframe? *Eight Principles for a Modern CBT* isolates the central concepts that form the foundation for clinicians to maximize the efficacy of this complex treatment model. The rich case illustrations provide readers with details on the full gamut of CBT applications with adults. The book should be seriously considered for any professional training clinicians in this approach. It is also an excellent resource for seasoned experts who need a quick reference for problems that might not be a routine part of their everyday practice."

Dean McKay, PhD, ABPP, *professor of psychology, Fordham University, past president, Association for Behavioral and Cognitive Therapies, and past president, Society for a Science of Clinical Psychology*

"This is a book that aspires to be the 'big tent' under which all the diverse forms of cognitive and behavioral therapies are described and integrated. And it succeeds. Although some may want a deeper dive into each—and ample references are provided for those readers— most will find the clinical integration of these approaches extremely useful. For teachers, this book provides the next step for students who struggle to make sense of how to navigate so many forms and waves of CBT without rigidly adhering to a specific school of thought. For clinicians, the book validates the need to do what works in complex clinical situations. I will use it with my PG4s."

Donna M. Sudak, MD, *past president, AADPRT, professor of psychiatry and vice chair for education, Drexel University, and general psychiatry residency program director, Phoenixville Hospital – Tower Health*

Eight Principles for a Modern CBT

Re-Visioning Cognitive Behavior Therapy in Clinical Training

Scott Temple and
R. Trent Codd, III

Routledge
Taylor & Francis Group

NEW YORK AND LONDON

Designed cover image: Getty Images

First published 2026
by Routledge
605 Third Avenue, New York, NY 10158

and by Routledge
4 Park Square, Milton Park, Abingdon, Oxon, OX14 4RN

Routledge is an imprint of the Taylor & Francis Group, an informa business

ISBN: 978-1-032-81830-6 (hbk)
ISBN: 978-1-032-81829-0 (pbk)
ISBN: 978-1-003-50558-7 (ebk)

DOI: 10.4324/9781003505587

Typeset in Bembo
by SPi Technologies India Pvt Ltd (Straive)

Contents

Figures

Series Editor's Foreword

Eight Principles for a Modern CBT is an important moment in the world of Cognitive Behavioral Therapies. This book has the power to revolutionize the way we practice CBT. I spoke with Scott Temple about this project many years ago and recall how deeply I felt at the time about the importance of this book. I have long thought of Scott Temple and Trent Codd as two of the most brilliant minds in modern therapy. Their knowledge of the intricacies of cognitive behavioral theories and associated protocols is unmatched. Further, they possess something that's quite rare. They understand the history, culture, and events surrounding the foundation and evolution of the cognitive behavioral therapies and also have a clear understanding of and competence with cutting edge innovations within the field. Their expertise spans generations. This book represents a distillation of their wisdom and knowledge. I was thrilled to hear about it, and I was even more excited to read it. I love this book, and I know that you will too!

As someone who truly loves therapy, I often think about the evolution of CBT. The earliest success of CBT for depression resulted in its proliferation. As it spread, it matured. CBT was adapted for a multitude of diagnoses including anxiety disorders, trauma, eating disorders, personality disorders, and psychosis. It also evolved in form. Some have spoken of the waves of CBT, those characterized as behavioral, cognitive, and mindfulness and acceptance based.

Different iterations of cognitive and behavioral therapies emerged, as did the alphabet soup that followed. Treatment developers and researchers focused on how the different branches of the CBTs compared to one another. Simultaneously, many therapists learned to move from branch to branch, capturing tools and strategies to help their clients (and themselves).

Over the decades, countless brilliant and passionate people have developed specialized approaches to CBT. Scientific work has shown that these approaches are effective in treating a wide variety of problems, including psychosocial stressors and resilience building. Millions of people have benefitted from these efforts.

From these conditions, many therapists developed competencies across the different related therapies like Beckian CBT, Acceptance and Commitment Therapy, and Dialectical Behavior Therapy. As we've learned these different approaches, we've yearned to know, "How might we go about combining these tools to best help the people we work with?" Certainly, several universals exist across these therapies. How do they fit together?

This book represents an integration of these differing models. CBT evolved as it spread, and now it's being gathered back together to represent a robust and pragmatic transdiagnostic therapy that is rooted in depth, compassion, curiosity, recovery, and empiricism. This book provides a framework for a psychological understanding of the factors that are implicated in the kind of suffering we see in our consultation rooms. And it shows how to create case formulations that allow for disciplined integration of the many techniques that have evolved across multiple models of Cognitive Behavior Therapy.

The authors wrote a book that is amazingly accessible and clinically oriented. The skills and ideas are immediately usable. This book represents the type of therapist I aspire to be. I thoroughly love this book, and I wholeheartedly recommend it.

This book also heralds in a new book series for Routledge. Modern Integrative CBT is a series developed specifically for books just like this one. The series is focused on shaping the future of CBT that is concentrated on high quality therapy and includes a robust integration of effective strategies and with a lot of heart. Keep an eye out for other great titles just like this one.

Scott Waltman, PsyD, ABPP
Editor, Modern Integrative CBT book series for Routledge
Clinical Psychologist
Board Certified in Behavioral and Cognitive Psychology
Fellow, Diplomate, Certified Trainer/Consultant, Academy of Cognitive & Behavioral Therapies
President-Elect, Academy of Cognitive & Behavioral Therapies
President-Elect, International Association of Cognitive Behavioral Therapy

Acknowledgements

ST: First and foremost, I am grateful to my friend and colleague Trent Codd, for his friendship, wisdom, trust, and collaboration these past 20 years. He's made the writing of this book more fun, more thoughtful, and more useful to readers than it would otherwise have been. To Aaron "Tim" Beck, and to my many valued colleagues in the Academy of Cognitive and Behavioral Therapies, my "home base" for nearly 30 years. My gratitude to the many dedicated clinicians I've trained throughout the United States, and in the Academy's CBT training projects in Los Angeles County and Mexico. They have helped me appreciate that the modal case in a clinician's daily schedule rarely conforms to a research treatment protocol: hence, this effort to create a disciplined, but flexible, model for delivering CBT in the "real world". My thanks to Alex Gamble, MD, for reading and commenting on an earlier draft of this manuscript. Much love to Ben, Melissa, Jesse, Jamie, and Jonah. And, as always, I am especially grateful to my wife, Rachel, for 52 years of marriage.

RTC wishes to acknowledge Scott Temple for his friendship and for the weekly conversations about this project that frequently went into deep, intellectually interesting clinical and theoretical areas. I will always cherish those conversations. To T.V. Joe Layng and Paul Andronis for introducing me to the work of Israel Goldiamond; to my friend, colleague and conversation partner, Keith Cox; to Tom Lynch for introducing me to the importance of biotemperament; and to countless colleagues and collaborators who contributed to shaping my development. I'm blessed that there are too many of you to name. Finally, to my loving wife of 22 years, Ginger, and my daughters Isabella and Caroline.

Part 1

Eight Organizing Principles for CBT

CHAPTER 1

Introduction

This book is written as a Cognitive Behavior Therapy training guide for both new and seasoned clinicians, and for teachers, trainers, and supervisors. We intend the book to be both scholarly and practical. We know there are many training manuals, some of which are quite superb. We have learned from many of them ourselves. What we offer here that is different is an integrative framework for understanding and applying modern Cognitive Behavior Therapy to real world cases. There are many therapies that cluster together under the broad umbrella of CBT. Each has evidence to support its efficacy. Each differs from the other. Yet we believe we have discerned common features, and ways of organizing competing theories and techniques into something hopefully resembling a well-made stew, in which all ingredients are blended in the cooking. To do this, we structure the book according to Eight Organizing Principles that we believe allow for a meaningful integration of the many strands of today's CBT movement. We offer the reader a deep dive, and it is our hope that they will emerge with a renewed commitment to becoming an expert in this evolving model of human functioning and freedom. We will have achieved our objectives if the reader views this book as a meaningful step on this journey.

Both authors have been practitioners and trainers for many years. We are steeped in Beckian CBT, Acceptance and Commitment Therapy, Dialectical Behavior Therapy, and Radically Open Dialectical Behavior Therapy. The first author has implemented and co-led Mindfulness-Based Cognitive Therapy programs in academic medical settings. The second author has led in the creation of innovative practice groups, dedicated to providing evidence-based CBT. This book is intended as a teaching tool for clinicians from multiple disciplines, seeking to understand the key

DOI: 10.4324/9781003505587-2

elements of modern CBT, and how to use them prescriptively in each therapy session. We will present vivid case vignettes, sample therapy transcripts that illustrate specific techniques, as well as diagrams and worksheets for use in practice. Our aim is to help clinicians draw on our Organizing Principles to use the tools and techniques within modern CBT in a disciplined and flexible manner.

We start with the acknowledgement that today's field of Cognitive Behavior Therapy can be bewildering to the novice and to seasoned practitioners alike. We have already likened modern CBT to an umbrella, under which are a myriad of related therapies, often known only by their acronyms: CBT, REBT, ACT, PST, DBT, RO DBT, MBCT, MCT, CFT, FAP. All Cognitive Behavior Therapies share a common commitment to science, and to testing both their theories and the outcomes of their therapies. But the therapies often differ from one another: in the populations they treat, in their theoretical postulates, in their central focus, in the way they view cognition, emotion, and behavior. No wonder it can be confusing for a newcomer to choose a model for practice.

We view the field as akin to a diamond, faceted in what is commonly called the 57-facet brilliant cut. Depending upon which facet one turns toward the light, the colors and the sparkle flash differently. There may well be as many facets in today's CBT as there are in that diamond. How to choose among therapies? Must you know them all? Or can you find ways to integrate in a disciplined and flexible manner?

Others have recognized the need for meaningful integration into therapy models that simplify and potentially unify the field (Hofmann, Hayes, &Lorscheid, 2021; Hayes & Hofmann, 2018; Barlow et al., 2017). This book builds on the first author's previous volume, *Brief Cognitive-Behavior Therapy for Cancer Patients: Re-Visioning the CBT Paradigm* (Temple, 2017). We will employ Eight Organizing Principles for a modern CBT, one applicable to the broad range of problems faced in clinical practice. The cancer book was written for practicing, seasoned clinicians, with a focus on a discrete clinical population. The *Eight Organizing Principles for a Modern CBT*, from the cancer book, are applied here to the broad range of clinical problems that mental health practitioners face in everyday practice. Those eight principles preserve the cognitive and behavioral core of CBT, integrated in a disciplined manner with what we believe is the best of new science and fresh clinical perspectives.

This book is intended to be practical, leaning heavily on clinical applications and skill building. We will draw on what we consider the most salient scholarship and science in our field, but our aim is for clinicians and trainers to leave with new skills that they can apply in practice.

Readers wishing to do a deeper dive into the clinical science that forms the foundation of our model will find that each chapter provides relevant references and, where possible, links.

We also invite the reader to apply the skills in this book in their personal lives. We have learned that the wisdom, perspectives, and techniques of modern CBT can be transformative, not just for our clients, but for us. The authors routinely apply the knowledge and tools in this book in our personal lives, in our practices, and in training clinicians. Modern CBT isn't just something we do to clients, like performing surgery or dispensing medicines. It becomes a way of looking at life's challenges, a lens for understanding the factors implicated in human suffering, and for evoking our own inner resources, while building the necessary skills to meet those life challenges. It's for all of us.

The Cognitive Behavior Therapies have always been integrative. From an initial core of radical behaviorism came an awareness that internal experience matters (Skinner, 1957, 1965). Though early behaviorists always recognized the importance of internal experience, it fell to later thinkers to develop more effective and pragmatic integrations of behavioral and cognitive factors (Beck et al., 2024; Ellis & Joffe-Ellis, 2019). Descartes famously declared "I think, therefore I am", and Beck introduced the idea that accessible cognition, in the form of language and visual images, provides keys to understanding and resolving many life problems. One's capacity to tune into one's thinking could be used to free one of mental traps. Beck's initial research addressed the treatment of recurrent major depression. Cognitive Therapy has integrated both the cognitive model Beck developed and behavior therapy. A behavioral focus, on activity scheduling, was an initial clinical target for the more severe depressive episodes. And Cognitive Therapy also targeted the specific types of cognition that are implicated in the onset and maintenance of depression. Beck drew on his psychoanalytic background to parse various types of cognition, in part based on accessibility to awareness. Those just on the edges of awareness, called automatic thoughts, became a more central focus of his new therapy.

And while early CBT perhaps overemphasized the role of accessible cognition, it always recognized the importance of emotion. That said, newer therapies within the CBT community, for example Dialectical Behavior Therapy (DBT), made emotion and emotion regulation a more central focus. This reflected the broader range of clinical problems that CBT began to treat, with each therapy tailored to match the features of the problems and diagnoses being addressed. In addition, it reflected the march of our scientific understanding of basic human psychological processes.

One of the great strengths of CBT is its commitment to building upon a foundation of psychological science. As science changes, so, too, does the therapy. One area where clinical science has had an impact is our understanding of cognition, and the role of cognitive interventions in CBT. Beck always eschewed the idea that we "challenge" dysfunctional beliefs. Instead, he developed a gentler form of inquiry, called Guided Discovery, which bypassed client resistance, and encouraged the client to be a co-explorer, sparking the kind of curiosity that a detective or a scientist might have about not only why one believes a thought, but whether there might be a more accurate or beneficial alternative. That said, a common misconception about Beck's CBT is that it forcefully attempted to make clients rid themselves of "bad" thoughts and replace them with "good" thoughts. As research continued, primarily in the UK and the US, newer models of cognition emerged. That included the finding that it isn't thought replacement that is central; it is the relationship one maintains to one's thoughts that matters. By that, we mean that we may well continue to notice the emergence of emotionally compelling beliefs, but that we become able to simply watch them, more dispassionately, while also recognizing potential alternatives that offer more flexible, adaptive potential.

Newer models of cognition in our field help us recognize that there are multiple avenues for intervention. One strategy, commonly employed by Beckian CBT, would be to take a careful look at the threat estimates, and to help develop a more realistic view of the threat, while also helping to reduce the catastrophizing if, in fact, the client does not get the job. A different strategy would be to recognize that such beliefs may well persist, and that they cannot be made to disappear through therapeutic interventions. Instead, one learns to watch such thoughts, with curiosity, compassion, and distance, while at the same time practicing the skill of throwing oneself wholeheartedly into the very situations that evoke avoidance and painful emotions (Hayes, 2019; Linehan, 1993, 2015). In the process, new learning forms alongside the older, less fortuitous learning. Rather than surrender to avoidance, the new learning brings with it an increased ability to engage in purposeful and necessary actions, even if painful thoughts, images, and emotions remain in the background. We are helping people build new learning, new ways of being, and new ways of experiencing life. They don't replace older modes. We don't unlearn. We build new ways of being in the world, ones that become stronger and more available, with practice.

The differences in these approaches may seem subtle. Yet they became the foundation for competing claims and different therapies within the CBT community. One CBT therapy, Beck's Cognitive Behavior Therapy, seeks to gently encourage the client to test the evidence for their beliefs, not just for the accuracy of their beliefs, but for the impact or function served by the belief. Then, the client is encouraged to test alternative perspectives, in session and in daily life. The other, chiefly represented by Acceptance and Commitment Therapy (ACT), doesn't seek to test or to specifically create an alternative to dysfunctional cognition, it seeks to change one's relationship to a thought, often through experiential exercises and by encouraging clients to step back and take less seriously their dysfunctional beliefs.

Who is right? A detailed discussion of the science and theories behind these competing models is beyond the purview of this book. For our purposes, we have come to view these perspectives as complementary to one another, not necessarily antagonistic. Both models work, though each works perhaps slightly differently from the other. Which one is best? *The one that works best for a given client and a given therapist.* We will show the reader how to think through and select from the broad spectrum of interventions available in competing models of CBT. To do that requires a familiarity with more than one theory, and the ability to synthesize, so that the choice of interventions is coherent, disciplined, and relevant.

This book reflects an effort to integrate these and other new findings in the field, including mindfulness and acceptance, radical behaviorism, cognitive science, affective neuroscience, personality theory of temperament, and evolutionary psychology. The contributions from these fields have deepened our understanding of both normative and dysfunctional human processes. The scientific fields above contribute to an understanding of transdiagnostic processes that we can draw on for our understanding of human suffering. We will show how to create a case conceptualization that draws on the above disciplines.

Besides new advances in the human sciences, there is another driver of our quest for a better clinical model. As newer therapies were evolving in CBT, the number of presumed psychiatric diagnoses has exploded in number, culminating in the newest iteration of the *Diagnostic and Statistical Manual* (DSM5) (APA, 2022). Clinicians have thus been faced with two dilemmas: First, our reliance on a medicalized understanding of human suffering has begun to buckle under the weight of the expanding DSM. This has amplified the already numerous challenges to the validity and reliability of the DSM (Hayes & Hofmann, 2020; Sauer-Zavala & Barlow, 2021). It is beyond the purview of this book to detail the current controversies about the *Diagnostic and Statistical Manual* (DSM5), and about the medicalized paradigm on which it is based. But for our purposes, we see the medicalized paradigm waning, one that posits our clients as necessarily having "broken brains" and presumed psychiatric "illnesses". This is not to suggest that brains are not implicated in human functioning and dysfunction, or to suggest that there are not disorders that have a stronger biological vector. It is to say that newer models are emerging, of which ours is one, which put the study of human suffering on a broader, and we believe, more credible foundation of understanding. In addition, we posit that our approach is potentially less stigmatizing, as well. In a subsequent chapter, we will briefly review the reasons for a transition from a medicalized, DSM approach to one involving transdiagnostic factors. Briefly, for now, transdiagnostic factors are the temperamental, behavioral, and psychological mechanisms that we think better explain psychological disorders. This suggests that those underlying psychological and temperamental variables are more parsimonious, closer to the emerging science in the field, less stigmatizing, and more pragmatic in their therapeutic applications.

As faith in the DSM began to erode, even as the number of identified disorders increased, the number of treatment manuals increased to an unwieldy number. This led to a second conundrum: must a skilled clinician learn dozens of manualized therapies in order to be competent as a CBTer? Realistically, how many manualized treatments can one clinician possibly hope to master, let alone even read about?

We're offering an integrative, pragmatic model, guided by Eight Organizing Principles for a modern CBT, and the chance to flexibly choose interventions and techniques from across the broad spectrum of CBT therapies. We view techniques as akin to a palette of colors used by a painter, from which the clinician can select interventions prescriptively, as dictated by the needs of the client and the creativity of the clinician.

At the same time, we are well aware of a debate in the field between "purists" and "integrators". Purists tend to argue for a one-size-fits-all model of therapy, as though that one model can accommodate all the people who seek help. To depart from this standard means that one is no longer practicing an evidence-based therapy. This notion is pinned to the early research in the field: manualized treatments for discrete DSM disorders. But as the field grew, a movement has developed towards a more flexible, principle-based approach, one that targets the maintaining factors of suffering, not just a DSM diagnosis, while using a spectrum of interventions that target those factors. We intend to provide a case conceptualization framework that allows for flexible adaptation to the realities of clinical work. And it allows the clinician to select techniques from the spectrum of available therapies, as long as they offer promise of moving the therapy towards the client's and clinician's therapeutic objectives.

Partly in reaction to these challenges, the field saw the emergence of an effort to target core processes that explain human suffering, rather than relying principally on DSM diagnoses. Rather than using the manualized treatment protocols that were de rigueur in the earlier randomized trials, CBT began to develop a more flexible approach to case formulation and therapy. Instead of trying to fit people into diagnostic categories, CBT increasingly fits the therapy to the individual client, based on a fresh understanding of the psychological processes that ensnare human beings. This also led to treatments that were based on those processes. Examples include Process-Based Therapy (Hayes & Hofmann, 2018; Hofmann, Hayes, & Lorscheid, 2021), and Barlow's Unified Protocol for Transdiagnostic Treatment (Barlow et al., 2017), the latter of which addresses primarily the temperamental trait of neuroticism, or disorders in emotional stability and regulation.

The debate continues between those who advocate fidelity to specific protocols and manuals, versus those who seek to identify principles that can be applied broadly to a wide range of clinical problems. We opt for the latter.

Let's now take a look at the landscape we find ourselves in as clinicians and researchers. Even before the COVID pandemic, we have witnessed a dramatic rise in unhappiness, in the United States and in many other developed countries. Rates of depression and anxiety for all age groups, particularly for young people, have soared (Haidt, 2024; Twenge, 2023). And suicide rates in America have now reached record proportions (CDC, 2023). Our Surgeon General warns of a "loneliness epidemic" that plagues America. This can't be attributed to "broken brains" or "chemical imbalances". There are a number of factors posited as contributors to this time of unhappiness. Political scientist Robert Putnam wrote an influential work that describes the steady erosion of social institutions in American life that provide connection and meaning (Putnam, 2020). Social scientists also note the dramatic rise in depression and anxiety in young people, related to at least several factors. One is the use of the internet by young people, especially Gen Z youth, often to the exclusion of actual face-to-face contact, play, and engagement with others (Haidt, 2024). Second, Lukianoff & Haidt (2019) posit that we are evolving a culture that fosters beliefs and practices that markedly contribute to depression and anxiety in youth. They specifically draw on the work of CBT in describing three key cognitive factors.

1. A sense of personal fragility, encompassed by the belief that "What doesn't kill me makes me more fragile."
2. "Always trust your feelings."
3. "Life is a battle between good people and evil people."

These beliefs mirror some of the common cognitive distortions we will present later, as a focus of psychotherapy: Catastrophizing; Emotional Reasoning; Black and White, or Dichotomous, Thinking. All are toxic when taken to the extreme, especially when stoked by the larger culture.

As for a biological paradigm, we do not contest the role that medications can play. We just think it's a hand that has been overplayed. According to the CDC, in 2020, 16.5% of American adults were prescribed psychiatric medication, while the number receiving psychotherapy had declined (CDC, 2023). We believe that new accounts are needed for understanding human suffering, and its resolution in psychotherapy. And modern CBT is, we believe, well equipped to serve a role in facing this challenge.

We aren't victims of our biology, though biology is clearly one factor that shapes us. We now know more about the roles of behavioral genetics, temperament, emotion processing, cognition, and evolutionary psychology in shaping who we are as human beings. Our CBT technologies provide us with tools to work with those givens in ways that increase our power to shape our own destinies. It's exciting. It's optimistic. And it's time. Sixty-five years ago, the famous Swiss psychiatrist Carl Gustav Jung, then in his mid–eighties, admonished viewers in a televised BBC interview of the dangers facing humanity, all because, he said, "we know nothing of man". Yet since his time, advances in science and in clinical practice are providing potentially exciting and hopeful answers to the following questions: What are some of the evolved features of our species, and why, in the face of abundance in developed countries do we see so much despair? We believe that modern CBT can help us not only understand ourselves better but can help us navigate the challenges we face in our lives. Those challenges include the twin tasks all of us as humans in our culture face: the need to get along with our fellow humans and the need to get ahead by finding a path that secures the necessary resources for us to live effectively (McAdams, 2016).

We will apply our model to some of the more commonly occurring situations we face in our consulting rooms. Rather than organize our clinical chapters by diagnosis, we will offer something novel: we will tackle head on the kinds of problems real clinicians and real sufferers face from the first encounter. And we believe those challenges often involve the struggle of human beings to make relationships work, to create a place in the world that secures adequate resources for themselves and loved ones, and to cope with the many bruises and occasional disappointments that life dishes out. In sum, this is about helping people live a life that matters to them.

In the book you are reading, we advocate a modern Cognitive Behavior Therapy that has the underpinning of science combined with the heart and soul of humanistic therapies. We believe in a modern CBT that has an answer for some of the common concerns about CBT that we hear from trainees. Among the most common concerns are the following:

1. CBT is a rigid model that feels too constraining and artificial. It doesn't seem humanistic and warm enough.
2. CBT was shaped by its adherence to a medical model. Most of my clients don't have psychiatric disease; they have problems in living.
3. CBT doesn't seem to pay attention to human emotions.
4. CBT feels like it just focuses on changing people's thoughts; my clients have real problems, not just distorted thinking.
5. CBT lacks depth. It seems concerned with superficialities in a person's life, not the deep core of disturbance that hides beneath the surface.

We will explain through discussions and case applications how and why we believe that each of these concerns is misplaced.

We offer a clinical model that we know is challenging to learn. Reading is a start. Case supervision is a next step. Expert status is achieved not through books or workshops, alone. Expert status is achieved through receiving direct performance feedback, from experts, and by modifying one's practice to increasingly conform to expert standards (Ericsson, Hoffman, Kozbelt, & Williams, 2018; Ericsson & Poole, 2019). Consider for a moment how one learns to play the game of tennis. One goes to a tennis court and watches how others play the game. One becomes familiar with the nets, the lines, the various kinds of playing surfaces, the mode of dress, the decorum, the rules. One begins to play, and if fortunate, one gets a coach. The coach instructs after observing the player and gives specific feedback about how to create a mechanically perfect backhand through repeated practice. The player learns by adjusting performance to meet the standards that will allow for winning. It's a slow process. And it's what works in tennis, in music, in surgical training; and it's how one learns to be an expert therapist, as well. We will provide resources for clinicians to achieve further training and supervision as we go.

Modern CBT isn't just about removing symptoms of disorders. It's about growth, about living worthwhile, dignified, and meaningful lives. We aim to help those we serve do just that. The science of our field increasingly teaches us about the forces in our lives that we don't control. We don't control our histories. We don't choose the color of our skins, or the parents who gave us life, or the social order in which we were born. Or the century of our birth. We don't control our genetics, or our temperaments. But we have this moment. And in this moment we can pause and take stock. And we can learn to choose wisely. As the neuroscientist Lisa Feldman-Barrett has written: "Sometimes we're responsible for things not because they are our fault, but because we're the only one who can change them" (Feldman-Barrett, (2021, p. 81).

Life is precious. It is filled with uncertainties and pain. It is filled with the potential for great joy and peace. We find ourselves in this moment, with the histories and the temperaments we carry, and the stories we tell ourselves. What if we can do as Feldman-Barrett suggests and take responsibility for taking steps towards a life that we intend, rather than feeling dragged by forces we cannot control. That is the challenge that modern CBT can help all of us meet, as therapists, and on behalf of those who seek our help.

To meet those challenges, we offer Eight Organizing Principles for a modern Cognitive-Behavior Therapy (Temple, 2017). The first three principles address "what" questions, in the sense that they focus on those factors that set the stage for understanding human suffering and its resolution or management. The remaining five factors are "how" factors, in the sense that they focus on the how of doing therapy:

1. Normalizing human suffering
2. A focus on transdiagnostic processes in psychological disorders
3. A focus on accessing and building on client strengths and values
4. The disciplined use of Guided Discovery and Validation Strategies
5. Balancing acceptance, mindfulness, and change processes
6. Balancing cognitive and experiential interventions in CBT
7. A focus on self-processes in therapy
8. A more contextual model of human functioning

We will explore each of these principles in subsequent chapters. And we will show how they are linked together. These principles are not orthogonal, or independent of one another. They are related in ways that allow for an integrated approach to understanding and treating our clients. We will show both aspiring and practicing clinicians how to use these principles in the challenges of daily practice. Briefly, then, for now, here are the principles.

1. *Normalizing Human Suffering*: We can't remove the inevitable pain of life, or the distress humans face as they meet life's challenges. We strive. We fail at times. We age. We become ill. We face loss and eventual death. Other sources of human pain lie in the mismatch

between our evolved natures and the environments we live in today. We have built a world that takes us far from the environments of evolutionary adaptation from which we came (Buss, 2025; Gilbert, 2017; Stewart-Williams, 2024), leaving us even more vulnerable to depression and anxiety. In addition, there seem to be properties of the human mind that both provide an evolutionary advantage, yet can also go awry: a tendency towards cognitive biases that lead to misappraisals of self, others, world; a tendency to be very sensitive to short-term consequences of our behavior, while being relatively insensitive to long-term consequences.

This is not to say we take a gloomy view of life. We don't. As part of normalizing the pain of life, we help our clients understand that it is not necessarily a sign of either a disease or a personal failure to struggle at times.

Paul Gilbert (2017; Gilbert & Simos, 2022) advocates helping clients understand that it's not their fault that they were born with the brains and evolved natures they contend with. But maybe Robin Williams said it best, when he played a therapist working with the tormented young genius, played by Matt Damon, in *Goodwill Hunting*: "It's not your fault". That said, it is nonetheless the responsibility of the client to face the challenges that brought them to therapy. They aren't alone in that struggle; the therapist is with them as a guide and a coach.

2. *A Focus on Transdiagnostic Processes in Therapy*: There is an increasing interest in the Cognitive Behavior Therapies in finding additions to, if not alternatives to, the DSM for understanding the core processes by which human lives can become derailed. Hayes and Hofmann's Process-Based Therapy is an example (Hayes & Hofmann, 2018). Barlow's Unified Protocol for Transdiagnostic Treatment of Emotional Disorders provides an overarching treatment for those high in the temperamental trait of neuroticism (Barlow et al., 2017). We share that interest. As we will describe in more detail, there are underlying factors that appear to provide a better account of human suffering than current psychiatric diagnoses, and lend themselves to developing treatments that target these processes. In truth, likely contributing factors to human psychological suffering are probably vast. There is so much that we do not and cannot yet know. That said, there are several candidates for a transdiagnostic model of psychological suffering that we think merit inclusion in that list. The factors we deem most relevant for our purposes are:

a.   cognitive and behavioral processes that are implicated in the maintenance of destructive vicious cycles

b.   Temperament, which involves the biological and psychological substrate of personality, and for which considerable empirical support exists.

We will show how these cognitive, behavioral, and temperamental trans-diagnostic factors are causally implicated in human suffering, and they become intertwined, such that cognition and behavior can amplify temperamental factors in producing dysfunctional patterns of living. We will also present ways to develop case conceptualizations that draw on these processes, allowing for DSM diagnosis only as a starting point. While we do not purport to provide an exclusive list of possible transdiagnostic factors, we believe that the three factors, above, provide opportunities for robust interventions, based on scientifically credible underlying factors that amplify, if not cause, human psychological suffering.

3.   *A Focus on Strengths and Values*: Aaron "Tim" Beck, the founder of Cognitive Therapy, taught the importance of focusing on strengths, and on "islands of sanity" in even the most psychologically impaired patients, those with psychosis. Many theorists, from a wide variety of therapy models, have emphasized the importance of strengths and resilience (Walsh, 2016; Boszormenyi-Nagy, 1999; Padesky & Mooney, 2012). These factors are important because they can be brought to bear on solving current problems. We'll see in the chapter on strengths that many clients come to therapy underestimating their own ability to deal with the problems they face. And yet, when we look with them into their histories, client strengths have nonetheless been used to meet the challenges of the past. Marsha Linehan, the creator of Dialectical Behavior Therapy, taught that within each person is the capacity for wisdom, or what she named "Wise Mind" (Linehan, 2015). We will teach how to help ourselves and our clients access that inner wisdom, as an ally in facing life's challenges. Finally, an emphasis on values, or what matters in a client's life, creates an opportunity to shift the focus, dignifying and energizing the therapy (Hayes, 2019).

4.   *The Use in Guided Discovery and Validation Strategies in Fostering the Treatment Relationship*: We often ask trainees new to CBT what images they have of the therapy relationship in CBT. Cognitive Behavior Therapy is often thought of as rigid, impersonal, and mechanical. We view CBT much differently. We teach and practice a CBT that is a rich, emotionally engaged, and collaborative process. We will teach

how to create treatment relationships that use two technologies, which we combine in a novel framework for intervening: Guided Discovery (from Beckian CBT) and Validation Strategies used in Dialectical Behavior Therapy (Linehan, 1997). In addition, we will show how ruptures in the treatment relationship can be spotted and repaired, using these tools.

5. *Balancing Acceptance, Mindfulness, and Change Processes*: Cognitive Behavior Therapy began with a strong technological core, rooted in Behaviorism. It is filled with tools and technologies for helping people change. But change technologies often only work when a client feels accepted, understood, and validated by the clinician. There is also a paradox of change: one must first accept the existence of a problem before one can change it. In addition to the clinician's acceptance of the client, we invite the client to adopt an accepting stance towards their internal states, and a tolerance for distress, while beginning to solve the problems they bring to therapy. Changing a problem situation often begins, paradoxically, by tolerating the distress associated with the problem itself.

Anxious avoidance is a great example. Learning to deal with social situations, because they are both necessary and potentially pleasurable, is not immediately easy for someone with a social phobia. Rather than ridding the person of their anxious arousal, we help the person focus on being fully present and engaged, in the moment, whether at a party, in the grocery store checkout line, or a job interview. By accepting the distress that may have long accompanied social encounters, the client learns to build a new repertoire, a new mode of being, if you will, much as a person learns to build muscle in workouts: with practice. That also provides a link to mindfulness. We will focus on mindfulness as a set of psychological processes, without leaning into the longstanding spiritual traditions from which mindfulness springs. Mindfulness is a set of psychological skills for being present with whatever shows up, increasing one's capacity for attention and focus, and creating a space to more calmly and wisely choose actions that meet the needs of the moment effectively. Part of the art and science of therapy is knowing when and how to focus on change, when to foster acceptance, and how to use the present moment to foster mindful engagement, as a bridge between acceptance and change.

6. *Balancing Cognitive and Experiential Interventions in CBT*: Humans process information in multiple modes (Kahneman, 2011; Teasdale, 2022). One of those modes is the more explicitly verbal, including the

capacity to more cooly and dispassionately employ reason to examine information within and from the world. But other modes are more rapid, emotionally and intuitively encoded, physical, even postural. So while the earlier models of CBT focused on helping people rationally appraise their thoughts, we also recognize that therapy works best when what is learned is emotionally compelling. As CBT has evolved, it has created an incredibly rich and engaging set of tools that make therapy alive, emotionally rich, and effective. Whether through the use of behavioral experiments (Bennett-Levy et al., 2004), experiential exercises in Acceptance and Commitment Therapy (ACT), guided imagery, body posture, or other experientially compelling tools, we broaden the focus of therapy. We have likened this to lowering the center of gravity in therapy, from "the head", to the "gut", in order to create cognitively and emotionally compelling change. We will show how to do that in case examples that are sprinkled throughout this book.

7. *A Focus on Self-Processes in Therapy*: We will tackle some of the complexities in talking about what is a "self". We characterize the "self" as a fluid set of processes, not a static noun, or a homunculus residing in some recess of the brain. These processes have a rich history in psychotherapy and have shown up in more recent elaborations of CBT, from which we draw.

For now, we hope you'll join us in an experiential exercise, one that we think gets at self-processes, experientially.

Take out a sheet of paper and a pen or pencil. Write the following at the top of the sheet: "Thoughts, Emotions, Urges". Now set the paper aside. Let yourself settle into your chair or your couch. Draw a breath. Let your eyes close if they wish, or if you prefer, keep them gently open, with a soft gaze at neutral space, perhaps the carpet or floor at your feet. Breathe gently. And imagine that you are the captain of a ship, in turbulent waters. A storm is coming in from the west. You can see a black line of low, fast-moving clouds over the western horizon, rippling your way. The waters are whipped into white peaks as the rains hit. Now imagine yourself as a scared little child, quivering, fearful and helpless at the helm. Stay with this, please, even if it hurts a little. Pay attention to your body. Notice what you feel in your body, and where you feel it. Stay. Notice any thoughts coming up. Notice what urges show up, and what emotions. Stay with it for a moment longer. Now come back to the breath.

Let's pause for a moment to process what just happened. On that sheet of paper you set aside, write down, under those words you wrote, the thoughts you noticed, the emotions and body sensations that came up, and any urges. Did fear show up? Helplessness, appropriate to a small child being asked to pilot a ship in a savage storm? Urges to flee or cry out for help, or look around for a grown up to take the wheel?

Okay, let's move on. Settle again. Draw a few breaths. Now, visualize yourself as a mountain, settled and rooted firmly. A storm moves in from across a desert landscape. Winds and rain begin to whip around the mountain. Imagine yourself as that mountain, impervious to the lashing of water and wind; focused, clear-eyed, calm, fearless. Notice carefully what you feel in your body. Now as we come back to the room and to this moment, we have a question: can you feel a difference, in your body, in your mind? Which "self" would you choose to bring forth to meet the challenges you face in life? A robust CBT is one that recognizes the importance of an embodied "self", which can serve as a platform to meet the challenges of life.

We will spend time focusing on how to access and build self-processes in therapy, linking this work to the acceptance, mindfulness, and change processes of CBT. And we'll try to do this without getting caught up in the ontological and epistemological conundrums that can trap people. What is a true self? How many selves compose us? We'll leave the deepest speculation to the poets, like Walt Whitman, and the philosophers, like William James. We aim to be practical and clinically relevant. We'll show you how as we go.

8. *A More Contextual Model of Therapy*: Lives unfold in multiple contexts, both inner and outer contexts. We have interior lives, including body sensations, emotions, thoughts, rules, beliefs, and images. And we are part of a much broader set of contexts, in which we are nested and with which we interact. We both provide and receive feedback that modifies and is modified by our behavior. And we are obliged to effectively manage our relationship to all contexts, sometimes simultaneously. CBT requires us to have a model for extending our therapeutic work into all relevant contexts of our clients' lives.

Theorists ranging from the biological sciences, including General Systems Theory (von Bertalanffy, 2015) to psychology (Hayes, 2019) have put forth models to account for behavior as it unfolds in these multiple contexts. So has the work of Goldiamond (Layng et al., 2022), whose Constructionalist model we draw on here. In fact, we have been struck by the way in which Goldiamond's work seems to have gently nudged other CBT models towards his Constructionalist approach. This contextual model helps the clinician and the client set a clear direction for therapy, based on client values and goals. We are then able to identify those factors from within our eight organization principles that may be derailing goal attainment, while helping to build patterns of living that align with client values. This allows us to develop a case conceptualization for each client that is context sensitive, and that allows us to bring in interventions that harness each of the other organizing principles. The model can and should be adapted to meet the specific needs of each client. We will show you how to do that in the following chapters.

The astute reader will already be noticing ways in which these principles are linked to one another. As we proceed, we will make each principle clear, including their clinical utility, in detailed case vignettes, sample therapy transcripts, and case discussions. We will focus on the kinds of cases and problems that clients bring to our clinics. Clinicians can always find a DSM diagnosis for a client. Indeed, doing so is the royal road to insurance payment and administrative happiness. That said, the real work of therapy often involves problems, more than diagnoses. These include relationship challenges, parent–child difficulties, work-related problems, problems dealing with life circumstances that seem unfair and unchangeable, loneliness, a lack of meaning, and a sense of fear and defeat; a struggle to cope with painful emotions, thoughts, memories, or images; problem-solving strategies that may have worked in the past, but are coming up short in current life contexts. Some of the clients in these vignettes will meet diagnostic criteria for a variety of DSM5 diagnoses. Some will not. In either case, what matters is how we conceptualize the case, how we create a shared formulation with the client, and how we mutually agree on a path towards agreed-upon improvement. We will re-visit these cases in Part II of the book. We hope to make this journey not only useful and pragmatic, but also fun and energizing.

CHAPTER OUTLINE AND CHAPTER ORGANIZATION

Part 1 is divided into chapters that provide detail about each of the Eight Organizing Principles for a Modern Cognitive Behavior Therapy. Chapter 2 focuses on what we mean when we talk about normalizing human suffering. Chapter 3 addresses how to access and build on client strengths and values in therapy. Chapter 4 outlines the use of Guided Discovery principles and techniques, as well as Validation Strategies in fostering the treatment relationship. It also details how to spot and manage rupture in the therapeutic relationship. Chapter 5 details how to balance Acceptance, Mindfulness, and Change Processes in Modern CBT. Chapter 6 details how to employ cognitive and experiential interventions to create intellectually and emotionally compelling and powerful interventions. Chapter 7 describes transdiagnostic factors in human suffering, which can be used as a complement to DSM diagnoses. We believe these factors account for important sources of variance in understanding the clinical problems that show up in our consulting rooms. Chapter 8 addresses the role of self-processes in therapy, including the use of guided imagery, behavioral experiments, posture, and other tools for accessing and building on stable, healing self-processes in therapy. Chapter 9 describes what we mean by contextualism, and how the principles derived from contextualism can be brought to bear on helping clients manage the ecosystems they navigate. Chapter 10 describes the case conceptualization framework that we will use in the case discussions that form Part 2 of the book.

Part 2 consists of clinical applications, including vivid case descriptions and sample transcripts. This second part of the book will be case-based. We will demonstrate how to apply the Eight Organizing Principles to the kinds of cases commonly seen in clinical practice. We will introduce several cases early in the book, in the first chapter, and will follow up on those cases throughout the rest of the book. We will provide diagrams and worksheets that can be used in session, and in self-practice. We aim to make this book practical, personally and professionally meaningful, as well as fun and energizing.

Chapter 11 The Case of a Desperate Mother: Rose is a 54-year old divorced Latina mother. Her daughter has a drug problem, yet retains custody of her own daughter, Rose's granddaughter. Rose is depressed, despondent, and guilt-ridden, believing that her own frailties as a mother contributed to her daughter's difficulties. She is desperate to create a better relationship with her daughter, while also protecting herself against her daughter's tendency to steal from her, run up credit card debt on Rose's cards, and distance herself for weeks or months on end, following conflict with Rose. At the same time, Rose is motivated by a wish to protect her granddaughter and preserve her ties to the girl.

Chapter 12 The Case of an Alienated Combat Veteran: John is a 44-year-old ex-Army Ranger, who did two tours of duty in Afghanistan. He is now an attorney, working in a prestigious law firm in corporate law. He does not have clear symptoms of PTSD. Yet he reports an ongoing sense of estrangement, irritability, and loneliness in his workplace. He says that he does not trust his partners, and that he does not fit into the culture, despite his intense wish to succeed at the firm. He comes in for therapy at his wife's urging. And he agrees with her assessment that though the marriage is strong, his irritability with work is spilling over into their home life. He cannot figure out what the problem is. By all accounts, he says, he should be happy. But he is not.

Chapter 13 The Case of a Lonely Cocaine User: A 34-year-old female, Kelly, has been struggling with a cocaine addiction for at least 16 years. She reports having made many failed attempts to discontinue cocaine use and to remain functional in work and family contexts. She's been to residential treatment twice and had many outpatient therapists over the years. She's also participated in NA on and off. She describes her use as sporadic. That is, she can go many weeks without any use, but then go on a binge which lasts "a week or so". She works at a local radio station on the weekends. She says this means she is working when her friends are off and that she is off when her friends are working. This leads her to struggle with loneliness, one of the antecedents to her cocaine use.

Chapter 14 The Case of the Powerless Parents and a Tormented Teenager: Barbara and Tom, whose 16 year old daughter, Jessica, has been struggling to adjust to the rigors of mid-adolescence. Her struggles are exemplified by difficulties managing her mood, substantial decline in academic performance, and frequent peer conflict. She has also started vaping and smoking cannabis. Perhaps most troubling to Barbara and Tom, she has been cutting herself when she becomes acutely distressed. Because Jessica is either withdrawn or when semi-engaged, arguing with her parents, they feel incredibly anxious because they believe they've lost parental influence with her and because this leaves them wondering what information about her struggles they do not know. It is this distress alongside their feelings of powerlessness regarding their parenting that led them to seek psychological consultation.

Chapter 15 When Life Seems Meaningless: Efran, a married, employed, 39-year-old male, sought services because he felt "nothing really matters". He described his mood as depressed and complained of little motivation. He described his life as one of just "going through the motions". He had been a devoutly religious person until around the age of 35 when he determined that he no longer believed in God. Efran described losing his faith as the precipitant to his current concerns. His faith had made the world and his place in it meaningful. Though he is not currently suicidal, he is struggling to determine how he can continue his life, despite being confronted with his conviction that it is meaningless.

CHAPTER SUMMARY

This chapter provides an introduction and overview of the book. We intend this book to be scholarly, and also practical. We set forth the challenges faced by clinicians either new to CBT, or for those steeped in one type of CBT, but puzzled over how that model fits with others in the

CBT community. We offer an integrative framework, rooted in what we consider the current science of psychology, and allowing clinicians to flexibly integrate techniques from multiple CBT, and other, therapies. The chapter concludes with a summary of the Eight Organizing Principles that are the focus of Part 1 of this book, and a description of case chapters that compose Part 2.

REFERENCES

APA (2022) *Diagnostic & Statistical Manual of Mental Disorders, Text Revision Dsm, 5-tr*. New York: American Psychiatric Association.

Barlow, D., Farchione, T., Sauer-Zavala, S., et al. (2017) *Unified Protocol for Transdiagnostic Treatment of Emotional Disorders*. Oxford: Oxford University Press.

Beck, A., Rush, A. et al. (2024) *Cognitive Therapy of Depression* (2nd edn). New York: Guilford Press.

Bennett-Levy, J., Butler, G., Fennell, M. et al. (2004) *The Oxford Guide to Behavioural Experiments in Cognitive Therapy*. Oxford: Oxford University Press.

Boszormenyi-Nagy, I. (1999) *Invisible Loyalties*. New York: Routledge.

Buss, D. (2025) *Evolutionary Psychology: The New Science of the Mind*. New York: Routledge.

CDC (2023) Vital Statistics Rapid Release. Report no. 34, November. https://www.cdc.gov/nchs/data/vsrr/vsrr034.pdf

Ellis, A. & Joffe-Ellis, D. (2019) *Rational Emotive Behavior Therapy* (2nd edn). Washington, DC: American Psychological Association Press.

Ericsson, A., Hoffman, R., Kozbelt, A., & Williams, A. (2018) *The Cambridge Handbook of Expertise and Expert Performance* (2nd edn). Cambridge, UK: Cambridge University Press.

Ericsson, A. & Pool, R. (2019) *Peak: Secrets from the New Science of Expertise*. New York: HarperOne.

Feldman-Barrett, L. (2021) *7½ Lessons About the Brain*. New York: Mariner.

Gilbert, P. (2017) *Living Like Crazy*. New York: Annwyn House.

Gilbert, P. & Simos, G. (eds.) (2022) *Compassion Focused Therapy: Clinical Practice and Applications*. New York: Routledge.

Haidt, J. (2024) *The Anxious Generation*. New York: Penguin Press.

Hayes, S. (2019) *A Liberated Mind*. New York: Avery Press.

Hayes, S. & Hofmann, S. (eds.) (2018) *Process-Based CBT: The Science and Core Clinical Competencies of Cognitive Behavior Therapy*. Oakland: Context Press.

Hayes, S. & Hofmann, S. (2020) *Beyond the DSM: Toward a Process-Based Alternative for Diagnosis and Mental Health Treatment*. Oakland: Context Press.

Hofmann, S., Hayes, S., & Lorscheid, D. (2021) *Learning Process-Based Therapy: A Skills Training Manual*. Oakland: Context Press.

Kahneman, D. (2011) *Thinking, Fast and Slow*. New York: Farrar, Straus, & Giroux.

Layng, J, Andronis, P., Codd, T., & Abdel-Jalil, A. (2022) *Nonlinear Contingency Analysis:Going Beyond Cognition and Behavior in Clinical Practice*. New York: Routledge.

Linehan, M. (1993) *Cognitive-Behavioral Treatment of Borderline Personality Disorder*. New York: Guilford Press.

Linehan, M. (1997) Validation and Psychotherapy. In A. Bohart & L. Greenberg (eds.). *Empathy Reconsidered: New Directions in Psychotherapy*. Washington, DC: American Psychological Association.

Linehan, M. (2015) *DBT Skills Training Manual* (2nd edn). New York: Guilford Press.

Lukianoff, G. & Haidt, J. (2019) *The Coddling of the American Mind*. New York: Penguin Press.

McAdams, D. (2016) *The Art and Science of Personality Development*. New York: Guilford Press.

Padesky, C. & Mooney, K. (2012) Strength-based Cognitive Behavior Therapy: A Four-step Model to Build Resilience. *Clinical Psychology & Psychotherapy*, July/August, 19 (4), 283–290.

Putnam, R. (2020) *Bowling Alone: The Collapse and Revival of the American Community* (Revised). New York: Simon & Shuster.

Sauer-Zavala, S. & Barlow, D. (2021) *Neuroticism: A New Framework for Emotional Disorders and Their Treatment*. New York: Guilford Press.

Skinner, B.F. (1957) *Verbal Behavior*. New York: Appleton, Century, Croft.

Skinner, B.F. (1965) *Science and Human Behavior*. New York: Free Press.

Stewart-Williams, S. (2024) *The Ape That Understood the Universe: How the Mind and Culture Evolve*. Cambridge: Cambridge University Press.

Teasdale, J. (2022) *What Happens in Mindfulness: Inner Awakening and Embodied Cognition*. New York: Guilford.

Temple, S. (2017) *Brief Cognitive Behavior Therapy for Cancer Patients: Re-Visioning the CBT Paradigm*. New York: Routledge Press.

Twenge, J. (2023) *Generations*. New York: Atria Books.

von Bertalanffy, L (2015) *General Systems Theory: Foundations, Development, Applications* (Revised edn). New York: George Braziller.

Walsh, F. (2016) *Strengthening Family Resilience* (3rd edn). New York: Guilford.

CHAPTER 2

Principle #1: Normalizing Human Suffering

America is the land of plenty. We have plenty of food. We have the most advanced technologies in the world: in healthcare, in computer sciences, in emerging technologies, in entrepreneurship, in wealth. We also have plenty of suffering. Rates of depression and anxiety, of confusion and loneliness are soaring, especially among the young (Twenge, 2023; Haidt, 2024; Lukianoff & Haidt, 2019). Suicide rates have hit an all-time high in the United States (Garnett & Curtin, 2025). And loneliness is rampant. Nearly half of us, in a land of 340 million people, report feeling lonely sometimes or always (APA, 2025). The health consequences of loneliness can be substantial, in the form of increased risk for heart disease and stroke, diabetes, depression and anxiety, addiction, suicidality and self-harm, dementia, and early death (CDC, 2023). The rise in loneliness prompted the Surgeon General of the United States, Dr. Vivek Murthy, to issue a report "to address the public health crisis of loneliness, isolation, and lack of connection" in America (Office of the Surgeon General, 2023). His policy prescriptions are intended to address loneliness in the context of a public health crisis, with a focus on those factors in American life that seem to be contributing to the problem. Those factors include the erosion of social institutions that once bound Americans together, providing social connection and meaning. Those factors are amply chronicled in political scientist Robert Putnam's work, *Bowling Alone* (Putnam, 2020). Social psychologist Jonathan Haidt adds to our understanding in his work examining the impact of the internet, and the erosion of play-based childhood, with decreased face-to-face contact for young people (Lukianoff & Haidt, 2019; Haidt, 2024). The upshot is that we may be living in a world for which we were not evolved. This contributes to social conditions once described by the French sociologist Émile

DOI: 10.4324/9781003505587-3

Durkheim, an erosion of shared meaning and connection, leading to loneliness, despair, and what he termed anomic suicides. We believe this is increasingly the landscape in which psychotherapists navigate today. Lest we too lapse into despair, we also believe that modern Cognitive Behavior Therapy provides the tools to both understand and more effectively deal with these conditions, both for our clients and for ourselves.

But human pain isn't a new phenomenon. Nor is it unique to America. It is also a part of the human condition, a condition recognized by world spiritual and wisdom traditions since the dawn of time. We age. We become ill. We die. The existential realities of life are iron clad. The passage of time and the recognition that life is fleeting form a backdrop to human existence, one that challenges us to remain resilient and engaged in the great dance of life.

Life also contains great bounties, and our role as psychotherapists is to help people turn their lives towards those bounties, while coping effectively with the existential realities that we all face. To quote Viktor Frankl, the creator of Logotherapy: "Our aim must be to help our patient to achieve the highest possible activation in his life, to lead him…to experience his existence as a constant effort to actualize his values" (Frankl, 1986, p. 61). Our aim in this book is to help clinicians develop the conceptual, analytic, and technical tools to understand the roots of human suffering and to help us all actualize those values of which Frankl writes, the deep values that point us towards a meaningful, well lived life.

Modern Cognitive Behavior Therapies increasingly recognize the ubiquity of human suffering and harness that awareness in the service of both energizing and dignifying our work (Hayes, Strosahl, & Wilson, 2016; Linehan, 2021; Gilbert, 2019). Our purpose in highlighting the ubiquity of suffering is not to bathe in despair. It's to help destigmatize the unhappiness that so many clients bring to the clinical encounter, and to reduce the shame that so many feel for life conditions that are no fault of theirs. Instead, we take the position that while we may not create the conditions of our existence or of the culture in which we find ourselves, we are nonetheless endowed with the inner resources to take responsibility for the lives we live. Contributing to that process is the privilege we enjoy as modern Cognitive Behavior Therapists.

In the early years in the development of empirically supported therapies, an effort was made to employ the research paradigm used in medication clinical trials. Hence, specific treatment protocols were created for specific psychiatric syndromes. Thus, Beck developed a protocol for Cognitive Therapy of recurrent major depressive disorder (Beck, Rush, Shaw, & Emery, 1979; Beck et al., 2024), to test the efficacy of his psychotherapy versus medication therapy. Psychiatric diagnosis was key. So was the specificity of the treatment protocol for that disorder. While we don't contest the utility of diagnosis, as an entry point, we believe the field has moved towards a much broader, more accurate, and potentially less stigmatizing perspective on human suffering. We recognize that the efforts to diagnose psychiatric illnesses were intended to destigmatize human suffering, by removing the moral censure and the sense of shame that sufferers experienced. But the medicalization of human suffering has created an immense industry, and has not succeeded in either accounting for, or stemming, the human suffering endemic to our culture. Thus, our efforts at normalizing human suffering take us in another direction.

We will focus on two factors that provide a richer framework for understanding suffering and for normalizing suffering in the context of therapy. These aren't the only factors. But they have generally not been given their due when it comes to understanding and reducing suffering in our culture: Those include:

1. The existential realities of life, as they contribute to human suffering.
2. Understanding the evolutionary mismatch between the environments in which humans evolved, and the environments in which we now live.

EXISTENTIAL REALITIES OF LIFE

Some 2,500 years ago, the Buddha observed, as a young man, that there were inevitable changes that overtake each life: we age, we are prone to illness, we die. He saw that there was no escaping these realities, and vowed to find a way to free human beings of the suffering that these realities could engender. Other spiritual traditions provide guidance in how to deal with these realities as well. The Book of Ecclesiastes, in the Hebrew Bible, teaches that all life is fleeting, and that rather than retreat into meaninglessness in the face of this ever-changing flow of existence, one is wise to throw oneself wholeheartedly into the moment. We point out these traditions not to advocate a religious resolution to life's existential dilemmas, though we respect that as one path our clients may choose, but to highlight the fact that humans have long wrestled with the life challenges that, sooner or later, affect us all, and from which there is no escape.

Here are examples of cases that may appear in your own office.

Case #1: A 33-year-old woman appears for a first appointment. She is with her nine-month-old baby. She starts to cry as she sits in your office, holding her baby on her lap. Looking up at you she says: "I can't believe it. I had childhood leukemia and was cured. Now, my doctor tells me that my heart was so damaged by the chemotherapy all those years ago that if I don't get a heart transplant, I'm going to die. I've been so scared and sad I haven't been able to think straight for the past two weeks."

Case #2: A 54-year-old plumber is referred to you for treatment of depression. He informs you that he is struggling to get his work done, after more than 30 successful years in his profession. He has hip, shoulder, and hand pain, all from arthritis. The effects of aging, and his years of physical labor are also taking a toll on his work performance. He is proud that he has been able to take care of his family all these years, and now fears that he will lose his job. But at the same time, he isn't sure how he can keep up with the physical demands of his work. He feels defeated, ashamed, and humiliated. He has life insurance, and has wondered whether his family would be better off, financially, with him gone. He owns a pistol but gave it to a friend to keep for him, for now.

Case #3: Mrs. Gonzales is a 45-year-old married mother of three adult children. She is from a large extended family. She was particularly close to her mother, who died three months ago. Since then, she has had difficulty sleeping and spontaneously cries for seemingly no reason. At night she sometimes hears her mother's voice calling out to her, which frightens her. She wonders if she is going crazy. But her husband tells her that she needs to get over her grief at the loss of her mother and focus on all the good things in their lives. She wonders if you can help her with her fears of going crazy, and with her depression. She has no prior history of mental health involvement and no history of psychosis or other severe psychological problems.

We don't pretend that these cases are easy to solve or that we have simple answers for them. But they are also not uncommon kinds of presenting problems. In the chapters that follow, we will apply the Eight Organizing Principles to these cases, initially showing how the management of the treatment relationship offers healing potential, through validation, and using acceptance and change strategies. First, though, take a moment to consider how it might provide relief for these clients to have their psychological responses normalized in the context of what we are focusing on: the impact of life's existential realities. At least as a start, we might validate the emotional pain and help each client feel understood and less alone. And we can intervene in ways that help destigmatize their suffering, diminish shame, and foster engagement in a therapy that may focus on two areas: reality acceptance and, at the right time, active problem-solving to deal with that reality as effectively as might be possible. Those areas will be explored further in a subsequent chapter, on balancing acceptance and change strategies, as well as in the cases that comprise Part 2 of this book.

EVOLUTIONARY MISMATCHES

Humans represent one link in the chain of being that extends to the dawn of our planet's history of life. As such, we are subject to the same evolutionary processes that govern other life forms. We are an evolved species, which suggests that it is wise to learn about the environments in which we arose, and the evolutionary pressures and demands that exert effects on our lives today. We live in a world of internet access, hand-held devices, and youth who spend five hours a day on social media (Haidt, 2024). We experience a loss of face-to-face interactions with peers, declining participation in religious and civic organizations, and increased social isolation. Technological change has increased at warp speed over the past 50 years, bringing with it social upheaval to which we struggle to adjust. To be sure, the benefits of our evolved brains and social organizations have provided bounties: food supplies are adequate to feed the planet, if we shared with one another; medical and other technological advances have improved the quality of life for many, such that there has never been a better time to be alive than now. And yet. As we noted, this is a time of deepening uncertainties and unhappiness in our culture. It is little wonder that mental health agencies and psychotherapists have long waiting lists. And the number of therapists well trained in evidence-based therapies is far, far too small to meet the burgeoning needs of those seeking their help.

Perhaps we have not evolved to deal with the world we have created, and in which we now find ourselves. Perhaps we are not the blank slate that some believe we may be, creatures of infinite adaptability, social and psychological plasticity. We may well have evolved for another way of living (Christakis, 2019; Gilbert, 2019; Pinker, 2003; Buss, 2025; Stewart-Williams, 2024). The impact of evolutionary biology and psychology is beginning to work its way into the field of modern Cognitive Behavior Therapy: in Rational Emotive Behavior Therapy (Abrams, 2020), in Cognitive Therapy (Hollon, Andrews, Thomson, 2021), in Compassion-Focused Therapy (Gilbert & Simos, 2022), and in Acceptance and Commitment Therapy (ACT) (Hayes & Hofmann, 2018; Hofmann, Hayes, & Lorscheid, 2021).

This isn't the place to provide a detailed description of either the field of evolutionary psychology, or of basic evolutionary principles. The interested reader is referred to the magisterial text on evolutionary psychology by David Buss (2025), and to a colorful, yet scholarly book by Stewart-Williams (2024). Both address the complex intertwining of evolutionary and cultural pressures that make us who and what we are as a species. We choose to focus on one key area of evolutionary psychology, which is the degree to which our clients' emotional pain may reflect the mismatch between the environments in which humans evolved, and the environments in which we find ourselves today. Gilbert (2019) suggests that this mismatch is "crazy making".

Our purpose in describing the evolutionary mismatch is best served by providing a brief description of the psychological and social mechanisms that evolved in our species tens of thousands of years ago, in another time and another place. That time and place is referred to as the "Environment of Evolutionary Adaptation (EEA)" (Buss, 2025). We can envision it as the savannahs and woodlands in which small groups of our species lived in bands of no more than 150 people. Everyone knew everyone else in the tribe or band. A "social suite" likely characterized these tribes or groups (Christakis, 2019), consisting of:

1. The capacity to have and recognize individual identity
2. Love for partners and offspring
3. Friendship
4. Social networks
5. Cooperation
6. Preference for one's own group (i.e. "in group bias")
7. Mild hierarchy (relative egalitarianism)
8. Social learning and teaching

Let's imagine for a moment what life might have been like under these conditions, as posited by Christakis. Hunters worked together in small groups, traveling as far as necessary to kill animals for their meat. The hunter groups that succeeded tended to display high reciprocity, which in turn fostered social cohesion. The result was the creation of a unit that was best able to flexibly meet the demands of the environment, and that fostered survival. Let's take a hypothetical example: When a hunter bagged an elk, he (and these were usually male hunting groups) did not regard the meat as exclusively his. In a socially cohesive group, he wouldn't consider hiding the meat and saving it only for himself and his family. It was the community's. This reciprocity served to enhance social cohesion. Today's successful hunter might fail the next time. Cooperation and reciprocity fostered the sense that each hunter, and each member of the community knew that the tribal members had one another's backs. A climate of cooperation and mutual trust ensued. Whatever the configuration of family and pair bonding, it was characterized by mutual love between partners, and it fostered loving caregiving of offspring. A high degree of social cooperation was fostered among the larger group. There were, of necessity, hierarchies. But the social hierarchy in effective groups was not characterized by dominance of others, but by reciprocity and a sense of mutuality, fostering in-group loyalty and security. The young played together in small groups, where, in the rough and tumble of play, social rules were established, and reciprocity was fostered. Lifelong friendships were formed beginning in early childhood. Social learning and teaching unfolded as elders and adults in the tribe taught not only relevant life skills, but the rules of the tribe, which were enforced when infractions occurred.

Sound idyllic? Well, perhaps in some ways, compared to the world we inhabit, yes. But it was also a brutal world. If you cut yourself, you could die from an infection. If a tooth cracked while biting into a seed, you were left vulnerable to pain and infection. If you broke a leg? You get the picture. And of course, competing tribes posed the hazard of death from clashes and wars. The dark side of our tribal nature was, and is, the tendency to form not only "in groups", but "out groups." Whether due to competition for resources, or for other reasons, the dark side of our tribal nature fosters at times a need to vilify others, dehumanize them, and to seek to dominate. We are capable of banding together to inflict horrors on members of out-groups that we see as threats, either to our supplies of necessary resources, or to our collective sense of ourselves. That is the stuff of wars, resource wars, religious wars, hatred of "the other".

Yet in these relatively small bands, we evolved psychological mechanisms that were adapted to those groups and to that pace of change. The consequences of departing from this evolved social suite can be damaging, though inevitable, given the pace of technological advancements in our world. These changes, and the fact that we may now be living in a world that is far from our environment of evolutionary adaptation at least partially explain the rise of loneliness and isolation that is rampant in our world. For example, we are in a world where young people spend up to five hours a day on handheld devices and social media. Instead of a social milieu that consists of a small band of friends, in face-to-face interactions, serious reciprocal friendships do not develop the same way on the internet (Haidt, 2024; Twenge, 2023). Young people may fail to learn the relevant social skills necessary for everything from pair bonding to establishing a cohesive identity, to finding a path in the work world. With diminished social cohesion and the erosion of engagement in civic and religious organizations, transmission of culture and knowledge becomes fragmented even further, to the potential detriment of young and old. And of course, when living in huge cities, rather than that 150-person tribe, we risk becoming strangers to one another, leaving us alone, vulnerable, afraid.

The factors producing today's higher rates of unhappiness are likely very complex, and not reducible to smart phones or anything else. Many small inputs can create big effects, leading up to complex psychological and social problems, in a non-linear manner (Layng, Andronis, Codd, & Abdel-Jalil, 2022; Feldman-Barrett, 2021). So we can't say we know precisely why there is such a dramatic increase in unhappiness; but we can posit that there is overall now a mismatch between our evolved natures and the environments in which we now find ourselves.

More than a century ago, the French sociologist Émile Durkheim, explored a concept he termed "anomie" (Lukes, 1972; Durkheim, Riley, Buss, & Sennett, 2007). In periods of rapid social transformation and upheaval, such as we are in today, the bonds holding people together can fray. Societal structures that hold people together include religious affiliations, trades groups, social clubs, civic organizations, political groups, for example. Once these begin to break down, humans tend to lose a sense of both meaning and social connection. These periods of rapid social transformation and upheaval were implicated, for Durkheim, in a personal loss of meaning, purpose, and connection. This, in turn, he found, related to suicidality, which he termed anomic suicide. We may be in such a period of time today, and clinicians who understand this are in a better position to help clients navigate the challenges of our time in ways that restore personal meaning and, hopefully, social connection.

To bring this back to the therapy process, we think it can be destigmatizing to help our clients understand a little bit about their evolved natures. We have evolved brains and behavior patterns that we did not ask for, and which may create dilemmas that are not our fault (Gilbert & Simos, 2022). It's easy, for example, to see the benefits conferred by evolution of having brains that can problem solve, communicate with others, think, reason, and try out problem solutions in the real world. But why, in addition to that, do those very same evolved cognitive and behavioral processes go off the rails? Why are we so prone to buying into conspiracy theories, or tormenting ourselves with rumination and worry? Why do we call ourselves names and berate ourselves to the point that some of us commit suicide for being a "bad me"? It may be that the benefits of our problem solving and communicating and thinking abilities have a dark side, one that is a by product of the primary function of our evolved natures. These by products have been described as "spandrels", a term borrowed from architecture, meaning "traits that weren't specifically favored by natural selection, but came along for the ride with traits that were" (Stewart-Williams, 2024, p. 58).

It's sobering, but potentially freeing, to consider the possibility that our evolved potentials include not only the ability to reason and communicate, but that the by products of those capabilities include a dark side. Misappraisals, cognitive biases, rumination, mental self-torture, may be "spandrels" of the mind, mental and behavioral stuff that goes along for the ride. So next time you catch yourself caught in a mental loop that leads nowhere, consider it just a "spandrel".

Along those lines, while it is not our fault that we are here in this environment, with this set of evolved psychological mechanisms and needs, it is nonetheless our responsibility to manage the conditions in which we find ourselves. In line with Gilbert's work, this perspective can not only destigmatize the emotional pain our clients come to therapy with, it can also help foster self-compassion and compassion for others. All of us are in this together, and the pain of the world today is a pain we all share. And finally, there is a humanistic core to modern CBT, in the sense that our evolved needs for affiliation, connection, meaning, and engagement with the world serve as guides to therapy. We can help people identify and move towards an unfolding of their potential, as they define it for themselves. In that sense, a modern, science-based CBT shares common features with the humanistic movement in psychology: one of helping people unfold their evolved potentials for affiliation, connection, love, compassion, and meaning, all while pursuing their interests in securing necessary resources for living in our society.

Let's consider two cases. We invite you to think about how these cases might reflect that mismatch between the environment of evolutionary adaptation (EEA), or the environment in which our psychological and social selves evolved, and the environment in which we find ourselves today.

Case #4: Jessica is a 16-year-old girl. She spends hours a day on her i-Phone and her computer. She is alone in her room, except when at school. She doesn't interact with her worried parents, except at meals, and for perhaps 10–15 minutes a day. She has little contact with either her older brother or her younger sister, each of whom spend time in their rooms, also on social media. Her world consists of few friends with whom she interacts face-to-face. Instead, she posts to anonymous others online, and checks constantly to see if her doctored photos of herself are "Liked" by peers. When a hostile remark is made about her, she broods, withdraws further, and eases the pain of her loneliness and emptiness by cutting herself. She has already had one psychiatric hospitalization. Her parents, Barbara and Tom, are deeply fearful, and seem unable to reach her. They are at wits' end.

Case #5: John is a 44-year old ex-Army Ranger, who did two tours of duty in Afghanistan. He is now an attorney, working in a prestigious law firm in corporate law. He does not have clear symptoms of PTSD. Yet he reports an ongoing sense of estrangement, irritability, and loneliness in his workplace. He says that he does not trust his partners, and that he does not fit into the culture, despite his intense wish to succeed at the firm. He comes in for therapy at his wife's urging. And he agrees with her assessment that though the marriage is strong, his irritability with work is spilling over into their home life. He cannot figure out what the problem is. By all accounts, he says, he should be happy. But he is not. He frequently thinks about his Ranger days, where everyone had one another's backs, and he knew who to trust. That isn't his experience of the firm in which he now works, and where his family is dependent upon his large and increasing income.

CLINICAL STRATEGIES FOR NORMALIZATION

SAMPLE THERAPY VIGNETTE: (CASE #3, MRS. GONZALES, THE VOICE HEARER OF HER DECEASED MOTHER)

CLIENT: I sometimes think I'm going crazy. My mom comes to me at night. I mean, I don't see her, but I hear her, and she's telling me she's okay and will see me again someday.

THERAPIST: You said it's at night? As in, when at night?

CLIENT: When I'm trying to get to sleep.

THERAPIST: Oh, I see. You know, if I might, there is a lot of research showing that it's rather common for people to hear the voice of a deceased loved one, especially when trying to get to sleep or when awakening. I'm not saying it's actually the person calling them. It's just that it's pretty common for our minds to have such a hard time letting go, that the memories, or voices come to people at those times. The fancy term for this is hypnagogic and hypnopompic imagery. Lots of research that it happens to people, and not an indication of being crazy.

CLIENT: I feel like it's her, though. Can that be?

THERAPIST: I know that in the culture you grew up in, a lot of people have believed that the dead can send messages to us. I personally don't know and have no experience of that. But that, too, isn't crazy.

CLIENT: (Breathes, settles into chair, appearing to be relieved as she reflects on what the therapist said)

CHAPTER SUMMARY

Normalization of suffering is a key principle of modern CBT. We employ this not to dismiss the severity of our client's problems, but to help people recognize that many of the concerns that bring people to therapy are reflections of the human condition. We focused on two sources of suffering that we believe are common in the presenting problems clinicians face these days:

Existential concerns: the problems associated with the inevitables of life, including loss, changes in health status, aging, changes in employment or social status.

Evolutionary mismatches: we are an evolved species, as are all life forms on our planet. As such, we face the challenges of adaptation that are common to other life forms, with an additional twist: we have created a world that differs in many ways from the world of our evolutionary heritage. We may not be evolved to easily deal with the challenges of that changed world; and one source of suffering occurs when we are compelled to deal with forces in our life for which we were not well equipped by evolution to cope with. This factor may be one key explanation for the ever-increasing rates of depression, anxiety, social isolation, and suicide in our modern society.

REFERENCES

Abrams, M. (2020) *The New CBT: Clinical Evolutionary Psychology*. New York: Cognella Academic Publishing.

American Psychological Association. (2025, February 16) New APA Poll: One in Three Americans Feels Lonely Every Week. https://www. psychiatry.org/news-room/news-releases/new-apa-poll-one-in-three-americans-feels-lonely-e#:~:text=Washington%2C%20D.C.%20 2D%20In%20May%202023,superficial%20(46%25)%E2%80%9D% 20relationships.

Beck, A., Rush, A., Shaw, G., & Emery, B. (1979) *Cognitive Therapy of Depression*. New York: Guilford.

Beck, A., Rush, A., et al. (2024) *Cognitive Therapy of Depression* (2nd edn). New York: Guilford.

Buss, D. (2025) *Evolutionary Psychology: The New Science of the Mind* (7th edn). New York: Routledge.

CDC (2023, March 30). *Health Effects of Social Isolation and Loneliness*. https://www.cdc.gov/socialconnectedness/riskfactors/index.html

Christakis, N. (2019) *Blueprint: The Evolutionary Origins of a Good Society*. New York: Little, Brown, Spark.

Durkheim, E., Riley, A., Buss, R. & Sennett, R. (eds.) (2007) *On Suicide*. New York: Penguin Classics.

Feldman-Barrett, L. (2021) *7½ Lessons About the Brain*. New York: Mariner.

Frankl, V. (1986) *The Doctor and the Soul: From Psychotherapy to Logotherapy*. New York: Vintage Books.

Garnett, M.F. & Curtin, S.C. (2025, February 15) *Suicide Mortality in the United States, 2002–2022*. CDC National Center for Health Statistics. https://www.cdc.gov/nchs/products/databriefs/db509.htm

Gilbert, P. (2019) *The Compassionate Mind*. London: Robinson.

Gilbert, P. & Simos, G. (eds.) (2022) *Compassion Focused Therapy: Clinical Practice and Applications*. New York: Routledge.

Haidt, J. (2024) *The Anxious Generation*. New York: Penguin Press.

Hayes, S. & Hofmann, S. (eds.) (2018) *Process-Based CBT: The Science and Core Clinical Competencies of Cognitive Behavior Therapy*. Oakland: Context Press.

Hayes, S., Strosahl, K., & Wilson, K. (2016) *Acceptance & Commitment Therapy: The Process and Practice of Mindful Change*. New York: Guilford Press.

Hofmann, S., Hayes, S., & Lorscheid, D. (2021) *Learning Process-Based Therapy: A Skills Training Manual*. Oakland: Context Press.

Hollon, S., Andrews, P., & Thomson, J. (2021) Cognitive Behavior Therapy for Depression from an Evolutionary Perspective. *Frontiers in Psychiatry*, 12:667592.

Layng, J., Andronis, P., Codd, T., & Abdel-Jalil, A. (2022) *Nonlinear Contingency Analysis: Going Beyond Cognition and Behavior in Clinical Practice*. New York: Routledge.

Linehan, M. (2021) *Building a Life Worth Living: A Memoir*. New York: Random House.

Lukes, S. (1972) *Emile Durkheim: His Life and Work*. New York: Harper & Row.

Lukianoff, G. & Haidt, J. (2019) *The Coddling of the American Mind*. New York: Penguin Press.

Office of the Surgeon General. (2023) Our Epidemic of Loneliness and Isolation: The US Surgeon General's Advisory on the Healing Effects of Social Connection and Community. https://www.hhs.gov/sites/default/files/surgeon-general-social-connection-advisory.pdf

Pinker, S. (2003) *The Blank Slate: The Modern Denial of Human Nature*. New York: Penguin Books.

Putnam, R. (2020) *Bowling Alone: The Collapse and Revival of the American Community* (Revised). New York: Simon & Shuster.

Stewart-Williams, S. (2024) *The Ape that Understood the Universe: How the Mind and Culture Evolve*. Cambridge: Cambridge University Press.

Twenge, J. (2023) *Generations*. New York: Atria Books.

CHAPTER 3

Principle #2: Transdiagnostic Processes

For at least 50 years, the main instrument for viewing human suffering in our culture has been the American Psychiatric Association's Diagnostic and Statistical Manual (2022). We recognize that the DSM-5 remains a starting point for many clinicians and for those who seek their help. Insurance doesn't pay without a diagnosis. Administrators require diagnoses of their clinicians. And much of the public speaks in the language of clinical disorders. We don't contest the historical importance of the medical model. It has served multiple purposes. It destigmatized psychological suffering by taking it from the moral to the medical realm. It led to a focus on evidence. And it spearheaded the proliferation of services for people in need of help. In addition, many of the empirically supported psychotherapies developed in response to psychiatric diagnosis: major depressive disorder, anxiety disorders, and so forth. Each diagnosis spawned separate treatment protocols, as we have discussed in earlier chapters.

But as we noted earlier, there are problems with this approach. First, it's categorical, in the sense that each disorder represents a discrete category of illness. You either have it or you don't. So if your presumed symptom picture otherwise meets criteria for a disorder, but duration is slightly lacking, you don't qualify. Second, the categories contain many combinations of potential symptoms, such that two people with the same diagnosis may have very different clinical pictures. Third, the DSM is based on an assumption, or hope, that the categories represent underlying medical disorders, for which in most cases there is scant evidence. Fourth, the number of diagnostic categories has increased markedly, raising questions about the validity and utility of these categories. Fifth, there is a problem

DOI: 10.4324/9781003505587-4

with co-morbidity. Clients often meet fully or partially the criteria for multiple disorders at the same time, which raises questions about the validity of the diagnoses, and also whether there are underlying factors that might more parsimoniously account for the clinical pictures (Sauer-Zavala & Barlow, 2021). And finally, the number of treatment protocols for each disorder reached the point that no clinician can be expected to learn them all.

But the trail of knowledge didn't stop with the DSM. Neither did the quest for a more thorough understanding of human suffering. As we've discussed earlier, a disease model is not sufficient for explaining the rise in suffering that we see in our world. Neither is the DSM. A full exploration of the frailties and limitations of the DSM is beyond the scope of this book. The DSM's reliability and validity has been questioned, as has its clinical utility. For example, two people can meet criteria for depression, yet have markedly different symptoms, raising the question of whether it is the same disorder. In addition, co-morbidity is so common that it raises questions about whether there are better, more parsimonious, explanatory factors for psychopathology. The factors that are emerging to explain psychopathology are considered transdiagnostic, in the sense that they represent temperamental traits and psychological mechanisms that cut across psychological diagnoses and better explain those clinical problems. In turn, they lend themselves to more targeted and effective treatments. For a more thorough exploration of the limitations of the DSM and the search for transdiagnostic factors, see Hayes & Hofmann (2018) and Sauer-Zavala & Barlow, 2021. The search for transdiagnostic factors began to yield new insights, which in turn, led to new therapies. In contrast to the binary, or categorical, nature of DSM diagnoses, transdiagnostic factors tend to be dimensional, occurring on a continuum. This fits with the normalizing approach we take to human suffering.

The fact is, there are likely hundreds of transdiagnostic processes that affect mental health. Some are well known. But there are others that seem quite distal to the emotional life of humans. For example, neuroscientist Lisa Feldman-Barrett describes "nudges", numerous small forces that add up to significant impacts on our psychophysiology. She describes how small changes in atmospheric CO_2, such as are attributable to global warming, can impact us: "Small changes in carbon dioxide, really small changes, can actually affect how you feel…does that mean that that's the cause of this epidemic (increased anxiety and depression in youth)? No, it's not the cause, but it makes certain things more likely and it nudges the system in a particular direction and not in another" (https://www.feedyourhead.blog/p/your-brain-is-not-for-thinking).

Feldman-Barrett's ideas of the additive effects of many small nudges, dovetails with the work of behavioral psychologist Israel Goldiamond, who describes the effects of non-linear contingencies on human behavior (Layng, Andronis, Codd, & Abdel-Jalil, 2022). We will draw on Goldiamond's work later, in chapter 10, on case conceptualization.

In looking for big, empirically supported nudges, we turn to two areas. One is the tendency of humans to display a variety of cognitive biases. These biases can affect problem identification, problem solving skills, mood, and behavior. The second area gets far less attention: temperament. The one temperamental factor that is frequently identified as an important transdiagnostic factor for mental health is neuroticism, as we have shown. Other temperamental traits have equal empirical support and are emerging as potentially important treatment targets for CBT.

Temperament, in particular, links biological and behavioral genetic domains of experience to the psychological domain. Cognitive and behavioral transdiagnostic processes are the evolved psychological mechanisms that, as we will see, functionally link temperament with the patterns in living that show up in our consulting rooms. Both temperament and the psychological transdiagnostic factors are deeply shaped by the personal, social, and cultural contexts in which we live. Transdiagnostic processes reflect dimensions of experience along which human functioning exists on a continuum. This represents the evolutionary process of variation, with points along the continuum representing adaptations for various challenges faced by the species. And since evolution creates variation in the species, transdiagnostic processes contribute to normalizing this richness of human experience. In addition, by definition, all transdiagnostic processes cut across the lines of specific psychiatric diagnoses or categories. Understanding those processes, rather than just focusing on the categories of presumed illness, not only seems closer to the emerging science, it allows for the development of new, more targeted, and hopefully more effective therapies. People can become caught in rigid patterns of functioning that impair their life development and cause pain. DeYoung and Krueger (2023) put forth a new theory of psychopathology in which "to be considered mentally ill, people must be persistently unable to move toward their important goals, due to failure to generate effective new goals, interpretations or strategies when existing ones prove unsuccessful" (p. 228). This definition of psychopathology comports with newer models of CBT therapy, including our own.

The search for transdiagnostic factors and the creation of attendant therapies are ongoing in the CBT community. Let's take a little deeper look at three of them. Acceptance and Commitment Therapy (ACT) is built on a transdiagnostic perspective that shows up in the ACT Hexaflex. The Hexaflex displays six interlocking, related processes, involving: Acceptance, Self as Context, Present Moment (Mindfulness), Defusion (akin to distancing and decentering in Beck's CBT), Values, and Committed Action. And at the center of the Hexaflex is Psychological Flexibility, the enhancement of which is a central objective of ACT (Hayes, 2020). While ACT can and has been applied to specific psychiatric diagnoses, it is done through the framework of the Hexaflex and psychological flexibility, not with the objective of the removing symptoms of a psychiatric syndrome.

Newer elaborations of the model reflect a joint effort of Steve Hayes, founder of ACT, and Stefan Hofmann, a Beckian-trained CBT researcher. In their search not only for common ground, but common elements that make therapy work, they co-created Process-Based Therapy (PBT) (Hayes & Hofmann, 2018). Shifting from a Hexaflex model to one that employs a "network" analysis, they create a framework that is intended to allow for integration of techniques, around a shared, coherent case conceptualization (Hofmann, Hayes, & Lorscheid, 2021). Online and in-person training are readily available for readers interested in doing a deeper dive into the ACT or PBT models.

A second therapy, transdiagnostic in its understanding of emotional problems and parsimonious in its treatment model, is the Unified Protocol for the Emotional Disorders (Sauer-Zavala & Barlow, 2021; Barlow, Sauer-Zavala, Farchione, et al., 2017). As noted earlier, this protocol targets problems that involve the personality trait of neuroticism, encompassing depression and anxiety disorders, and the management of strong emotions, more broadly, such as bipolar disorder and borderline personality disorder. It is highly parsimonious in its theory, and based on years of research into transdiagnostic factors. Sauer-Zavala & Barlow (2021) posit that:

> In our model, individuals with a trait-like propensity for negative affect (personality), who find these emotional experiences aversive (intermediate dimensional mechanism), engage in behavioral strategies to escape or avoid these experiences (e.g., leaving a feared situation; engaging in nonsuicidal self-injury; DSM disorder symptoms such as checking and worry).
>
> (p. 125)

The Unified Protocol is a single therapy model, which can be flexibly applied for people who meet diagnostic criteria for any of 35 DSM-5 diagnoses. Those disorders share the common feature of difficulties managing strong emotions. The treatment consists of five core components. Those include training people in mindful awareness of emotions. Like other mindfulness-based therapies, this includes non-judgmental awareness while remaining anchored in the present moment (Kabat-Zinn, 2016: Linehan, 2015; Hayes, 2020). Other components include training in identifying and managing problematic automatic thoughts, reducing behavioral and emotion avoidance in the face of emotion-eliciting stimuli. Final components include exposure to internal (interoceptive) and situation cues (exteroceptive) that elicit the problematic emotions, cognitions, and behaviors. Sauer-Zavala, & Barlow (2021) note that their model targets the trait of neuroticism, with the intention of extinguishing features of neuroticism that are problematic. The therapy can be group or individually administered.

There are differences between these two approaches, in terms of theory, case conceptualization, and, potentially, range of applicability. The Unified Protocol was developed for one temperamental trait: neuroticism. And while that encompasses many, perhaps most, of the people who seek mental health help, there are other relevant personality traits, which we will briefly review. Last, the therapies differ at the technique and delivery levels. ACT and PBT are very idiographic in their case conceptualizations and in the range of techniques they draw on. The Unified Protocol, though it can be adapted for individual work, based on an individual case conceptualization, is modular in nature. While this may contribute to ease of delivery and ease of training mental health personnel, it may also limit the flexibility of the model, in our opinion.

We believe our Eight Organizing Principles, as well as our case conceptualization contribute to the effort to identify relevant transdiagnostic processes, to incorporate those processes into a case conceptualization format that applies to most cases that appear in clinical settings. In addition, our model allows for flexible integration of a wide range of therapy techniques. Let's turn to the transdiagnostic factors that we have found most compelling:

COGNITIVE BIASES

The tendency of humans to experience cognitive biases is not the exclusive domain of any specific psychiatric disorder. The common illusion of control, which is the human tendency to believe we have more control over our destinies than warranted, is one example. You don't have to be depressed or manic to experience this bias. We are all potentially subject to this illusion, to varying degrees and at varying times and circumstances in our lives. Similarly, we can all be affected by the tendency to believe what we want to believe, rather than what the facts dictate. This is called the confirmation bias, and it, too, isn't the property of any specific psychiatric disorder. When Beck developed CBT, his observations of patient "thinking errors" were clinically derived, not derived from cognitive science. Yet he was prescient in many ways, as cognitive science has shown that some of the common thinking errors he described in depression and anxiety have been borne out by research. Harvey et al. (2004) concluded that there is strong empirical support for the following transdiagnostic processes that commonly occur in depression and anxiety disorders (Temple, 2017):

1. Selective attention: the tendency for attention to be directed towards specific, concern related outer and inner stimuli and safety resources.
2. Reasoning biases: these include biased interpretations of ambiguous stimuli, biased inferences about causal outcomes in life, various biased interpretations and heuristics, including seeking data that confirm one's pre-existing beliefs (confirmation bias).
3. Memory biases: this involves both explicit selective memory and recurrent memory, as the mind involuntarily selects memory that is biased in the direction of specific concerns, such as loss, diminishment, and threat.

The above biases comport with many of Beck's clinical findings. For example, an anxious person may direct attention to the real or perceived anticipated threat, scanning the inner and outer environment for signs of that threat, and excluding evidence to the contrary. In depression, memory becomes highly selective of painful experiences, which also become more emotionally salient to the person than pleasant or happy memories. This in turn can lead to prediction errors, such as "I'll always be like this. Nothing will ever get better." Other transdiagnostic cognitive and behavioral factors identified by Harvey et al. (2004) include:

4. Rumination and worry, with rumination tending to involve repetitive negative thinking about the past, and anxiety involving repetitive negative thinking about anticipated future threats, as well as intolerance of uncertainty. These processes tend to be experienced as involuntary, and when they dominate thinking they can impair the very problem solving that the client sometimes believes worry solves. Watkins (2018), a co-author in the Harvey et al. (2004) volume, has developed a clinical protocol specifically for repetitive negative thinking.

5. Positive and negative metacognitive beliefs are beliefs about the "operating system" of the mind. This can include the belief that repetitive negative thinking is causing the mind to spin dangerously out of control, or, alternately, that rumination and worry are necessary, functional strategies.
6. The use of avoidance or safety behaviors, which are covert and/or overt behaviors that foster avoidance of internal or external cues that are presumed to be "dangerous". Paradoxically, this avoidance of such cues actually impedes effective problem solving and it prevents new learning that might show the cues are either harmless or tolerable.

Newer work in cognitive sciences and information processing has produced voluminous evidence of many types of commonly occurring cognitive biases or heuristics. The work of psychologist Daniel Kahneman is especially prominent (Kahneman, 2012), and garnered him a Nobel Prize in Economics, for work relating to the field of Behavioral Economics. Recall that we briefly described Kahneman's theory about System 1 and System 2 thinking. System 1 is the rapid, automatic processing that may often be effective. Yet it is prone to certain heuristics, which Kahneman defines as "a simple procedure that helps find adequate, though often imperfect, answers to difficult questions" (p. 98). There are now literally dozens, if not hundreds, of cognitive biases that have been identified. It is important to note that these are not necessarily properties of psychological disorders. They are the way the brain has to make sense, in real time, of complex and uncertain information. Fitting new data into pre-existing patterns often works. Until it doesn't. These heuristics and biases are omnipresent in humans, particularly when the allostatic load, or the emotional burden of stress, runs high. Considering that many people who seek help are stressed, the astute therapist will be familiar with these common cognitive biases and will be prepared to help clients identify them, step back from them, fit the facts to the situations they face, and make better decisions.

Here are a few of the more common and clinically relevant cognitive biases and heuristics.

The Sunk Cost Fallacy: Originally applicable to cost accounting, this bias leads people to keep throwing good money into a lost cause, rather than accept a loss and close out a failing business. However, it applies to many other situations. For example, a person who has a difficult time letting go of a bad job might say, "I can't leave now, because I've put so much into this." Think of how this applies to relationships, as well, especially relationships that are failing and beyond redemption.

Confirmation Bias: We believe what we want, fit the data to our pre-existing belief, and screen out data that disconfirms what we believe. When in the grip of the confirmation bias, a person experiences bias in their search for information, such as only watching news outlets that confirm their beliefs. It can bias our interpretation of information, also, such as interpreting news we dislike in a way that confirms our own beliefs. And finally, our recall can be biased, so as to confirm what we want to believe.

The Availability Heuristic: We tend to make estimates based on immediate retrieval of available information. So for example, despite the fact that murder rates have declined, someone watching the news and seeing stories and images of homicide, is likely to overestimate threat based on the availability of recent information.

The Hindsight Bias: When we look back and see the consequences of our earlier decisions, all the uncertainty of the moment the decision was made disappears. It seems we can now predict, after the fact, how the decision would turn out. Now we know what the right answer was. Unfortunately, not only can we not go back, but if we wallow in that hindsight bias, it's a formula for regret (Leahy, 2022).

Loss Aversion: This was one of the early biases discovered by Kahneman & Tversky (1979). Humans seem more sensitive to loss than to equal gains. The pain of losing is often far greater than the prospect of gaining. Loss aversion can show up in our clinical work when clients have difficulties making decisions involving potential loss. This can occur in work decisions, relationship decisions, any situation in which the prospect of a loss stops someone from moving forward by taking a risk.

Harvard cognitive psychologist Steven Pinker adds more biases, which also show up in clinicians' offices (Pinker, 2021).

Motivated Reasoning: This is similar on the surface to confirmation bias. While confirmation bias tends to be unconscious, motivated reasoning is at least partially, if not completely conscious. It occurs when we actively reject information that clashes with something we want to believe. Pinker writes "the obvious reason that people avoid getting onto a train of reasoning is that they don't like where it takes them. It may terminate in a conclusion that is not in their interest." Sometimes, as Pinker notes, people terminate an entire line of reasoning by brute force (pp. 289–290). Motivated reasoning often shows up in our consulting rooms. How? Anyone ever worked with couples? In addition, people can be motivated to tenaciously hold on to core beliefs, including powerful beliefs about self, in the face of all evidence to the contrary. This is where Guided Discovery comes in handy.

The My-Side Bias: When seeking to understand why smart people believe stupid things, Pinker concludes that smart people can spot biases in others easily. And they can spot biases in their own thinking better than less intelligent people. But if tribal affiliation is invoked, then information is readily accepted when it makes one's own side look good, while putting "the other side" in a bad light. This bias is unfortunately very common in today's cultural and political landscape. It also shows up at the Thanksgiving dinner table, as family members deliberately or inadvertently trip wire the "my side" bias in others, resulting in unpleasant interchanges and memories.

The wise and ethical therapist refrains from engaging in debates with clients. That's why we advocate the use of Guided Discovery and Validation techniques. However, we do have an obligation to help clients spot their biases when failing to do so results in adverse consequences to them, or to those with whom they wish to maintain a relationship. Marsha Linehan rather famously asked of clients who were tightly wedded to harmful beliefs about self, others, and world: "Would you rather be right, or would you rather be effective?" The skilled therapist learns when and how to do this. The client's future adaptive functioning may hinge on their ability to use some of Kahneman's System 2, or deliberate, rational thinking, in order to make life and relationships work.

TEMPERAMENT

The second set of transdiagnostic processes we want to emphasize involves temperament, which is a point at which biology and behavioral genetics can meet CBT. *The American Psychological Association Dictionary of Psychology* defines temperament as "the basic foundation of personality, usually assumed to be biologically determined and present early in life, including such characteristics as energy level, emotional responsiveness, demeanor, mood, response tempo, behavioral inhibition, and willingness to explore" (https://dictionary.apa.org/temperament).

Personality psychologist Dan McAdams describes personality as comprising "the broad dispositional traits that give your performances (as a social actor) their recognizable social and emotional brand" (McAdams, 2018, p. 5). Those dispositional traits are well established in the research literature and are best encapsulated in a theory known as the Five-Factor Theory of personality. The Five-Factor Theory is the most widely used and researched organizing framework of personality in existence (DeYoung & Blaine, 2020). The five traits in this theory are dimensional, meaning that they exist along a continuum, rather than the binary, categorical nature of psychiatric diagnoses. In DSM, you either do or do not have a disorder. In the Five-Factor model, as in many areas of human functioning, traits are manifested along a wide continuum. The five traits most studied are: Neuroticism, Extraversion, Agreeableness, Openness to Experience, and Conscientiousness. This suite of personality traits sets parameters on many areas of our functioning. But the parameters are flexible. McAdams (2018) shows that temperament is subject to a wide range of contextual influences, including culture, life history, and personal choice. The debate about free will is beyond the scope of this chapter, though it continues to be hotly contested (Sapolsky, 2023). We choose to accept the proposition that humans have the capacity for choice, and that choice may be limited by a variety of parameters. These include, but are not limited to, the transdiagnostic elements in this chapter: cognitive blinders and temperament. So while it is true that we humans do not enter the world as a blank slate (Pinker, 2003), free to choose such things as our emotional reactivity to stressors, we do have the latitude to shape our own destinies. The good news is twofold: by understanding the role that temperament plays in our lives, we have the tools to exercise choice about how to work with our temperaments in a way that lets us pursue valued life objectives. It's important to recognize that these temperamental traits are not the sum total of a human personality. We see them as akin to biopsychosocial building blocks, which set the stage for our emotional and interpersonal functioning, as well as our ability and willingness to engage with the world we enter. Their importance shows up in a number of ways. For example, "most people's life satisfaction is highly consistent with their personality traits, even across many years" (Mottus et al., 2024, p. 676). Life satisfaction is especially strongly predicted by emotional stability, extraversion, and conscientiousness. The other end of the continua for these traits predicts unhappiness: feeling misunderstood, unexcited, indecisive, envious, bored, used, unable, and unrewarded (Mottus et al., 2024). The personality traits with which we come into the world matter. So, too, does what we do with them.

As we will briefly describe, the traits that compose temperament are subject to modification over the course of the life cycle (Sauer-Zavala & Barlow, 2021). That modification occurs, for McAdams (2018), as we seek to meet the twin demands of our development, getting along with others, and getting ahead in the world. Or, as psychoanalyst Erik Erikson described it, the adult demands of creating relationships, including intimate relationships, and of forming an identity. That identity involves finding a path towards securing resources, such as a career path that gets the bills paid and contributes to society. The traits that compose our overall temperament frequently bend to accommodate those demands, with such traits as neuroticism declining as we enter adulthood, and other traits, such as conscientiousness increasing. The how and why of that malleability is, as we noted, where biology meets the broader context, including life history, culture, work demands, relationship management, and the capacity for individual choice. Modern CBT can help.

Let's take a look at a broad-brush view of temperament, using the Five-Factor mode. Each factor represents a trait, and each trait exists along a continuum. For example, extraversion is not a binary phenomenon. One isn't either all extravert or its opposite, introvert. Again, we lean a bit or perhaps a lot more in one direction than the other. Yet context counts, as does our own ability to shape temperament based on our selection and accommodation to the contexts of our lives. We'll explore clinical examples as we go. First, let's take a look at what research has shown regarding the five basic temperamental traits that help compose part of our personalities. In addition, further research has identified two aspects for each trait, which will also be briefly described. For this, we draw on the work of psychologist Colin DeYoung, at the University of Minnesota, and others (DeYoung, Quilty, & Peterson, 2007; Widiger et al., 2019; Allen et al., 2019).

Neuroticism: This trait reflects a propensity for negative affect, such as sensitivity to threat and loss of reward. Those higher in neuroticism experience a heightened sense of threat sensitivity. They are often chronically tense, worried, and stressed, and face challenges with a dread of uncertainty. Behaviorally, they lean towards finding safety, even when there is no objective, clear threat, or they withdraw from engaging with situations they fear will lead to humiliation and loss. Their avoidance behaviors can sabotage their efforts to engage productively with others and with their life trajectories, generally. Others scoring high on this trait can become unpredictably volatile, angry, and emotionally dysregulated. They often lack the ability to quickly restore calm, to stabilize, and to behave effectively in an emotionally charged situation. Beck's CBT is built on the assumption, derived from Stoic philosophy, that it is not the events, but our interpretation of events, that determines our response. Those high in the trait of neuroticism react with greater emotional intensity, and with greater distress to a wide range of situations. Their life outcomes, not only in satisfaction, but in health and in mental health are unfortunately compromised. It's important to note that the "Big Five" traits interact with one another, amplifying or moderating the effects of one another at times. For example, neuroticism, extraversion, and conscientiousness exert a moderating influence on one another in ways that predict depression in normal populations (Allen, et al., 2018). A deeper dive by that research team found that aspects of those traits, withdrawal, industriousness, and enthusiasm predicted depression.

While people do not choose their temperament, with the right life experiences, including therapy, they can learn to take responsibility for managing their lives more effectively. That includes dampening the impact of negative affect, while engaging productively in key domains of their lives. As DBT teaches, the purpose of DBT is not suicide prevention or removal of borderline personality, it is having a life worth living (Linehan, 2015). DBT is an example of a therapy that targets the most extreme of those high in neuroticism.

These emotionally driven responses, which high neuroticism individuals do not choose to experience, can become building blocks for depression and anxiety, and the behavioral propensity for withdrawal in the face of either threat or perceived punishment or failure. At its extreme, neuroticism takes the form of extreme emotional volatility, such as seen in borderline personality disorder. Caspi et al. (2014) suggest that high scorers in neuroticism are at risk of emotional disturbances, and that high neuroticism is at the core of most psychiatric disorders. Neuroticism is frequently evident early in life, in the form of irritability and difficult to soothe infants and young children. It is, as noted, a biologically driven trait. At the other end of the continuum (and we emphasize this is a continuum), are those who are generally calmer, composed, stable, secure, and less emotionally reactive. Think Astronaut Neil Armstrong, as his Gemini 8 space craft started a forward roll, which if unchecked, would send the craft spinning out into infinity and certain death. His co-pilot, David Scott, admitted later to being clueless about how to prevent catastrophe. Armstrong, by contrast, knew which thruster was responsible for the forward roll, calmly reached up, turned the offending thruster off, and gently guided the craft back to stability, and to earth, safely. Scott would later say it was his lucky day to have Mr. Neil Armstrong as his pilot. Armstrong's temperament was one among many factors that contributed to his success in an endeavor that would leave most people, us included, quivering in helplessness and fear.

Those higher on the trait of neuroticism tend to experience more intense anxious and/or depressive affects in response to life stimuli. And at more extreme ends of the continuum, to dysregulate quickly and to stay dysregulated for longer. Not the stuff of astronauts. More the stuff of entry into a Dialectical Behavior Therapy program. DBT is one of the therapies most adapted to the trait of neuroticism, at its extreme, in borderline personality. But as we saw, many of the clinical problems that show up in our clinics involve neuroticism. To wit: the Unified Protocol for the Emotional Disorders.

Most people are not at the extreme ends of the spectrum. Instead, most are what is called "bivalent", meaning that we are more in the midrange on neuroticism. And depending upon social context, allostatic loadings for stress, physical illness, we can lean more into calmness or dysregulation depending upon those factors. We aren't all one or the other. And as we adapt to the demands of the world we live in, we temper that trait, reducing the volatility and tendency to withdraw that untrammeled neuroticism can bring. Does that mean that we cease to be sensitive to cues to prompt painful affects? No. But we often do learn to "get our butterflies flying in formation". That's what allows us to form and preserve relationships and to find a path in the world. When those "butterflies" interfere sufficiently with the developmental task of getting along or getting ahead, that becomes the stuff of many of our caseloads. The good news is that with the proper understanding, some self-compassion, and the right tools, we can alter within limits our emotional responses to life stresses and challenges. We may not all be able to become Neil Armstrong, but we can learn to improve our ability to tolerate distress and to counter the tendency to dysregulate or withdraw in the face of those challenges.

The trait of Neuroticism is a complex, multifaceted dimension, incorporating as it does the wide mixture of painful emotions and the behaviors to which they are linked. Although the research on the Five-Factor model is longstanding and voluminous, we draw on the work of Colin DeYoung, a psychology professor and personality researcher at the University of Minnesota, for a framework to understand the Five-Factor model. Clinical applications of the Five-Factor model are most richly detailed in the treatment of neuroticism developed by Sauer-Zavala & Barlow (2021). Let's briefly start with the personality theory DeYoung offers, and we'll pivot to the clinical model linked to this theory that Barlow and his team developed.

DeYoung has developed measures of the Five-Factor model (also known as The Big-Five), which appear at the end of this chapter. Of particular importance here is the work he did parsing the five-factors of temperament into what he calls aspects. He has used factor analytic and other statistical methods to define two aspects for each trait. For neuroticism, he identifies the aspects of "withdrawal" and "emotional volatility". In addition to scoring anywhere on the continuum for overall neuroticism, people score along a continuum on the two aspects of each trait. The aspect of withdrawal maps onto the experiential avoidance characteristic of depression and anxiety. One of the core modules of the Unified Protocol targets these very processes. It is important to note that the Unified Protocol clearly identifies the psychological mechanisms that are functionally linked to neuroticism, producing the impairments for which clients seek help. Those psychological mechanisms map onto the cognitive and behavioral transdiagnostic factors we have already identified in our model, as well. That primarily consists of strong emotional responses to real and perceived threats; a tendency to avoid both emotion arousal and situations that may give rise to threat arousal; a tendency to underestimate one's capacity to manage both emotions and threats. The second aspect DeYoung identifies, besides withdrawal, is emotional volatility. Emotional volatility is the tendency to become defensively angry and to dysregulate rapidly in the face of real and perceived threats or losses. This, too, is targeted by a module of the Unified Protocol. It is also a key target of Dialectical Behavior Therapy.

Importantly, this trait, neuroticism, is the primary focus of many of our psychotherapies, and for good reason. As noted, high neuroticism accounts for a big chunk of the clients we see in our clinics. Well-regulated people, those on the lower end of the neuroticism spectrum, don't need the skills provided in DBT, for example. Two other points, for now: first, neuroticism exerts an amplifying effect on some of the other traits. Those who tend to withdraw and/or become emotionally volatile may also struggle with conscientiousness, and they may become more interpersonally disagreeable. This creates a spiral of dysfunction, affecting multiple life domains: relationships, work, educational attainment, among others. Second, we emphasize that one's level of neuroticism is not chosen. It is a biological given, amplified by the social contexts of one's life, and by one's behavioral repertoire. It's not our fault. Recognizing this helps destigmatize temperament. At the same time, the continuum of emotional responding serves evolutionarily adaptive functions. Those early humans who were prone to negative affect were more likely to scan the environment for threats, and perhaps less likely to be eaten by saber-tooth tigers. Those low in neuroticism imparted a sense of stability and calm to the group. Linehan's DBT understands this, as do other CBT therapies. At the same time, it must be noted that neuroticism is not destiny. It's not completely immutable. As McAdams (2018) demonstrates, neuroticism tends to decline as we face the demands of life. Our contexts pull for more effective behavior. We learn to do what works. That said, those higher in neuroticism may experience a greater burden of stress in the face of life challenges. While they may learn to manage those challenges effectively, they can pay a price for the heightened allostatic load, which is the cumulative effect, physically and emotionally, of exposure to stress. Therapists who understand these processes can help clients learn to tolerate stress more effectively, and to build in practices that reduce the allostatic load and allow for regeneration.

Let's take a look at the four remaining traits of the Big-Five factors. These will be broad-brush descriptions of the factors. The literature on personality traits is rich, complex, and evolving. The interactions of traits are also complex, including their intertwinement with life circumstances. What follows is just a brief introduction. This chapter is not the place for a deeper dive, though the interested reader is encouraged to do further reading (Clark & Watson, 2022; Clark, Ro, Vittengi, & Jarrett, 2024; Allen et al., 2018; DeYoung & Blaine, 2020 Little, 2017; Sauer-Zavala & Barlow, 2021).

Extraversion: The first psychologist to study and define the trait of extraversion was actually the famous Swiss psychiatrist, Carl Jung. The Five-Factor Model, however, defines extraversion in a way that is different from the popularized notions of Jung's. Where neuroticism is one's tendency towards experiencing what we commonly consider negative emotions (fear, rage, sadness, dread), extraversion is our propensity for experiencing the more positive emotions. Such emotions tend to foster approach behaviors. Extraversion tends to include a big embrace of life and its possibilities. The two aspects of extraversion are labeled Enthusiasm and Assertiveness. Those scoring lower on these dimensions may be more reserved, pensive, and less willing to embrace or take on leadership roles. A more introverted person, especially if also burdened by higher neuroticism, would not be likely to thrive in a sales position, for example, especially one requiring frequent cold calls, with its attendant likelihood of rejection. The assertiveness of an extravert may lead them to embrace leadership positions, while an introvert might prefer to hang back from such challenges. Once again, these traits are not fatalistic and inevitable destinies of ours. An introvert whose only prospect of a job is sales may well learn to do what's necessary to support themself and a family. The skilled clinician will recognize that people higher in introversion, especially when fueled by neuroticism, may need strategies in place to manage the allostatic burden of the stress associated with behaving somewhat out of character (quiet time in the woods, meditation, massages, etc.). This may be especially true if introversion is amplified by neuroticism. That combination of high neuroticism (emotion sensitivity + experiential avoidance + low sense of ability to manage threat) and introversion (tendency towards withdrawal) is also a risk factor for depression (Sauer-Zavala & Barlow, 2021).

Agreeableness: Agreeableness and its polar twin, disagreeableness, each contain benefits and potential problems at the extremes. Agreeable people are "nice". They may be nurturing, trusting, and kind in their dealings with others. But they can be too nice, in the sense that they avoid conflict and are ill equipped to face and deal directly with problems, especially interpersonal problems (Burns, 2010). Disagreeable people tend to be more blunt, dominant, and stubborn in their dealings with others. At their worst, they can be vindictive, cruel, and willfully harmful to others. Those high on trait Disagreeableness are overrepresented in prisons. The two aspects of agreeableness that have been identified in studies are compassion and politeness. It is possible to be higher on one or the other. For example, consider a compassionate person, whose compassion extends to a marginalized group, and who scores lower on politeness, such that he or she is willing to take on powers that be. Being overly polite may work against one's ability to stand up for oneself appropriately. Yet polite people, also high in compassion, can be interpersonal magnets for others.

Therapies such as Dialectical Behavior Therapy may target also improvements in the trait of Agreeableness, by helping people develop theory of mind, improved empathy, and an improved ability to trust and cooperate with others (DeYoung, personal communication). Skills such as the DBT interpersonal effectiveness skill of DEAR MAN may improve agreeableness. At present, there are not strong data supporting the efficacy of CBT specifically for agreeableness, though as noted above, it appears to be a logical choice.

Conscientiousness: Conscientious people get the job done, and they often do it with meticulous attention to detail. They are able to make plans and carry them out in an organized manner (DeYoung & Blaine, 2020). They are dutiful, and they do not put off until tomorrow what they see needing to be done today. They are able to delay gratification, in the service of obtaining long term goals. Of the Big Five, Conscientiousness is typically the best predictor of positive occupational, academic, and health outcomes (DeYoung & Blaine, 2020). Conscientiousness predicts better occupational outcomes, social and interpersonal outcomes, and better health outcomes (Javaras, Williams, & Baskin-Sommers, 2019). Across cultures, these are people who do well academically and in careers, especially if they also are highly intelligent. Carried to an extreme, there can be an obsessional need for order and precision that is both off-putting to others and renders them ineffective. Highly conscientious people are often made anxious by failure and can be subject to a sense of guilt, shame and despair when their life projects fail. The two aspects of conscientiousness that have been identified are industriousness and orderliness. Industrious people are dutiful and get the jobs done in a timely manner. Orderly people believe that everything has a place, and they may brook no deviation. Interestingly, political conservatives tend to be higher on trait aspect orderliness than are liberals. While being orderly has an important place, too much can constrain creativity, which when combined with openness to experience and high intelligence, it can give us a Mozart. But creativity can also be messy and disorderly at various stages.

Those lacking in trait conscientiousness may be at risk of academic, career, and health problems. Low conscientiousness poses risks for substance use disorders and antisocial behavior (Krueger et al., 2007; Sauer-Zavala & Barlow, 2021). Studies suggest that conscientiousness can be improved by interventions aimed at improving organization, freedom from distraction, and delaying gratification (Roberts et al., 2017; Javaras, et al., 2019).

Openness: Those high in openness to experience tend to be creative, bright, and even potentially visionary. However, at the extremes, openness can correlate with psychotic experiences, and diffuse identity formation. At best, those high in openness become constant learners, who hate being stuck in careers that require routinization and repetition. Openness to experience correlates with political liberalism, much as conscientiousness correlates more with conservatives. The two aspects identified for this trait are intellect and aesthetics. Little work has been done or even conceptualized in altering this trait. It is not clear how modifiable it would be, in any case. A therapy such as Radically Open Dialectical Behavior Therapy (RO-DBT) (Lynch, 2018) has been developed for disorders characterized by overcontrol. And while it would superficially appear to target openness to experience, it focuses more on improving trait agreeableness and reducing the impact of neuroticism. Those lower in openness prefer predictability, and routine, and when combined with orderliness, from trait conscientiousness, are content to plow the same field over and over. Those high in openness may struggle to define a self, and to maintain a focus for long enough to achieve at the level of their capabilities. This is particularly true for those high in openness, who are also high in trait neuroticism, and lower in conscientiousness. Remember, just as there is a continuum, a broad spectrum, for each trait, so, too does each trait confer strengths and potential weaknesses on the individual. For now, one can either admire or vilify the visionaries who are often at the forefront of revolutionary changes, or the Mozarts, Mahlers, Margaret Atwoods, and poets in our midst. They tend to be high in both aspects of Openness, Intellect and aesthetics.

The two sets of transdiagnostic factors we explored in this chapter are not intended to paint a complete picture of a human personality. They do, however, convey important information about the people seeking our help. And they point towards potential therapy options and targets. We see the two factors as intertwined. People who are temperamentally inclined to view the future and its attendant uncertainties as threats will likely be more prone to a particular set of cognitive, emotion, and memory biases, as well as behavior patterns. Those who embrace the future as filled with interesting challenges may be prone to others. And rather than seeing ourselves as victims of either our cognitive biases or our temperaments, we see humans as co-creators of the realities we live in. Our temperaments set parameters for various types of emotion processing, engagement with others, and with the world. Our cognitive templates are both shaped by and help shape the realities of our lives. Rather than being inevitable victims of either biology or social factors, our temperaments and the nature of our cognitive processing help us shape the environments with which we engage and are in turn shaped by. Not only are we affected by environmental contingencies, but our temperament and cognitive biases help prepare us to "select" our environments, creating a self-reinforcing pattern of functioning.

To the degree that we can learn more about these and other transdiagnostic factors, we can increase our potential for freedom. If we can learn to step back from the waterfall of thought, emotion, and environmental contingencies, just for a moment, our opportunity for choice, and to shape our destinies, increases. That is one of the key tasks of therapy.

CHAPTER SUMMARY

This chapter explores two key transdiagnostic factors implicated in contemporary human suffering. We believe a search for transdiagnostic factors is important, given the frailties of the more medicalized perspective on human suffering that has largely defined our field since its inception. The factors we chose are: 1) evolutionary factors, including the mismatch between the environments in which we evolved, and the environments we now live in; and 2) human temperament. We briefly reviewed some of the evolutionary psychology literature, including a description of the environments in which we likely evolved as a species, and the disconnect between the demands of those environments and the current contexts we live in. We also reviewed temperament, chiefly focusing on the Big-Five Personality Theory, including its five temperamental factors, and the further refinement of that theory into subfactors. The utility of these two domains was demonstrated in case examples, including sample transcripts of therapy sessions.

REFERENCES

Allen, T., Carey, B., McBride, C., Bagby, R., DeYoung, C., & Quilty, L. (2018) Big Five Aspects of Personality Interact to Predict Depression, *Journal of Personality*, 86, 714–725.

Allen, T., DeYoung, C., Bagby, R., Pollock, B,. & Quilty, L. (2019) A Hierarchical Integration of Normal and Abnormal Personality Dimensions: Structure and Predictive Validity of Heterogeneous Sample of Psychiatric Outpatients. *Assessment*, 27, 643–656.

Barlow, D., Sauer-Zavala, S., Farchione, T. et al. (2017) *Unified Protocol for Transdiagnostic Treatment of Emotional Disorders: Workbook* (2nd edn). Oxford: Oxford University Press.

Burns, D. (2010) *When Panic Attacks: The New, Drug-Free Anxiety Therapy That Can Change Your Life*. New York: Harmony Books.

Caspi, A., et al. (2014) The P Factor: One General Psychopathology Factor in the Structure of Psychiatric Disorders? *Clinical Psychological Science*, 2, 119–137.

Clark, L., & Watson, D. (2022) The Trait Model of the DSM-5 Alternative Model of Personality Disorder (AMPD): A Structural Review. *Personality Disorders: Theory, Research, and Treatment*, 13, 4, 328–336.

Clark, L., Ro, E., Vittengi, J., & Jarrett, R. (2024) Longitudinal Prediction of Psychosocial Functioning Outcomes: Diagnostic and Statistical Manual of Mental Disorders, 5th Edition, Section-II Personality Disorders Versus Alternative Model Personality Dysfunction and Traits. *Personality Disorders: Theory, Research, and Treatment*. Advance online publication. https://dx.doi.org/10.1037/per0000673.

DeYoung, C., Quilty, L., & Peterson, J. (2007) Between Facets and Domains: 10 Aspects of the Big Five. *Journal of Personality and Social Psychology*, 93, 5, 880–896.

DeYoung, C. & Blain, S. (2020) Personality and Neuroscience. In P.J. Corr & G. Matthews (eds.), *The Cambridge Handbook of Personality Psychology* (2nd edn; pp. 273–291). New York: Cambridge University Press.

DeYoung, C. & Krueger, R. (2023) A Cybernetic Perspective on the Nature of Psychopathology: Transcending Conceptions of Mental Illness as Statistical Deviance and Brain Disease. *Journal of Psychopathology and Clinical Science*, 132, 3, 228–237.

Diagnostic and Statistical Manual of Mental Disorders (DSM-5), 5th edn (2022) Washington, DC: American Psychiatric Association.

Hayes, S. (2020) *A Liberated Mind: How to Pivot Toward What Matters*. New York: Avery.

Hayes, S. & Hofmann, S. (eds.) (2018) *Process-based CBT: The Science and Core Clinical Competencies of Cognitive Behavioral Therapy*. Oakland, CA: Context Pres18.

Harvey, A., Watkins, E., Mansell, W., & Shafran, R. (2004) *Cognitive Behavioral Processes Across Psychological Disorders*. Oxford: Oxford University Press.

Hofmann, S., Hayes, S., & Lorscheid, D. (2021) *Learning Process-Based Therapy: A Skills Manual*. Oakland, CA: Context Press.

Javaras, K., Williams, M., & Baskin-Sommers, A. (2019) Psychological Interventions Potentially Useful for Increasing Conscientiousness. *Personality Disorders: Theory, Research, and Treatment*, 10, 1, 13–24.

Kabat-Zinn, J. (2016) *Mindfulness for Beginners: Reclaiming the Present Moment and Your Life*. Boulder, CO: Sounds True.

Kahneman, D. (2012) *Thinking Fast and Slow*. New York: Farrar, Straus, & Giroux.

Kahneman, D., & Tversky, A. (1979) Prospect Theory: An Analysis of Decision Under Risk. *Econometrica*, 47, 263–291.

Krueger, R., Markon, K., Patrick, C., Benning, S., & Kramer, M. (2007) Linking antisocial behavior, substance use, and personality: an integrative quantitative model of the adult externalizing spectrum. *Journal of Abnormal Psychology*. 116: 645–666.

Layng, J., Andronis, T., Codd, R., & Abdel-Jalil, A. (2022) *Nonlinear Contingency Analysis: Going Beyond Cognition and Behavior in Clinical Practice*. New York: Routledge Press.

Leahy, R. (2022) *If Only: Finding Freedom From Regret*. New York: Guilford Press.

Linehan, M. (2015) *DBT Skills Training Manual* (2nd edn). New York: Guilford Press.

Little, B. (2017) *Who Are You, Really?* New York: Simon & Schuster.

Lynch, T.R. (2018) *Radically Open Dialectical Behavior Therapy: Theory and Practice for Treating Disorders of Overcontrol*. Oakland, CA: New Harbinger Publications.

McAdams, D. (2018) *The Art and Science of Personality Development*. New York: Guilford Press.

Mottus, R., Realo, A., Jüri, A., Liisi, H., McCrae, S, & Vainik, U. (2024) Most People's Life Satisfaction Matches Their Personality Traits: True Correlations in Multitrait, Multrater, Multisample Data. *Journal of Personality and Social Psychology*, 126 (4), April, 676–693.

Pinker, S. (2003) *The Blank Slate*. New York: Penguin Books.

Pinker, S. (2021) *Rationality: What It Is, Why It Seems Scarce, Why It Matters*. New York: Viking Press.

Roberts, B., Luo, J., Briley, D., Chow, P., Sui, R., & Hill, P. (2017) A Systematic Review of Personality Trait Change Through Intervention. *Psychological Bulletin*, 143, 2, 117–141.

Sapolsky, R. (2023) *Determined: A Science of Life Without Free Will*. New York: Penguin Press.

Sauer-Zavala, S., & Barlow, D. (2021) *Neuroticism: A New Framework for Emotional Disorders and Their Treatment*. New York: Guilford Press.

Temple, S. (2017) *Brief Cognitive Behavior Therapy for Cancer Patients: Revisioning the CBT Paradigm*. New York: Routledge Press.

Watkins, E. (2018) *Rumination-focused Cognitive-Behavioral Therapy for Depression*. New York: Guilford Press.

Widiger, T., et al. (2019) Personality in a Hierarchical Model of Psychopathology. *Clinical Psychological Science*, 7, 1, 77–92.

CHAPTER 4

Principle #3: A Focus on Client Strengths and Values

Before CBT, there was William James. In fact, before most of American psychology there was William James. His work is important here for two reasons. First, we think James would have appreciated CBT's relentless focus on creating an evidence-based psychotherapy. That includes evidence that CBT is effective as a treatment, and evidence that its theories are grounded in science. That said, James also knew that there were some beliefs that couldn't be tested. Only the effects of those beliefs could be observed when lived and acted upon in the world. The next idea we present from modern CBT comes from Marsha Linehan, and her notion that all people have wisdom. If it can't be tested experimentally, to either validate or invalidate that belief, perhaps there's another way of testing it: its utility as an assumption. Back to James.

In James' famous lecture "The Will to Believe" (James, 1896; 1992), he states that the truth of a proposition is not always contingent upon prior evidence. Sometimes we act as though something is true, even when it cannot be proven empirically.

So here's the question: Do all people possess hidden reserves of wisdom? Do humans possess self-actualizing capabilities and inner resources that can be brought to bear on managing or solving the problems they bring to therapy? Take a moment to reflect on these questions and see what comes up for you.

We encourage a "yes" to these propositions. And we encourage therapists to adopt the assumption that within everyone there is the capacity for wisdom and strength in the face of the adversity and challenges that life sometimes gives us. Is that a provable hypothesis? Is there a "brain circuit" that lights up when we access wisdom inside an fMRI machine? Not exactly. But as clinicians and clinical scientists, we can observe what

DOI: 10.4324/9781003505587-5

happens when we assume that clients have within themselves such. And perhaps more to the point, we can see what happens when we help clients access those inner reserves in therapy. Rather than treat our clients as helpless victims, or passive spectators of life, we offer an "anti fragile" option, one that empowers clients to collaborate as active agents in moving their lives forward.

STRENGTHS

A focus on mobilizing reserves of strength in the service of change was a key feature of the early family therapy movement (Boszormenyi-Nagy & Krasner, 1986; Walsh, 2016; Lindblad-Goldberg, Dore, & Stern, 1998; Speck & Attneave, 1974). It is also central in the humanistic psychology movement, which fosters the idea that self-healing and self-actualizing properties are an inherent part of the human experience (Rogers, 2004; Bugental, 1992; Frankl, 2006 Maslow, 2014).

Within the field of CBT, Padesky and Mooney (2012) describe a four-stage model that includes strengths in the case formulation and the treatment protocol. Their focus is less on relieving distress than it is on building resiliency. Bennett-Levy et al. (2015) also include a focus on strengths in their manual on self-practice, using CBT. Acceptance and Commitment Therapy (ACT) fosters a resource mobilization approach in their emphasis on client values (Hayes et al., 2016 Dahl et al., 2009).

Marsha Linehan coined the term "Wise Mind" to reflect the belief that all people have wisdom, though it is often obscured by the heat of emotions, by powerful, but destructive, action urges, by flawed problem-solving strategies, or by willfulness or despair. She encourages therapists to not "fragilize" clients, by which she means treating clients as though they cannot possibly face their painful inner experiences and life histories or learn the skills necessary to live a life that matters. However well intended the therapist, no favor is done clients by viewing them as too fragile to collaborate in improving their lives. We think that conveying that faith in client strengths helps invoke strength in our clients. Take a moment to try a little exercise:

Think back to a time in your life when you felt demoralized or defeated. Maybe you suffered a setback or an unexpected loss or failure. Take a moment to remember the sting of that experience, where you felt it in your body, what thoughts came up. Now consider if there was someone there, someone important in your life, who conveyed a complete belief in your ability to deal with this setback. We hope there was such a person. If not, take a moment to imagine someone kind and wise, coming to you in that moment to not only soothe you, but to convey that belief in you. What emotions do you feel? Where in your body do you feel those emotions? What thoughts come up? What state of being do you notice?

We hope you can connect with that deep sense of being validated by another. Because it's what we seek to provide our demoralized clients. It's not a trick. It stems from a deep faith in the inner strength and potential within each of us. If you aren't so sure, try acting as though this is true for a while. See what happens. Somewhere, inside the most painful life story you can find examples of strength shown in the face of adversity. Helping clients connect to those strengths is a core of our approach to CBT. But there are challenges.

It's common for clients coming in for therapy to have what the narrative therapist Michael White (Epston & White, 1991) called "problem-saturated" narratives, or stories about themselves. ACT therapists use the term "conceptualized self" to describe a process in which one's sense of self becomes fused with a problematic story (Hayes et al., 2016). In addition, we know that memory is altered by depression, such that it is easier to retrieve painful memories, which become more salient to the client than are the pleasant ones. For clients with long histories of adaptive difficulties, compounded by, or intertwined with, emotion and behavior regulation problems, there may truly be a long string of painful and humiliating defeats. Clients may come in without being able to remember or identify strengths and resources with which they addressed prior challenges. We'll show you how, using Guided Discovery, we can help clients identify the strategies and skills they employed to manage previous challenges. This serves to both deepen the therapy relationship, by conveying to clients our trust in their ability to change their lives, and to counter demoralization.

Here are some examples of what we mean by strengths and resources. Oftentimes, these strengths and resources occur in non-problem areas, and can be brought to bear on addressing the problems for which the client seeks therapy:

1. Times when the client displayed effective problem-solving skills
2. Indications of times when the client was able to regulate strong emotions and emotionally driven urges, in order to achieve objectives that required acting opposite to the urges
3. The ability to display conscientiousness.
4. Displays of interpersonal caring and compassion
5. Displays of moral reasoning and moral actions
6. The ability to reach out for emotional support and/or problem-solving help from others

Here are some examples of the kinds of questions we might weave into our session, to both elicit and highlight such strengths.

"When you were suicidal, what kept you going? Something led you to reach out to your friend, right? What do you think that was?"

"You're describing your life as a total failure. Yet I'm also hearing you talk about managing the family's finances during this tough time, and keeping food on the table and lights on in the house. What does that say about you?"

"I have to tell you, I'm impressed by something you just said: as depressed and hopeless as you were that night, you said you looked over at your little girl, saw that her diapers were dirty, and then you hugged her and changed her. Is there a message inside that act?"

"Can you walk me through the process you went through, that led to your decision to finally end that destructive relationship?"

The bicycle story: Most clients learned in childhood how to ride a bike. As adults that seems like no big deal. But we can use a guided imagery process to remind them, assuming they learned to ride, how this connects to their strengths: "Remember when you first saw other kids riding bikes, and you thought "how will I ever learn to do that"? You got on, maybe first with training wheels, and you started moving. Maybe you fell the first time or two, or even more. But something inside you said "keep going". And you did. Until finally, you rode on your own. What if the challenges you face today are like that?

A FOCUS ON CLIENT VALUES AND GOALS

The first author (ST) helped develop a psychiatric inpatient program for suicidal and self-injurious teenagers. In group after group, when asked what they wanted their lives to be about, these demoralized, despondent, angry young people commonly said similar things. They wanted their lives to involve taking care of others in some way. Some wanted to become nurses or doctors. A surprising number wanted to become veterinarians, or at least work in a veterinary practice, where they could extend take care of animals. And yet, many of these young people were struggling to stay safe, to remain in high school, to get passing grades, to get along with adults (especially their parents), and to regulate their mood, attention, and behavior. They were heading in exactly the wrong direction, just the opposite of the direction they deeply wished their lives were going.

Harnessing client values helps turn the therapy towards what matters in a client's life, whether that involves the management of one particular situation in the present, or the long-term challenge of becoming a veterinarian. This represents a turning point in our thinking about CBT. We believe that older models of CBT tended to focus on the removal of presumed psychiatric syndromes. This was a necessary focus, given the demands for funding clinical research. Depression, anxiety disorders, personality disorders, psychotic disorder, all were subject to treatment in clinical trials, using manualized protocols. In contrast, we join with newer efforts, by focusing on building new repertoires that aim to improve quality of life. We don't just organize therapy around removal of symptoms. Values work is a major doorway into this change in focus. A focus on meaning and values has long been prominent in psychotherapy (Frankl, 2006). We believe that therapies that target symptom or syndrome removal miss a golden opportunity to help clients live richer and more engaged lives. A number of CBT therapies now focus increasingly on values as a compass for therapy. DBT emphasizes a life worth living. Once suicidality and self-injurious behavior are no longer treatment targets, the therapy can begin a focus on quality-of-life concerns. Layng, Andronis, Codd, and Abdel-Jalil (2022) build on psychologist Israel Goldiamond's work. Rather than focusing therapy on the removal of problematic patterns of behavior, they focus on building new patterns that essentially take the client where they want their lives to go. Acceptance and Commitment Therapy also emphasizes values. Hayes describes values as freely chosen, verbally constructed processes that serve as guideposts for organizing and directing behavior. A technical term used is "motivative augmental", from Relational Frame Theory (Hayes et al., 2001). This refers to the way that a focus on values can strengthen and increase the effort to bring one's behavior in line with the intended direction of therapy. The purpose isn't to turn those young people on the first author's inpatient unit into veterinarians, though a few might do that. It's to get people focused and moving towards valued directions in life. In chapter 10, we will provide a case conceptualization format that accomplishes this.

Values versus Goals: Values are not the same as goals, however (Hayes et al., 2016). Let's go back to those young people in the Iowa inpatient unit. If the value, or what they really want to stand for in life, is caretaking, or being kind, that can be done now. One needn't be a veterinarian to live in alignment with that value. One can drop breadcrumbs in the back yard for neighborhood birds; or pick up one's clothing and put it in the basket, so other family members won't have to do the work; or simply pet the dog. The opportunity to live one's values are actually endless, and can be scaled up or down, depending upon the circumstances. Even someone confined to a wheelchair, in a nursing home (to go to the other end of the developmental spectrum) can pick up a phone and offer encouragement to a friend, thus living the value of "giving".

Goals, however, are different from values. You'll notice that values don't have endpoints. As ACT creator Steve Hayes notes, they are like "going east". One never finally arrives at "east". One can always move toward the direction. A goal has an endpoint. And as important as goals are in therapy, values can help determine the goals. As an example, for the young people who want to be vets, a good goal is being able to finish homework, attend class, graduate from high school, find alternatives to self-injury, etc. And along the road of their lives, they may discover that they don't want to be vets. But they can still honor their value of "giving to others". The goals mentioned above, once accomplished, can serve these young people well, no matter what educational or career path they eventually take.

Values can provide the direction. Goals can point to the steps one takes as one "walks East" towards those cherished values. Knowing how to work with clients around both their values and the goals we set in therapy is vital. As we describe in chapter 5, behavioral repertoires must be practiced enough to be robustly accessed in all relevant life contexts. Values can energize the therapy and help set a course, serving as those "motivative augmentals" that Relational Frame Theory posits. We teach clients to keep those values in mind for a number of reasons. One of those reasons is that life is challenging, and the ability to sustain and build life skills requires real courage, persistence, and discipline. There are no shortcuts.

Once you identify a list of problems that become treatment targets, you can begin to explore the following. These kinds of questions can help:

1. How has the client tried solving or managing this problem?
2. What seems to be maintaining the problem? What are the cognitive, emotional, behavioral, and contextual features that maintain the problem?
3. If it appears likely that the problem will require acting opposite to the barriers that maintain it, explore what's in it for the client to do the work. The latter is often entailed with client values. For example, if a client has social anxiety, yet wants to be able to meet people, the client will be required to tolerate the anxiety and eventually put him or herself into social situations, to practice the skill of engaging with people. Values come in to play when we simply ask what's in it for the client to do this work? Oftentimes, we'll hear heartfelt desires to "be connected", to find partners, to show up for a family member's wedding

anniversary, and so forth. The goals can then be established in a step-wise fashion, depending upon the willingness and tolerance of the client to engage in the exposure work. A client who comes in saying "I want to find someone to marry", but can't approach anyone for a conversation, has some preliminary work to do, some skills to build and some anxiety to learn to tolerate, practiced in many situations, all in the service of creating relationships that matter to the client.

CLINICAL EXAMPLE

Christina is a 36-year-old Hispanic female, living in LA. She is divorced from her alcoholic, abusive ex-husband, and lives with her mother and her two children, ages 13 and 10. She has an associate's degree from a California community college but hasn't worked since her marriage ended. She is depressed. She is conflicted about her desire to return to the work force, while also caring for her two children. She feels guilty about living with her mother and being financially supported by her. She wants to become independent, which first means finding a job, while collaborating with her mother to provide after school childcare, cooking, and home maintenance activities when Christina returns to work. Christina is scared that no one will hire her. If she does get a job, she fears being a bad mother for not being home when her children return from school. But she also fears that she will be a bad mother if she doesn't become a role model of female independence. Dealing with her depression is a treatment target, including her depressive self-appraisals of being a failure. Returning to work is also something she wants to focus on in therapy.

THERAPY SESSION VIGNETTE: FOCUSING ON CLIENT STRENGTHS VIA COGNITIVE INTERVENTIONS

CLIENT: I don't seem to be able to do anything right.

THERAPIST: (Focusing on negative self-appraisal and lack of focus on strengths) Would you be willing to take a look at that with me?

CLIENT: Yes. How?

THERAPIST: Well, you're saying you don't do anything right. May I ask something? (Client nods). How does that idea fit the following facts? You finally stood up to your ex-husband, after years of violence and alcoholism. You left. You ensured that your children were safe and remain safe. You worked with your mother to arrange for you and the kids to stay with her for now.

Your kids are in school. You help them with their homework and you help
do housework, to take as much of the burden off your mom as you can.
And you're ready to start exploring re-entry into the work force. Did I
miss anything?

CLIENT: (smiles). No. I guess not.

THERAPIST: What do those facts say about you?

CLIENT: That I'm a survivor. That I don't tolerate danger to my kids. But still, I just
feel like a failure so often.

THERAPIST: I get that. Sometimes, old thoughts and feelings linger and take some time
to work with. We'll get there. How about in the meantime we keep in mind
some of those strengths you show. Those are a big part of who you are, too.

CLIENT: (Nods). Yeah. They are. I lose sight of that sometimes.

A focus on client strengths in the above vignette utilized primarily
cognitive interventions, helping the client cast a wider beam of light on
her sense of herself, seeing a fuller picture of who she is. We will see in
future chapters how we can work with strengths in other ways: behaviorally, through guided imagery, and self-process work, for example.

Now, let's briefly take a look at how client values can be brought to the
fore in this case, as a means of setting a course for therapy and boosting
motivation to do the hard work of change. In this case, change means
effectively mobilizing the client's social network, to provide care for children while she works. It also means doing the scary work of applying for
jobs, interviewing as well as possible, and, hopefully, dealing with the
everyday demands of the workplace, while also juggling responsibilities as
a mother and daughter.

CLIENT: I'm scared to even think about applying for jobs. My resume has big gaps
in it. I don't have up-to-date computer skills. I'm afraid that any employer
I'm interested in will just laugh at me.

THERAPIST: You just had a look on your face that made me wonder if you were pictur-
ing being laughed at.

CLIENT: Yes. I can see it in my mind's eye. And it just stops me cold.

THERAPIST: Yes. Pictures in the mind can be frightening. And I get that when it pops
into awareness it stops you in your tracks. So what keeps you from just
giving up the struggle to get back into the work world?

CLIENT: (settles back in her chair and thinks). That's a great question. I guess a
couple of things. First, I need the money. And second, I just want to get
back to work. But I'm scared. Scared I'll fail. Scared no one will hire me,
except for a crappy job. Even that would worry me.

THERAPIST: If we set a course towards getting a good job, I get that you'll have to face down some fear. It's like, you'll most likely be scared AND go through all the steps it takes to get a job. So what's really in it for you to do that scary work? Money is one thing, you said. But that's only one reason.

CLIENT: I want my kids to see that if you work hard and have courage, you can succeed. I want them to be proud of their mom and draw strength from her courage and her example, like I do my mom.

THERAPIST: So you want to be a role model for your kids. You want to be a kind of lamp lighter for them, showing them the way to be a grown up in this world?

CLIENT: (sits up in chair, looks at therapist). Yes. I want my kids to be proud of their mom, and to draw strength from her example.

THERAPIST: So if it takes walking with some fear to be that, would it be worth it?

CLIENT: Yes. Yes. It would. I've handled scary things before. This is just one more.

THERAPIST: So, as we go forward in our work, which includes helping you get back into the workforce, how about we keep in mind what all this is really about. Yes, the money will help. And, at heart, this is about something that really matters to you. Being that mom you're here in this world to be.

When the work of therapy becomes tough, and scary, and demanding, a course has now been set. That key value can be referenced as a means of dignifying the work and helping the client stay motivated to face her fears, while doing what she must, to get back into the workforce. Both values and her strengths will be resources in facing this challenge.

CHAPTER SUMMARY

We focused on the Organizing Principle of Strengths and Values in this chapter. The case example demonstrates how we can highlight and bring to the fore the client's inner strengths and resources. They can be brought to bear on meeting the challenges the client faces in therapy. In addition to inner strengths, resources available in the client's social network can also be highlighted and worked with. Finally, we focused on helping clients identify the deep values that can guide their lives in tough times. As the case example hopefully demonstrates, values can help set a course for therapy. And values can also be sources of motivation during the challenging process of change.

REFERENCES

Bennett-Levy, J., Thwaites, R., et al. (2015) *Experiencing CBT from the Inside Out: A Self Practice/Self Reflection Workbook for Therapists.* New York: Guilford Press.

Boszormenyi-Nagy, I. & Krasner, B. (1986) *Between Give and Take.* New York: Brunner/Mazel.

Bugental, J. (1992) *The Art of the Psychotherapist.* New York: W.W. Norton & Company.

Dahl, J., Plumb, J.C., Stewart, I., & Lundgren, T. (2009) *The Art and Science of Valuing in Psychotherapy.* Oakland: New Harbinger.

Epston, D., & White, M. (1991) *Narrative Means to Therapeutic Ends.* New York: W.W. Norton.

Frankl, V. (2006) *Man's Search for Meaning.* New York: Beacon Press.

Hayes, S., Barnes-Holmes, D., & Roche, B. (eds.) (2001) *Relational Frame Theory: A Post-Skinnerian Account of Human Language and Cognition.* New York: Springer.

Hayes, S., Strosahl, K., & Wilson, K. (2016) *Acceptance and Commitment Therapy: The Process and Practice of Mindful Change* (2nd edn). New York: Guilford Press.

James, W. (1896; 1992) The Will to Believe. From *William James: Writings (1878–1899).* New York: Library of America.

Layng, J., Andronis, T., Codd, R., & Abdel-Jalil, A. (2022) *Nonlinear Contingency Analysis: Going Beyond Cognition and Behavior in Clinical Practice.* New York: Routledge Press.

Lindblad-Goldberg, M., Dore, M., & Stern, L. (1998) *Creating Competence from Chaos: A Comprehensive Guide to Home-Based Services.* New York: W.W. Norton & Company.

Maslow, A. (2014) *Toward a Psychology of Being.* New York: Sublime Books.

Padesky, C., & Mooney, K. (2012) Strength-based Cognitive Behavior Therapy: A Four-Step Model to Build Resilience. *Clinical Psychology & Psychotherapy,* July/August, 19 (4), 283–290.

Rogers, C. (2004) *On Becoming a Person: A Therapist's View of Psychotherapy.* New York: Constable.

Speck, R. & Attneave, C. (1974) *Family Networks.* New York: Vintage Books.

Walsh, F. (2016) *Strengthening Family Resilience* (3rd edn). New York: Guilford.

CHAPTER 5

Principle #4: The Use of Guided Discovery and Validation Strategies in Fostering the Treatment Relationship

The balance of acceptance and change has already been described as a central feature of our version of modern Cognitive Behavior Therapy. That need for balancing acceptance and change extends into understanding and managing the therapeutic relationship (Norcross & Lambert, 2013; Temple, 2017). We will highlight two strategies that offer the therapist a toolkit for enhancing the therapy relationship and for creating a matrix for therapeutic change: *Guided Discovery*, employed in Beckian CBT, and Dialectical Behavior Therapy's (DBT) *Validation Strategies* (Beck, Rush, Shaw, Emery, DeRubeis & Hollon 1979; 2024; Waltman, Codd, McFarr, & Moore, 2020; Linehan, 1997; Temple, 2017).

We have already noted in an earlier chapter a common misconception about CBT: the idea that it is a mechanical, rigid therapy, applied in too-cold a manner to suit the tastes of the humanistically inclined. In our view, that is not what good CBT looks or feels like. Whether it is Aaron "Tim" Beck, Steve Hayes, Marsha Linehan, or other CBT treatment developers, the humanistic core of the models is absolutely prominent. It's not uncommon in CBT manuals to find that Carl Rogers is referenced. Marsha Linehan described Rogers as her hero, which may surprise people who see DBT as rigid and directive. Good therapy is a balancing act between compassionate listening and equally compassionate advocacy for change. And the bedrock of good Cognitive Behavior Therapy, as with other therapies, is the person of the therapist interacting with the person of the client. What we propose is to integrate Guided Discovery/Socratic Questioning and Validation Strategies in a way that can be incorporated into the person of the therapist, without being manipulative, tricky, or

DOI: 10.4324/9781003505587-6

mechanical. It is a tribute to the genius of Beck and Linehan that they found a way to create a technology of both Guided Discovery/Socratic Questions and Validation, without sacrificing the humanistic core of the work. We turn to that technology now.

GUIDED DISCOVERY AND SOCRATIC QUESTIONING

"Do I only ask questions when I'm doing CBT?" No. But it's a good place to start. Maintaining a gentle, questioning style serves multiple purposes. First, it helps elicit relevant clinical information, including the client's stream of images, thoughts, physical sensations, and emotions. Those provide some of the data necessary first to formulate a case, then to intervene in ways that effect change. Second, staying in what Beck called "questioning mode" fosters collaboration, and diminishes the likelihood of the therapist lecturing the client or leaning too hard into persuading a client what they think, should think, or what they should do. Kennerley notes that the use of this method ensures that we are focused on "guiding discovery, not changing minds" (Kennerley, 2020). Again, this doesn't mean that there isn't a place for therapists to quite actively engage, even at times being directive. Guided Discovery is a method that increases the likelihood that our clients feel understood, respected, and brought on board in the process of self-understanding and change.

Beginning and intermediate CBT therapists often struggle to figure out *which* of the plethora of presenting situations, cognitions, emotions, and behaviors to target. When Beckians target "hot cognitions". they mean those that are the most emotionally powerful and resonant, the ones connected to key situations that are implicated in the client's problems. Here's a way to think about this: the first author once fished with a wise trout guide, who understood that most casts into a trout stream are wasted effort. Trout congregate in richly oxygenated water, or in deeper pools. To find the trout, he said, "follow the bubbles in the stream". The bubbles in the stream of therapy are those that are linked to emotion (Temple, 2017).

There are several excellent frameworks for thinking about Guided Discovery and Socratic Questioning (GD/SQ). We review three in this chapter.

Wills (2015) provides the following sequence, one that summarizes the entire process of GD/SQ:

1. Accessing information about current problems and maintaining factors, of which the client may be unaware
2. Reflecting back what we have heard, in order to insure our accurate understanding

3. Summarizing the material we have gathered in session
4. Synthesizing and helping generate new alternatives for thinking, experiencing, and acting

Waltman et al. (2020) also describe a four-step framework for Socratic Questioning that begins with helping the therapist see the client's life from the client's perspective, before focusing on expanding that perspective together.

The first step involves *focusing*. In this step the therapist selects a target focus for inquiry. That target focus is often cognitive, yet it can also involve emotions or behavior. Since Beck's CBT primarily addressed problematic cognition, we will focus on Guided Discovery and Socratic Questions to illuminate cognitive processes implicated in clinical problems. Humans have an endless array of internal experiences, some of which relate more directly than others to the problems that are the object of therapy. The therapist must hone the skill of selecting the most emotionally salient or "hot" cognitions for a focus.

The second step is referred to as *phenomenological understanding*. As you will see, this dovetails with key validation strategies in Dialectical Behavior Therapy (DBT), in the sense that the therapist must understand the hidden logic of the client's predicament. We accept the principle, also articulated in DBT, that clients are doing the best they can (though they must be encouraged to work harder, in order to change their lives for the better). In that sense, we validate the logic of the client's interpretations of their circumstances, and their coping strategies. By learning to do this step properly, client's feel understood, and the stage is more readily set for taking a look at how those strategies are "working" for the client. This step often includes the therapist making brief summaries of what they have heard the client say, in addition to wondering about what the client may not have said. The therapist helps elicit a clear view of the client's inner life, and how that plays out in their problem situations, cognitively, emotionally, and in behavior.

Step three involves fostering *collaborative curiosity*. We are asking ourselves "what is the client not seeing here" that is maintaining the problem? Sometimes this is tricky, because client blind spots, when challenged, can spark resistance, due to feeling misunderstood or due to a premature effort by the therapist to effect change. So the focus is on mutual curiosity, rather than telling the client what they are not seeing or understanding about themselves. For example, a client who blames external factors, including others, for painful life problems may not see their own contributions to these problems. A depressed client may be focusing on personal failings to the exclusion of noticing the many strengths, the relationships, the successes being displayed in their daily life. By helping the client become curious, and by gently guiding the client to explore, we can test a variety of hypotheses together. It is important in this step for the therapist to not assume she knows precisely what is maintaining the client's problems. Instead of having iron clad convictions about that, we encourage therapists to notice what their hunches are, and to test them collaboratively, with the client. Like the other steps, this step requires considerable patience and tact. In the process of engaging in mutual curiosity, the client is encouraged to widen the lens of their thinking, to explore alternative possibilities for viewing and dealing with the problems and challenges that brought them to therapy. In addition, therapists may also wonder aloud about alternative possibilities, ones that the client perhaps has not considered. Again, these are offered as hypotheses to be evaluated, not ironclad certainties imposed by the therapist on the client.

The final step, or step four, is creating a *summary and synthesis*. In this step, after having explored a variety of hypotheses, or an array of evidence, the therapist guides the client to consider whether an initial assumption or a newer assumption serves the client's interests best. We aren't striving to find the "objective truth" about a client's life here. We're not attempting to get people to think "true" thoughts or "happy" thoughts. Instead, we focus on a realistic appraisal of a problem situation, and an outcome that will allow for a more functional engagement by the client in managing their life challenges.

For example, the client who is repeatedly losing jobs after blowing up at bosses, may come to see that they have a role in their job difficulties. And if the therapist has done her work properly, the client may understand a hidden logic in their anger, for example they can take a careful look at the thought: "I don't like being told what to do." Yet if the client wants to keep their job, they may conclude that despite a sensitivity to being controlled or told by others what to do, it is in their interests to figure out how to deal with bosses differently. Now you have a clear agreement with the client about their dilemma and can collaborate in practicing some new strategies for managing life in the workplace.

Kennerley (2020) and Padesky & Kennerley (2023) also offer a four-step process of Guided Discovery. Notice here the emphasis not just on intervening, but on listening:

1. Asking informational questions, whether about factual information, or about the meanings.
2. Empathic listening, which is similar to Waltman et al.'s emphasis on phenomenological understanding. The therapist tunes in to client language, adopts that language at times, listens for meaning, and for

unarticulated experiences of the client, i.e. things not said. Here the therapist is formulating hypotheses, using their knowledge of the science of psychology and psychotherapy, and of case formulation. Those hypotheses are tested in session before moving to the next step.

3. Summaries: as Waltman et al. describe, this step is where the therapist shares what she has heard, using the client's language, making sure that her understanding comports with the client's experience. This sets the stage for both collaboration and for change.

4. Analytical/Synthesizing questions: Like Watman et al., this is where the therapist has the opportunity to foster a new perspective with the client. "How might we check the facts on this?" "What would be another way of looking at this?" "If this were your best friend, what would you tell her?" "Now that we look at the experiment we did for last week's homework, what would you say you learned from this?" Those are all examples of such questions.

We will provide case examples and sample transcripts later in the chapter, to show you how to put these ideas into practice. As you'll see, we don't *just* ask questions. We seek to skillfully weave in questions, summaries, psychoeducation, alternative ways of thinking, and strategies for trying out new ways of thinking and behaving.

VALIDATION STRATEGIES

Validation strategies were developed by Linehan in an effort to address the extreme emotion dysregulation of borderline personality disorder (Linehan, 1993). Based on the principle that before seeking to change a client, the therapist must convey understanding, these strategies help calm, settle, and regulate, thus opening a door for both self-understanding and change. As noted earlier, one of Linehan's "heroes" was Carl Rogers, and she took the most heartfelt, compassionate qualities of Rogers' work and created a technology of validation (Linehan, 1997). Importantly, the technology works best when it is not treated as a technology, but as a way of being. When validation strategies are implemented effectively, clients not only experience the sense that they are understood, but also that their own puzzling emotions begin to make sense to them. This alone is psychophysiologically calming, thus making it more probable that the door will open to consider alternative ways of thinking and behaving. Kelly Koerner (2011) wrote, "When you validate, accurately and with precision, you not only reduce arousal but also trigger competing responses" (p. 116).

Temple (2017, p. 55) notes that:

> A therapist who uses DBT validation strategies and Guided Discovery in a disciplined, targeted manner, may help down-regulate painful emotions and reduce emotional and psychophysiological reactivity, in session. This, in turn, promotes the therapy relationship and aids in cueing more adaptive emotions and responses to distress. Emotion regulation is related to and is facilitated by interpersonal validation. Laboratory studies, by Shenk & Fruzetti (2011), demonstrate that validating and invalidating responses in experimental conditions are related to heightened and sustained reactivity involving negative affect and increased heart rate and skin conductance in non-clinical samples.

The effective use of validation strategies involves walking a dialectical tightrope, between acceptance and change, which is at the heart of Dialectical Behavior Therapy. That dialectic can be employed to good effect in virtually any form of therapy, certainly any form of CBT. This involves learning how to validate the person, though not necessarily the problematic patterns of thinking and behaving the client brings to therapy. Instead, the therapist uses these strategies to help the client feel accepted, while understanding the hidden logic of even their most maladaptive patterns of behaving. When delivered in tandem with Guided Discovery/ Socratic Questioning, the client more readily collaborates in creating alternative patterns of thinking and behaving.

Linehan describes six levels of validation:

Level 1: Listening with full attention. This level, along with Level 6 validation, should be present at all times in every session.

Level 2: Acknowledging that one has heard the patient, through one's words, gestures, and posture. This involves showing the client, behaviorally, that we are listening fully. That may involve leaning in as the client speaks, nodding our heads, or providing verbal signals to show that we are fully present and attentive.

Level 3: Giving voice to the thoughts, emotions, urges, or behavior patterns that the patient has not yet verbalized. This level of validation involves substantial intuition as well as an understanding of the kinds of experiences common to certain kinds of clinical problems. For example, clients with a history of sexual abuse may experience shame and avoidance but may find it hard to put those experiences into words. Similarly, a client whose friend committed suicide may convey great anger at the friend, but not be able to put into words their grief. The therapist may bring forth that grief, for therapeutic work, by wondering aloud if, in addition to anger, the client might also feel sadness and loss.

Level 4: Validating current emotions, thoughts, and behavior in terms of their historical causes. All behavior has causes. And helping clients understand that even the most problematic of behaviors may make sense in light of the historical causes of those tricky emotions, thoughts, or behaviors.

Level 5: Validates thoughts, urges, emotions, and behavior as valid in the current context. So, for example, a client who is disconnected from their own anger, or who self-invalidates their own anger, may be helped to recognize that their anger is valid in the context of a current abusive relationship.

Level 6: Radical Genuineness validates and affirms the person, his or her worth as a human being, without regard to the emotions, thought, or behavior patterns that the person brings to therapy.

The astute reader and therapist will already notice the many areas of overlap between these two methodologies, GD/SQ and Validation. Mindful listening, at every moment in each session, paired with genuineness, are common elements of both. The "reflecting" and "summarizing" elements of GD/SQ are isomorphic with DBT Level 2 Validation. And these reflecting and summarizing functions can be amplified by the validation levels that help clients recognize the logic of their thoughts, emotions, and behaviors, in the light of both their histories and their current life contexts.

Another common element in the two technologies is when to depart from being in questioning mode, to step more into "change" mode. DBT validates the person and the logic of even their most problematic of cognitions, emotions, and behaviors. But it does not validate patterns of functioning that are "invalid". which means patterns that contribute to, or maintain, the problems. So, for example, while a client's anger may be valid in both the context of their life history and a current situation, acting on that anger by punching one's boss is not likely to be a behavior the therapist will validate. Thus, it is possible simultaneously to validate the person, while invalidating a behavior. In both GD/SQ and validation, we set the stage for the client to experience themselves as fully understood first, thus setting the stage for a consideration of alternatives going forward. We provide psychoeducation, and we explain the reasons, where indicated, for the procedures and skills that will be required to help the client change. And Radical Genuineness sets the stage for not only acceptance of the client, but for the therapist's need to say things the client may need to hear and understand. In the words of the novel about the psycho-analyst Frieda Fromm-Reichman, *I Never Promised You a Rose Garden*, we promise our best efforts at understanding the client, while also recognizing that the process of change can be challenging and at times difficult. Change often requires courage, persistence, and the ability to tolerate distress, even the occasional thorns of life. The fortunate client knows that they have a trusty ally, coach, and guide with them for the journey.

CLINICAL APPLICATIONS

Let's use the case of John, the 44-year old ex-Army Ranger, to explore Guided Discovery. We will present this case in greater detail in Part 2 of the book.

You will recall that John did two tours of duty in Afghanistan, and is now an attorney, working in a prestigious law firm in corporate law. He is struggling at work because he does not trust his partners, and that he does not fit into the culture, despite his intense wish to succeed at the firm. He is irritable, and confused about how to deal with his emotions and his role at the firm.

Guided Discovery/Socratic Questions:

1. Accessing information about current problems and maintaining factors, of which the client may be unaware.
2. Reflecting back what we have heard, in order to insure our accurate understanding.
3. Summarizing the material we have gathered in session.
4. Synthesizing and helping generate new alternatives for thinking, experiencing, and acting.

Here is an example of how to use Guided Discovery to elicit facts as well as information about maintaining factors.

THERAPIST: Can you tell me about the last time you got really angry at work?

CLIENT: Yeah. I was in a partner's meeting. It was my first meeting since becoming a full partner. We were talking about opening a new office in central Jersey. I was tasked with leading this effort, and when it came time for discussion no one said one effin' thing. They were all just looking down at their shoes, like they didn't want to be involved. And I'm out there riding point, all alone.

THERAPIST: What went through your mind and your body right then?

CLIENT: Rage. Just rage. And some fear. Like I'm all alone here.

THERAPIST: Different from what you experienced in combat, right? (A reflecting question, leading up to a synthesizing question later.)

CLIENT: Oh yeah. When I led the platoon, we were in synch. Totally. We had each other's backs 100%.

THERAPIST: (Summarizing questions) OK. So it sounds from what you're saying that maybe you can handle big responsibilities, if the team shows up with you? If they don't, you feel maybe, what, betrayed, isolated, alone? And that leaves you both angry and scared? And you dealt with it by remaining silent, until you got home. Then you got angry with your wife, drank too much scotch, and fell asleep on the couch? Did I get it right?

CLIENT: (Looking into therapist's eyes and nodding slowly). Yes. You got that right, as in spot on. I hate how I handled it. My wife is golden. She doesn't deserve to be on the receiving end of my rage.

THERAPIST: (Synthesizing and generating alternatives). So in a way, it feels like being in combat, but without a band of brothers, or sisters, as the case may be in your law firm. I'm guessing that when you led a platoon, people followed orders and you were all together. But it doesn't work like that in the law firm. So it makes a kind of sense that in this situation, you feel hung out to dry. Alone. And since you can't just give orders, and you don't want to take it out on your wife, or your liver (client laughs), maybe we can find some other ways to deal with this situation. Especially since you want to remain at the firm, right?

CLIENT: 100%. Let's do that. I think you get the picture.

Now if we think about how validation fits in, notice that the therapist in the above vignette ties the current situation in with a prior time in the client's life, his combat experience. And the therapist speculates about some things that perhaps the client hasn't voiced in session. Level 3 validation encourages the therapist to be ever on the alert for the unspoken. Level 4 validates in the context of the client's history. Level 5 validates in the context of the present. Both of these levels can be validated in this case., as in the follwing example.

THERAPIST: You're a combat veteran. Not just that. You were a leader in combat, an officer. And you had a close-knit unit from everything you told me. You lived in a self-contained world where everyone had everyone else's back. You all knew you could trust each other. In fact, you'd die for one another. And if anyone fell in combat, you'd die trying to get them back to safety, right?

CLIENT: Yeah. And that's the one thing I miss. Not killing or hurting anyone. But that sense of trust. That bond.

THERAPIST: And that's not like the law firm. So it makes sense that in this situation, which in some ways feels a little like, maybe not combat, but leading a charge to take a hill for the firm, you feel left all alone. In that way, don't your emotions, your anger, and fear make sense?

Now, we've added Levels 4 and 5 of validation, to create a more seamless, integrated picture of the client's dilemma. This ensures that the client feels completely understood and validated in this situation, while we are also setting the stage for finding alternatives for handling the dilemma.

One might also add in some psychoeducation, as a means of normalizing the client's distress in this situation and deepening the use of Level 4 and 5 Validation.

THERAPIST: You know, we humans evolved long, long ago in small bands, or tribal groups. Kind of like your platoon. We hunted together. We stood watch for each other in the night, while our families slept. We sang songs around campfires, since fire was probably discovered almost 1.5 million years ago. We knew who had our backs, and who didn't. Those who didn't have other people's backs probably got booted from the tribe. So even though it was a primitive time, not one where I'd want to live today, especially if I broke a leg, it was a time where we all knew one another in the group, and we worked together. It sounds like that's different from how big law firms work today. I think what you experienced in Afghanistan was like dropping back into our tribal heritage, the world we evolved in, around those campfires. We have a deep need for that kind of bonding. But it's hard to find in the world now. Maybe in some ways we're in a world that we weren't evolved for. In this world we live in, it sometimes doesn't feel safe. But if we understand all this, we can find some ways to navigate this world, as is now. We can find some ways that will let you stay close to the wife you love, while also staying grounded in the law firm. Shall we find some ways to do that together?

CLIENT: Wow. I never thought of it like that. But it makes sense. It makes a lot of sense. Yes. Let's do that.

MANAGING THERAPEUTIC RUPTURES WITH REPAIRS

Marsha Linehan observed that "all therapists are jerks". She didn't mean that therapists are irretrievably doomed to fail or harm their clients. Rather, it was her provocative way of stating an essential truth: despite our best efforts as therapists and as human beings, we're going to fail sometimes. That includes failing to fully understand or to properly validate our clients. We also select techniques that don't work for a particular client in a particular moment. Or we home in on a problem less central to the immediate needs of the moment. There are many ways that therapy can fail. And when that happens, therapy can hit rupture points, which can potentially lead to a premature and unpleasant termination of therapy, or an opportunity to renew and deepen the therapy relationship. Long ago, the British pediatrician and psychoanalyst Donald Winnicott reminded both parents and therapists that we needn't be perfect, we just need to be "good enough" to meet the needs of those in our care. Part of being a "good enough" therapist is to be alert to failures in validation and technique, and to do our best to repair those moments when we fail. Safran and Segal (1990) provide an early guide to the role of interpersonal processes and therapeutic repairs in Cognitive Behavior Therapy. The first step in managing ruptures in the alliance is to recognize one when it occurs, and to non-defensively address it.

We offer the following principles:

1. By sticking closely to the use of GD/SQ and Validation strategies, we minimize the likelihood of ruptures.
2. The use of summaries, as we demonstrated above, is one way to make sure that our understanding matches the experience and intentions of the client.
3. When a summary is met by an objection or correction by the client, we embrace that correction and welcome it.
4. When an effort to validate falls flat, we notice that, tactfully bring that awareness into the therapy session, and encourage the client to collaborate in repairing the breach.
5. When the therapist suggests an avenue for change and the client is not on board, rather than push our agenda, we explore the client's response, maintaining a sense of collaborative curiosity. We can then modify or titrate our intervention to match the client's needs and their willingness to change.
6. As we will focus on in later chapters, we help clients change relevant behaviors in all important contexts of their lives. This is the reason that CBT employs "homework" assignments. When a client doesn't do the homework, rather than punish the client, we try to learn what got in the way. Sometimes, we discover that we are the reason the homework didn't get done, either because it was too big a task for the client, or the wrong task, or the rationale wasn't properly explained. We own our part, and encourage the client to consider they can't fail, even though therapy might fail.

Here's a therapy vignette to illustrate the management of therapy ruptures. Let's go back to the case, above, John.

THERAPIST: I'm wondering if you've considered that perhaps you are overly sensitive to the opinions and behavior of partners. Might that have been what happened in the meeting you're talking about? (Here the therapist departs from being in questioning mode, gathering information, and exploring options, and instead is experienced by the client as opinionated and directive in ways that anger the client. In sum, the therapist is inadvertently proving Linehan's point!)

CLIENT: You're saying that it's my failing? It's all on me?

THERAPIST: Oh my. Can we take a step back for a moment? I sense that I made you angry and wasn't at all helpful here.

CLIENT: That stung me. For God's sake, I'm in charge of a major project, and my colleagues are twiddling their thumbs, leaving me riding point alone.

THERAPIST: And what I said felt like I was one of them. Sometimes I miss the mark. I was hoping that I might help you find some ways of dealing with this situation a little differently, so you protect your relationship with your wife and keep your job at the firm.

CLIENT: Yes, I felt attacked in that moment. And yes, you put your finger on what I want help with. We're back on track.

It's important not to become overly apologetic or defensive. Just stick with the unpleasant facts, which sometimes point to therapist failings in session. We will focus more on how this plays out in therapy, particularly in Part 2 of the book, when we talk about creating effective homework assignments.

CHAPTER SUMMARY

This chapter focused on developing a conceptual and practical took kit for managing the therapeutic relationship. We began by exploring Guided Discovery and Socratic Questioning (GD/SQ), which was first developed by Beck, for use in Cognitive Therapy. Then we explored ways in which Validation Strategies, pioneered by Marsha Linehan, in Dialectical Behavior Therapy (DBT), can be combined to good effect with GD/SQ. Finally, we briefly explored the management of breaks, or ruptures, in the therapy relationship.

REFERENCES

Beck, A., Rush, A., Shaw, B., Emery, G., DeRubeis, R., & Hollon, S. (2024) *Cognitive Therapy of Depression* (2nd edn). New York: Guilford.

Kennerley, H. (2020) *The ABC of CBT*. London: Sage.

Koerner, K. (2011) *Doing Dialectical Behavior Therapy: A Practical Guide*. New York: Guilford.

Linehan, M. (1993) *Cognitive Behavior Therapy for Borderline Personality Disorder*. New York: Guilford.

Linehan, M. (1997) Validation and Psychotherapy. In *Empathy Reconsidered: New Directions in Psychotherapy* (A. Bohart & L. Greenberg, eds.). Washington, DC: American Psychological Association.

Norcross. J. & Lambert, M. (2013) Evidence-based Therapy Relationships. In *Psychotherapy Relationships that Work: Evidence-Based Responsiveness* (2nd edn), 3–21 (J. Norcross, ed.). Oxford: Oxford University Press.

Padesky. C. & Kennerley, H. (eds.) (2023) *Dialogues for Discovery: Improving Psychotherapy's Effectiveness*. Oxford: Oxford University Press.

Safran, J. & Segal, Z. (1990) *Interpersonal Processes in Cognitive Therapy*. New York: Basic Books.

Temple, S. (2017) *Brief Cognitive Behavior Therapy for Cancer Patients: Re-Visioning the CBT Paradigm*. New York: Routledge.

Waltman, S., Codd, R.T., McFarr, L., & Moore, B. (2020) *Socratic Questioning for Therapists and Counselors*. New York: Routledge.

Wills, F. (2015) *Skills in Cognitive Behavior Therapy* (2nd edn). London: Sage.

CHAPTER 6

Principle #5: Balancing Acceptance, Mindfulness, and Change Processes

In our earlier discussion of normalizing suffering, we focused on the process of Acceptance. Acceptance is a stance, or a posture, an experience. It is a lightening up in the face of a reality that we may not wish for. It isn't resignation and it isn't passive. It's just a willingness to let reality be what it is, without getting caught in judgments and without all the emotional turmoil of fighting that reality.

We can't "will" acceptance. And there aren't easy techniques to make it happen. It is an experience that can be invited and fostered. Acceptance can't be made to show up in therapy rooms through the use of any specific technique. And unlike the more behavioral techniques to which we will turn later, fostering acceptance is not a technology. It is an invitation to begin a process. Willfulness, the opposite of Willingness, is effortful and can be exhausting (May, 1982). Saying "NO" to reality wears one out and stokes pain. It also, paradoxically, blocks effective and flexible problem solving. As Marsha Linehan was fond of saying, you can't change reality if you don't accept it in the first place. That reality includes not only our life histories, the external events in our lives, it includes everything that goes on in our skins: thoughts, images, emotions, body sensations, memories. Some of that stuff is painful. Pushing it away seems to just increase the pain. Does this mean we're asking clients to wallow in pain? Certainly not.

Marsha Linehan has said that one cannot change a problem without first accepting that it's there in the first place. She taught Radical Acceptance, deep down, all the way, in mind and in action, as a process that we could not force, but could commit to nonetheless (Linehan, 2015).

Here's an example: the first author has tinnitis. Once, while taking a ride in the country with his wife, we passed a thickly wooded area, with a stream behind it. It was summer. The woods were abuzz with sound.

DOI: 10.4324/9781003505587-7

Crickets, and thousands of cicadas chirped wildly. I pulled over, turned off the engine, and said "This is what I hear in my head 24/7. It never stops."

When it started, it drove me literally crazy. I could not stand the sound, believed it would ruin my ability to take pleasure in life, and sought every avenue to make it stop. I went to ENTs and audiologists. There were no cures. Well, actually, it turns out there is one, just not the one I originally wanted. The cure, if it can be called that, is what Linehan notes as Radical Acceptance, a deep down commitment to wholeheartedly accepting reality as it is, and working with it effectively. And that means letting the sound be there, without fighting or judging it. It doesn't mean liking it or being glad for the benefits it brings. Although now that I write this, I realize that tinnitus did, in fact, bring me a benefit: it taught me something about acceptance. I learned to just let the sound be there, without fighting it. And I learned to just shift my attention to the present moment, to whatever I was engaged in. Soon, the problem began to disappear. For long stretches, I'm so focused on what's going on in my life that I don't know I have tinnitus. Until the next time I notice it, fight it a little, and turn my attention to music, conversation, a book, writing. And just like the eternal buzzing in my head, we can learn to bring some curiosity and awareness and acceptance to all the other things in our heads: thoughts, images, memories, emotions, body sensations, wanted and unwanted. It is freeing. But it can't be willed. We'll explore some experiential exercises in Part 2 of the book that help our clients step into a more accepting posture towards life, focusing on the specific areas of importance in advancing their therapy objectives.

In our clinical work, as another example, we rarely help people who are facing just one problem. Many of our clients have multiple problems to juggle at the same time. So we set up a list, as you'll see later, and we begin to work our way through the list together. But that means accepting that while we are working on problem #1, problems 2–6 are still there, and we have to tolerate them, opening up to an accepting posture, trusting that we'll get to them when we do. Not an easy dance, but one we teach the client to do with us.

EMOTION

To parse the key change components of CBT, let's begin in an unusual place: human emotion. We don't customarily think of starting there, in terms of our interventions. Still, emotion is a vibrant facet of the human experience, and the regulation and dysregulation of emotion is implicated in both a rich life and the derailment of a life. Let's start in this quest by saying what emotions are, and are not, and how we can fit emotions into a case conceptualization that can utilize specific techniques and skills to assist in the understanding of emotions, and what to do with and about them. Let's start with a definition of emotion, one offered by Hofmann:

> An emotion is (1) a multidimensional experience that is (2) characterized by different levels of arousal and degrees of pleasure–displeasure; (3) associated with subjective experiences, somatic sensations, and motivational tendencies; (4) colored by contextual and cultural factors; and that (5) can be regulated to some degree through intra-and interpersonal processes.
>
> (Hofmann, 2016, p. 2)

Let's take a moment to unpack this set of ideas about emotions. First, the definition includes the totality of an emotion, i.e. it is a deeply embodied, felt, subjective experience, one that also contains urges towards motivated action. It recognizes the spectrum of pleasure and unpleasure associated with emotions. It recognizes that while there are "bottom up" urges and motivations energized by emotions (i.e., they appear to be driven by evolutionary forces in our neurobiology), emotions are also shaped by psychological, interpersonal, and cultural factors. Finally, we regulate emotions in multiple ways: within ourselves (a target of therapy at times) and by interpersonal contact (therapist validation; soothing by significant others; punishment by significant others).

The value of this definition is two-fold: first, it offers a reasoned blend of multiple, sometimes competing, scientific models in affective neuroscience. Secondly, it is clinically rich and useful. We will show ways in which these principles can be applied to teach clients about their emotions, and to work with them in a way that lets them feel more empowered, balanced, and effective.

But contemporary advances in affective neuroscience present us with a remarkable challenge. To wit: the science is not settled. Theorists have data supporting multiple alternative conclusions about emotions, their evolutionary function (Gilbert & Simos, 2022; Panksepp, 2012; Davis & Panksepp, 2018), their malleability, whether they are "bottom up" or "top down" processes (LeDoux, 2016), whether they are socially constructed (Feldman-Barrett, 2018a). They argue about different epistemological frameworks, which suggests that we are in an early stage of development in our scientific understanding of these key, raw, primary building blocks of human functioning. And yet, without a framework for understanding emotions, therapy is haphazard and faltering, subject to fads, bad science, and potentially damaging ideologies.

We take a mid-point in this debate. We are in general agreement with those who see both an evolutionary and a socially and psychologically constructed component to emotion regulation and dysregulation (Hofmann, 2016; Papa & Epstein, 2018).

Here are some key points to consider, clinically.

We regard emotions as signals, and we teach clients to pay attention to the signals, and to delay, when appropriate, reacting to emotions until the motivated urge towards which the emotion pushes has been identified. If it is wise to act, we foster a thoughtful response, one that "works" in the context of the client's life and purposes. If it is wise to refrain from acting on an emotionally motivated urge, we teach how to watch, rather than fight, the urge, while behaving opposite to the urge, itself.

Let's try an example: Janelle is a 40-year-old African American college professor, sitting in a faculty meeting, listening to the departmental executive officer, a White male, list a new set of "productivity" standards. There is no input sought by faculty, and no discussion. Janelle experiences a knot in her stomach, and notices that she is becoming red and that her hands are clenching into a fist. She identifies fear as a key emotion, and also notices anger. She asks herself a key question here: "What is the threat?" She settles into her chair, breathes, thinks. The threat is twofold. Her research career may be derailed by the intensity of the new demands being placed on her by the university. She fears the loss of her professional dreams and ambitions. And she notices something else. She is angry at being treated in what she regards as an unfair and demeaning manner, one that echoes many life experiences as an African American. She is aware of an urge to act on her rage by speaking out in an angry and challenging manner. Should she speak? Should she remain silent for now? Should she sort the facts of the complex situation before deciding on a course of action?

What is important about this clinical vignette is the way in which so much of the threats are socially and psychologically constructed. Yet there is a core of evolutionarily driven emotion perhaps, in being thwarted from accessing necessary resources from the world, and in being subjugated by superiors in the social hierarchy. Complex? You bet. But understandable and creating a framework that can lead to thoughtful choice about what to do, or what not to do in the moment, in order to preserve status, if possible, and to secure necessary rewards and resources in the environment, also if possible.

Now, let's try a conceptually simpler example. The first author was walking his dog in an urban neighborhood abutting an open field, near a park and a stream. Suddenly, a dog-like creature appeared at the edge of the tree line. Before the form could be clearly identified by the author, the hairs on his neck stood up, fear welled up, and he tightened the leash on his small dog. Pure fear coursed through him. It took a moment to recognize that a coyote was peering at him and his dog from the other side of a street, at the edge of the tree line. First the fear. Then the conscious, verbal recognition of the threat. Human threat detection systems are prone to very rapid responses, just milliseconds long (Gustafson, 2005; Panksepp, 2012). This suggests that evolution has prepared us to experience threat detection before any conscious process has necessarily occurred. The first author tightened the leash and prepared for defense before even experiencing a clear emotional state (LeDoux, 2016). Then the fear hit. Which comes first, the threat response or the emotion? Depends on the theorist you read. For LeDoux, fear and anxiety are conscious experiences, but the body's response to danger is quicker, automatic, and often eludes consciousness…until the fear hits later. For LeDoux, one treats the conscious fear separately from the systems that are detecting and responding to threat (LeDoux, 2016). Complex? Yes. That's why it's wise to do as Linehan suggests, to pause and ask oneself "What is the threat?" at times, before acting on the real or perceived threat. Of course, if a tiger is jumping out at you, or a coyote, one cannot afford to wait too long. In the social world, however, and the world of psychological, or imagined, threat, it's often wise to delay. But in either case, our central nervous systems are designed to rapidly respond to environmental threats, and those appear to be prepared for some rather specific types of threat. We don't customarily respond with a fear response to bunny rabbits, but we do to snakes and spiders. Why? Evolution has selected a fear response to clear sources of danger, not necessarily to harmless animals.

That said, as the first example shows, our emotional responses contain highly complex psychological vectors and social vectors. And that leads to our second point about emotions.

Marsha Linehan said that "emotions love themselves". This gets at the mechanisms by which our own psychology and our interpersonal contexts "pull" for, or stoke, certain emotions. One of the curious things about us, as human beings, is that we feed our emotions, even when they are painful. That gets us connected with other components of "mind", i.e. cognition, emotion-driven urges, actions, attentional processes, social contingencies, etc. We get caught up in vicious cycles whereby, if we aren't very careful, we stoke the very emotions, and their attendant cognitions, attentional processes, and behaviors that cause mischief. And it can even feel weirdly good to do so.

Humans are prone to what Greenberg (2016) describes as a difference between primary and secondary emotions. Linehan draws on this distinction when she notes that two especially painful emotions to experience are shame and grief. When we sense that a client is stuck in anger about a humiliating situation and may be avoiding the more primary and painful emotion of shame or grief, we need the conceptual and technical tools to intervene. As you will see, we utilize strategies to foster the client making safe contact with body sensations, images, thoughts, so as to label emotions and track those that are more readily available to awareness and those that may end up being less so, even though they are more salient for purposes of advancing the therapy.

Finally, it is common to experience what our minds consider two or more conflicting emotions about the same person or situation. One can love the same person who evokes intense anger. People can become trapped in dichotomous thinking about their emotions: "I should only feel love. There must be something wrong with me." So we take the position that problematic emotions, those entailed with the problems for which the client seeks help, are both evolved mechanisms that support human existence, safety, and thriving (Gilbert & Simos, 2022; Panksepp, 2012) and that they are constructed actively out of the personal meanings and cognitions of individuals, and the shaping of those meanings by our social and cultural contexts (Feldman-Barrett, 2018a, b).

In closing this very brief tour of emotion research and its use in modern CBT, we think it's worthwhile to read the words from a TED Talk by Lisa Feldman-Barrett (2018b) as a summary of how we conceptualize and deal with emotion in therapy:

> Emotions that seem to happen to you, are actually made by you. You are not at the mercy of mythical emotion circuits which are buried deep inside some ancient part of your brain. You have more control over your emotions than you think you do. Your brain is wired so that if you change the ingredients that your brain uses to make emotions, then you can transform your emotional life.

Linehan has something profoundly right here. So does Hofmann (2016), in the sense that evolution prepares us to respond to environmental stimuli that pose both threats and opportunities. Mind and culture shape the nature and perception of those threats and opportunities, through the development of language and the ability to imagine the past and the future. Humans are capable of feeling threatened by the very things we want and need, such as social connection, sex, and engaging vigorously in the seeking of rewards and resources from our environments. We fear being judged, and step back from engaging with the world to avoid feared judgments. We fear violating rules that exist only in our heads, or in specific social contexts, such as the families in which we grew up, but no longer live in. We fly into rages and grievances that we stoke repeatedly, for infractions that only exist in our minds, and we punish others accordingly. And still, we may think we are victims of our emotions. But we can learn to work with them in a way that allows for a smoother response, with less wear and tear on our systems. It's not always easy. We'll explore in greater detail the steps we take in therapy, some of which have been explored earlier.

1. Pause before acting, when feasible, as emotion is aroused.
2. Bring awareness to the body, to thoughts and images, and, with some curiosity, label the emotions, beginning, if necessary by finding the areas of the body where we feel the emotion. This has the effect of downregulating emotion and attendant urges, providing some of that "top down" regulation of those "bottom up" processes.
3. See if a suite of emotions show up, and see if one is more primary and hidden, while another is more easily accessible, though being "fed" by our own stoking.
4. Ask what the threat or opportunity appears to be in the moment.
5. Determine if the emotion fits the facts of the moment.
6. See if the urge you are experiencing is wise to act on.
7. Do what works! Sometimes that means to act fully and wholeheartedly on the emotion-driven urge. Sometimes it means acting exactly opposite to the urge.
8. And in all cases, the emotions are to be tuned in to in a friendly, self-compassionate, curious manner, not denied, feared, or cut off by drugs, alcohol, compulsive spending or other avoidance maneuvers that block learning.

It's worth noting here that as you think about the above steps, we are actually blending a variety of CBT intervention domains. We're not *just* focusing on emotions. We're also working in the appraisals of those emotions, and we're fostering a behavioral strategy of exposure to emotions, as well as considering a disciplined use of mindful deployment of attention to suspend flight from, or indulgence in, those emotions. All the components of the model can and do work together at any given time. That's why we ask for patience and a commitment to gaining expertise in this treatment. It not only gets easier, it gets results.

Now let's take a moment to think through how you might work with Janelle, in the case above, using these principles to help her make sense of her experience of the faculty meeting, and how to respond wisely and effectively.

COGNITION

Humans are meaning-making creatures. As the great writer Joan Didion famously said, in her book *The White Album*: "We tell ourselves stories in order to live" (Didion, 2019). In psychotherapy, Viktor Frankl built a therapy around the human need for meaning. We are a species evolved as languaging beings, and as such, the search for order, meaning, certainty are vital to us. The paradox is that we are also prone to great uncertainty, as the future is always indeterminate. And just as we create order, so, too, can things fall apart. When meaning is shattered, or merely jumbled, and life is uncertain, we may become anxious and fearful, or enraged and seek to assign blame.

In addition, we are prone to experiencing certain cognitive biases in our processing of information. This, too, appears to be an odd evolutionary facet of our makeup. In our quest to map the world, cognitively, we fill in the blanks and respond as though what we think is how the world is. It brings comfort, up to a point. We are prone to overestimate the control we have over our destinies, overestimate our virtues, and underestimate our ability to deal with uncertainty. And are prone to a host of prominent cognitive biases that can render us less flexible, and less able to meet the world as it is (Kahneman, 2011). These tendencies toward biased cognition may be exacerbated by the pressure of both emotion and by the social contexts we inhabit. This is not always maladaptive. There is a certain economy in having a mental map, versus processing the world afresh moment by moment, which would be exhausting and redundant. Most of the time, even with the blinders our evolved natures have prepared us to wear, things go fine. But when the blinders no longer serve us well, we may need help, if we are willing, to examine the lenses through which we view the world, and find new, broader, more flexible perspectives for adapting to life.

It was part of the genius of Aaron "Tim" Beck to generate a useful model of cognition, not specifically from the cognitive neurosciences, but from the laboratory of his clinic. We find his overall framework to be highly useful, in terms of spotting the common cognitive biases that are implicated in many forms of human suffering, including depressive and anxious states, anger problems, relationship difficulties, and adjustment to key life contexts. It was a part of his clinical genius to recognize that the traps our minds set for us were often hovering just on the edges of awareness, accessible with training, and taking the form of not only verbal thought, but visual and auditory imaging. Thus, one could experience the internal dialogue of "I'm such a loser." Or, alternately, one might imagine oneself as a small child, being scolded and called "loser" by their angry parent. Same effect. As therapists, we learn to track such processes in both verbal and sensory modes. And we train clients to join us in showing some curiosity about these processes, as well. More on that later, also.

BECK'S COGNITIVE DISTORTIONS

Early on in his work with depression, Beck identified a series of common "cognitive distortions" associated with depressive states (Beck et al., 2024). They include the following.

1. Arbitrary Inference: interpreting events in ways for which there is no evidence, or where the interpretation is contrary to evidence.
2. Selective Abstraction: selecting one detail in a situation, without regard to other features of the situation, and using that detail to describe the entire situation.
3. Overgeneralization: reaching a general conclusion, based on a single incident.
4. Magnification and Minimization: making mountains out of psychological molehills vs ignoring or minimizing important information pertinent to one's functioning.
5. Labeling: name calling, for example: "I'm a moron!"
6. Personalizing: making external events about oneself, in the absence of any basis for such a belief.
7. Dichotomous thinking: Black and white thinking; either one is perfect or one is totally, irredeemably flawed, for example.

In addition to the more frank distortions and biases in human cognition, humans are also easily ensnared by arbitrary rules. These often take the form of "should" or "must" statements about how oneself, one's intimate relationships, and the world "should" work. And we can become very punishing of others, or demoralized, when those rules aren't followed by the universe. In fact, humans have a tendency towards "rule governed" behavior, even when the rules cease to work in the real world (Hayes, 2004).

In some ways, the dark side of cognition, especially with rules, is that humans can be slower to adapt to changes in the actual contingencies they face than are pigeons in a lab experiment. That's humbling. We will provide clinical examples of this, and how to deal with this phenomenon in Part 2 of the book.

Finally, there are what are sometimes referred to as "core beliefs". These tend to be akin to automatic thoughts in several ways, certainly in terms of their content ("I'm defective", for example). But whereas automatic thoughts tend to have an ebb and flow to them, core beliefs are more durable, often linked to either earlier eras of our life development, or dramatic, sometimes traumatic events in later life. We will show ways to work with both.

Beck's work was popularized in 1980 with the publication of David D. Burns' *Feeling Good: The New Mood Therapy* (Burns, 1980). He lists a variety of other common cognitive distortions people are prone to, especially in depressive and/or anxiety states. It's important to note that the early Cognitive Therapy work, done by Beck and, later, Burns, was largely based on clinically derived observation. Newer work in cognitive neurosciences, identifies other biases or cognitive heuristics that are often ubiquitous, easily observed in others, yet capable of blinding oneself (Kahneman, 2011). These include the availability heuristic, in which we assume the greater likelihood of an event's occurrence, based on its availability in recent memory; confirmation biases, in which we seek information that confirms our beliefs, while screening out evidence contrary to those beliefs. Think about the information silos that now dominate American news cycles and online platforms: all designed to confirm biases of readers and listeners, and to stoke emotions, as well.

The most commonly used clinical strategies for dealing with these cognitive processes is helping the client examine the evidence for them, and seeking a more adaptive, if not necessarily more accurate, alternative. That involves the use of things like Thought Records, or the use of Guided Discovery and Socratic Questioning. The latter will be covered in greater detail when we talk about the therapeutic relationship.

Unfortunately, as is often the case when treatments become popular, they can be used badly. And a common stereotype of early CBT was that it inadvertently could make things worse, by getting into arguments with clients about their beliefs; by trying to wheedle or harangue the patient into thinking "happy" thoughts, thus inadvertently strengthening the very beliefs that were problematic in the first place.

It's true. These are hazards. But we'd stipulate they are hazards especially for those who are poorly trained. That's why in our effort to encourage the journey to becoming an expert, we advise getting some top-notch case supervision, so that the model is used effectively, humanely, wisely. More on that later.

A second line of criticism of Beck's Cognitive Therapy suggested that Beckian cognitive interventions were simply unnecessary, and added little to treatment outcome (Longmire & Worrell, 2007). In response to emerging science and multiple critiques of Beckian cognitive approaches, significant refinements to Beck's model emerged with the work of Zindel Segal, John Teasdale, and others in the UK and Canada (Segal, Williams, & Teasdale, 2012). At heart, Teasdale and company proposed that it is not the change in cognitions that counts, as much as the change in the way the person relates to those cognitions. So for example, a common Beckian strategy is to help clients examine evidence for and against a particular biased cognition: "I'm a complete failure". By doing so, ideally a newer, more flexible, perhaps accurate, and functionally more useful alternative emerges: "I blew that exam. That hurts. That doesn't make me a failure. It just means I need to work a little harder for the next test."

Again, notice how the downside of this effort might be the creation of a tug of war, trying to force a new belief on a client, rather than allowing for a gentler exploration, without a challenge made to rid her of "bad" thoughts and replace them with "good" ones.

What Teasdale discovered is that we do not "get rid" of thoughts (Teasdale, 2022). They remain. In fact, it is a well understood fallacy to believe that we ever erase or extinguish any form of new learning (Brewin, 2006). Instead, as you'll see in our section on behavioral interventions, we build new repertoires that are more readily available in situations where they are more functional than an old behavior or an old cognition/image. This creates what Brewin (2006) refers to as competition retrieval, not in the sense that we promote an inner fight, but that we gradually help clients build new ways of functioning in situations that previously elicited an automatic, and dysfunctional, pattern. In terms of cognition, therefore, rather than expunge the "bad' thought", we encourage the client to change how they relate to those thoughts. And that changing of one's relationship to thought, rather than thought erasure, is a key insight of Teasdale. So: "I'm noticing that I'm having the thought 'I'm a failure' again. Interesting how that pops up at times like these. I'm just going to watch without reacting for now." There may be a dampening of believability of the thought, a weakening of its emotional pull, and perhaps, without forcing it, a more flexible alternative may emerge without a struggle.

A further challenge to Beck's model came from Steven Hayes, founder of Acceptance and Commitment Therapy (ACT), who initially took a much more vigorous stance against the use of Beckian techniques (Hayes, Strosahl, & Wilson, 2016), claiming that they could promote the very "fusion" with maladaptive cognition that they sought to fix. By contrast, Hayes developed a new model of human cognition called Relational Frame Theory (Hayes, Barnes-Holmes, & Roche, 2001), or RFT. So instead of "challenging" thoughts aggressively, which by the way is something Beck never advised we do, a raft of often brilliant and creative experiential exercises were designed to help people create a sense of distance from their thoughts. And clients were then encouraged to recognize when certain beliefs pulled them away from the direction they wished their life to move vs moving them toward their life values.

We lean towards the models of cognition pioneered by Teasdale, though we acknowledge the achievements of RFT. We find the experiential exercises in ACT to be especially useful, fun, energizing, and evocative of therapist creativity. Such exercises often employ enactments, including two-chair work, as well as guided imagery, of which we consider Hayes to be a master designer. So, too, was the Oxford Cognitive Therapy Centre team (Hackmann, Bennett-Levy, & Holmes, 2011). We find that the use of guided imagery exercises can tie together work in more than one of the eight Principle domains in a single intervention. Effective guided imagery work may simultaneously involve mindful awareness, cognition, emotion, behavioral rehearsal, exposure, self-processes, and therapist validation in one exercise. The limits are the needs of the client in any given moment, and the therapist's ability to improvise in a creative and disciplined manner. We aim to help the therapist create coherent case conceptualizations that will allow us to choose among the entire treasure trove of CBT cognitive techniques, based on what works for a given patient, in a given clinical context. We will teach a generally gentle, collaborative style of working with dug in cognitive processes, that help people spring free of their mental traps, through their own process of discovery.

BEHAVIOR

Behavior is influenced by its environment. More specifically, environmental events that precede and immediately follow behavior determine whether a behavior has an opportunity to occur and whether it will happen more or less frequently over time. This describes the essence of operant conditioning. To a large degree, intervening in client behavior involves changing their environment, meaning the environmental events that surround their behavior. We will teach a method of chain analysis (also known as functional assessment or analysis) to help identify important antecedent and consequent events, revealing important intervention targets and facilitating client and clinician understanding of how the pieces of the puzzle fit together.

Behavioral intervention also involves teaching skills (e.g., social skills) and making use of behavioral processes (e.g., habituation) in the service of desired client outcomes. The former involves a thoughtful process of identifying skills that are absent or underdeveloped in a client's repertoire and that will likely lead to positive clinical change, and effectively training them up. The latter involves the implementation of clinical procedures, such as exposure, that are designed to take advantage of learning processes.

Problem-solving skills can be effectively trained and are useful in a wide range of clinical problems (Nezu & Maguth Nezu, 2019). It is useful to think of problem-solving as referring to a composite skill comprised of two component skill classes: 1) Problem Orientation and 2) Rational Problem-Solving skills. When training clients in these skills, they are initially taught separately but as they acquire these skill sets, they are taught to use them simultaneously as they work to master life's problems.

Problem Orientation (PO) refers to how a client views their problems. This is important because their mental posture relates to their problem-solving effectiveness. We can think of PO as falling on a continuum, with "negative" and "positive" as end points. The goal is to increase the frequency with which clients approach their problems as close to the positive side of the continuum as possible, while keeping in mind that no one resides there permanently. We facilitate this by helping clients learn to recognize problems more quickly and to develop a healthy approach style. We also do this by helping expand their focus from the threatening aspects of their problems to an awareness of the opportunities that simultaneously reside in the problem. Finally, we accomplish this by helping a client recognize that the experience of problems is a normal part of life and not reflective of something uniquely defective with them. In line with our principle of normalizing human pain, we help clients recognize that problems are inherent in living, and pose not only a challenge, but an opportunity for growth.

Once a client has been taught PO skills and is working to sharpen their fluency with them, we begin teaching the sequence of steps necessary to resolve problems. These rational problem-solving skills include: 1) Stating the problem, 2) Brainstorming solutions, 3) Evaluating those solutions, 4) Identifying a solution, and 5) Implementing the solution and confirming it led to a successful resolution. This phase of instruction involves teaching step-specific strategies, one step at a time, and progresses to educating clients in using them in combination.

When helping clients build new behavior it is often unrealistic and unnecessarily stressful to them for us to expect them to emit the target behavior immediately, or even very quickly. In these circumstances we often *shape* behavior. By this we mean we start with an approximation, or a sub-step of the goal behavior, and gradually work from there through a series of other approximations until we reach the desired behavior. For example, if a shy client wants to learn to initiate and maintain conversations with strangers, we might first help them start conversations with people they know without regard to how long the conversation continues, then add a focus on duration, followed by initiating conversations with strangers without regard to conversation length, and culminating in initiating and maintaining conversations with strangers. Effective shaping entails starting at the first available step rather than at the earliest approximation possible. Many clinicians make the error of working through unnecessary approximations. To illustrate this point, consider our shy client example but this time assume he can already start conversations reasonably well. His difficulty begins when he must maintain interactions. In this circumstance, it would likely be an inefficient use of clinical time to begin with conversation starting.

Exposure is a robust clinical procedure, classically used with anxiety disorders but increasingly applied to a range of unwanted internal experiences such as thoughts, emotions, memories, urges, and bodily sensations. Exposure has been available as a procedure for decades, though the models underlying it have evolved. Currently there are three broad models of exposure: Emotional Processing Theory (Foa & Kozak, 1986), Inhibitory Learning Theory (Craske et al., 2014), and the Psychological Flexibility Model (Hayes et al., 2016). All three are supported by strong scientific evidence but we have a preference for the psychological flexibility model as articulated in Acceptance and Commitment Therapy (Hayes et al., 2016). It is important to understand the model because it will inform many aspects of exposure, including the goals of your exposure exercises and how you will implement them. As a broad example, exposure based on Emotional Processing Theory seeks to produce habituation (i.e., reduction in anxiety) whereas Inhibitory Learning and ACT-based exposure explicitly do not try to reduce anxiety. Instead, the goal is more one of increasing distress tolerance (Inhibitory Learning) or increasing the breadth of a behavioral repertoire that becomes narrow and rigid when it encounters certain stimuli.

Earlier we mentioned that behavior is a function of the environmental events that follow it, its consequences. There are two types of consequences, punishers and reinforcers, with the former decreasing and the later increasing the future occurrence of the behavior it follows. Science has taught us a lot about how these consequences impact behavior and we will illustrate how to use this knowledge to effectively influence behavior. For example, though punishers reduce behavior they do so at a cost. Punishers teach an individual what not to do rather than what to do. What emerges instead might be more undesirable than what was previously occurring. Punishers also tend to elicit anger from the recipient, an undesirable side effect. Yet another difficulty is that punishment delivery often reinforces the punishing behavior. This can lead to an overreliance on punishment. This is not an exhaustive list but hopefully underscores the importance of being thoughtful about the use of punishment. Furthermore, reinforcement is to be preferred because it builds desired behavior more quickly and does so without the previously articulated side effects. Some behaviorally oriented clinicians believe it should never be used. That isn't our position though we do agree that reinforcement is to be preferred and any use of punishment should be done briefly, mildly, and in combination with reinforcement. We will illustrate how to use reinforcement effectively, including in circumstances where it can be difficult to envision its use and it may seem punishment is the only option.

Let's look at a clinical example to see how some of these pieces come together in the clinic.

Alexis is a 35-year-old mother of three. She entered therapy because of distress related to what she describes as severe relationship conflict with her 16-year-old daughter, Samantha. After reviewing the finer details of these conflictual episodes with her therapist, Alexis discovered that many instances occur when she asks Samantha to participate in household chores (i.e., they discovered a common antecedent to the episodes of conflict). The following dialogue illustrates how the therapist worked with Alexis to identify some effective solutions to this problem.

THERAPIST: Alexis, it would help me get a better understanding of what's going on with this dynamic between the two of you if you can show me what it looks like. Would you be up for a brief role-play in which I play the part of Samantha and you approach me about participating in chores exactly the way you normally would?

ALEXIS: Okay, sure.

THERAPIST: Great, but first briefly set the stage for me. What am I (Samantha) likely to be doing and where am I likely to be?

ALEXIS: She's always in her room on her darn phone. Always!

THERAPIST: Okay, I'll pretend I'm in her room and on my phone. What is she typically doing on her phone?

ALEXIS: She's always scrolling through social media.

THERAPIST: One more question. What does her response to you look like exactly when you ask her to help? I think it would be best if you can show that to me now. Can you briefly demonstrate a typical response from her?

ALEXIS: Acting out Samantha's typical response – "In a minute." To which I'll say "you have one minute." I come back in a minute and ask her again and she responds "I told you – one minute! Take a chill pill." She always says this and it's never just a minute. I must nag her over and over!

THERAPIST: I think I have enough to work with now. Let's go ahead and role-play this. (Therapist pulls out her phone and starts scrolling through social media.)

ALEXIS: Samantha, I need your help cleaning the kitchen.

THERAPIST: (Remaining focused on the phone) – In a minute! I'm in the middle of something.

ALEXIS: You always say that and then you never come. I need you to help me now.

THERAPIST: Damn. Chill out! I've had a long day and I'm trying to unwind. I told you I'll help in a minute.

ALEXIS: Give me a break about having a long day. I've truly had a long day and I need your help in the kitchen. You are always on that damn phone.

THERAPIST: Out of role – I think I have a sense of the interaction now. Was this fairly representative?

ALEXIS: Yes, except it just escalates from there.

The therapist did a couple of things here. She didn't rely on a mere description of how Alexis approaches Samantha. Instead, she asked her to demonstrate it. This will almost always provide a more accurate picture. Also, though there are several variables at play she chose to begin by examining part of the context in which the problematic interactions emerge. It's important to emphasize that, though not illustrated here, a detailed investigation into the *full* context is necessary for effective clinical action.

THERAPIST: I can see why that is so distressing to you. I imagine it must be discouraging too.

ALEXIS: Nods head in agreement and appears sad.

THERAPIST: Do you always approach it in this way? Or have you tried to approach her any differently?

ALEXIS: What other way is there? I don't see another way. Besides, I'm the adult and she should do what I ask her to do.

THERAPIST: Can we try a brief exercise? I'd like to see whether we can come up with a list of alternative approaches to get a sense of the options we might have. I'm wondering whether if you stop to think about it a bit that you might see some new options. What other ways can you think of to approach her about her chores?

ALEXIS: I could tell her that if she doesn't help I'll take away her phone.

THERAPIST: Okay, that's one way. I'll write that down. What else?

ALEXIS: I could threaten other things I'd take away though her phone is what she cares about the most.

THERAPIST: I've added threatening the removal of other privileges to the list. What else?

ALEXIS: (thinks for several minutes) – I can't think of anything else.

THERAPIST: Is this like you? That is, when you try to come up with solutions to your problems do you have a difficult time coming up with several options?

ALEXIS: Yes, I guess so.

THERAPIST: I'm remembering when we've tried to do this with the problem we were discussing last week that you also stopped after you mentioned two options. It also sounds like your sense is that this happens a lot for you. We should celebrate this a bit because we might have found one of the things that has kept you stuck. It turns out that we are generally more effective at solving our problems when we come up with as many solutions as possible and when we come up with solutions with a decent amount of variety. Let's try an exercise to begin developing some brainstorming skills.

There were a number of ways the therapist could have gone with Alexis. For example, she could have chosen to educate Alexis on how to use prompts more effectively. Here, the therapist decided to focus on the rational problem-solving skill of brainstorming solutions. She only made this decision after seeing several instances of the difficulty and after Alexis confirmed this was a common difficulty.

THERAPIST: (walking up to a white board) – We're going to try some brainstorming. I'll write down everything you think of on the white board. Since our brains are not good at being creative and judgmental at the same, we want to separate these two from one another. Effective brainstorming involves being creative so I want you to say anything that comes to mind. It doesn't matter how silly or unlikely you think it is to work. What are all the creative uses you can think of for a pencil?

ALEXIS: You can write with it obviously. You can also draw. And you can tap it on furniture or a glass to make music.

THERAPIST: Good (recording these on the board). What else?

ALEXIS: I guess you can erase with it too. Oh, and you can tap someone on the shoulder to get their attention.

THERAPIST: (Continuing to record) – Good. Anything else?

ALEXIS: That's all I can think of.

THERAPIST: Okay, first you did a good job not judging any of your solutions. You also came up with more than you normally do. It looks like you came up with five solutions whereas you typically come up with two or three. Great job! There was also some variety in your solutions too. Let me teach you some techniques for growing your options even more. If you were to place "you can draw with it" in a category, what category might that be?

ALEXIS: Art?

THERAPIST: Yes! Let me ask you this: What are the artistic things you can do with a pencil?

ALEXIS: I guess you could paint it. Maybe you could glue several pencils together to make something.

THERAPIST: (adding these solutions to the list) – what else?

ALEXIS: You could pin some things into the eraser to create something interesting.

THERAPIST: Great. Do you see what we just did here? Placing solutions into categories and then asking what other solutions are possible in that category often helps us generate more ideas. So that's one strategy. Here's another: Who do you know who is good at art?

ALEXIS: My aunt. She's real artistic.

THERAPIST: What would your aunt do with a pencil when she's being artistic?

ALEXIS: She might stick many of them in her garden kind of like a fence around her plants or she might use them kind of like a scarecrow. I could also see her crushing it into many pieces, almost like sand, and creating some kind of sand sculpture.

THERAPIST: It looks like we've discovered another possible strategy for identifying additional solutions. We can ask ourselves "who do we know who ____" whatever the category is and then ask ourselves what they might do. Now, let's see whether we can use some of these strategies to help you identify additional ways of approaching your daughter.

This dialogue could have been greatly extended, prompting many additional solutions. We limited its length only because of space limitations. In clinical practice it's important to continue this process for a while as it signals to clients that sometimes, it takes time to come up with useful solutions. Not every problem can be solved quickly. As a general rule, we like clients to continue until they've identified at least ten solutions to their problem. Also, it would be important to highlight the variety, not just the quality, of solutions that were generated and to ask the client to provide a summary statement of what they learned. Such summations help you check their understanding and also help deepen their learning.

MINDFULNESS

Mindfulness, while placed at the end of this chapter, is nonetheless a foundational skill for the successful application of cognitive and behavioral strategies. At its simplest and most pragmatic level, mindfulness involves the ability to regulate emotions and behavior in a way that allows for flexible deployment of attention, as well as the ability to step back as needed from the stream of experience, so as to be able to respond appropriately in the moment. That can involve cultivating a gentle curiosity about one's thought processes, emotions, and action urges, so as to change response patterns when they have been identified as problematic. Fostering mindful pauses at strategic moments in sessions can help regulate intense emotions, and can open a space for clarity of thought and purpose. In the clinical applications in Part 2, we will describe and show how to implement specific, targeted strategies and techniques, which can be applied as indicated by the client's needs and the therapist's judgment. For now, let's unpack a little more the psychological processes we mean by, and target, when we employ mindfulness practices in CBT.

We should begin by saying what we even mean by mindfulness. The ideas and practices associated with mindfulness are now everywhere in our culture. Yet there isn't even a clear, agreed upon definition of what it is. The one definition of mindfulness that is perhaps most accepted as a starting point in the psychological community is Jon Kabat-Zinn's: "Mindfulness is awareness that arises through paying attention, on purpose, in the present moment, nonjudgmentally" (Kabat-Zinn, 2003, p. 145).

The American Psychological Association (APA) defines mindfulness thusly: "Mindfulness is awareness of one's internal states and surroundings. Mindfulness can help people avoid destructive or automatic habits and responses by learning to observe their thoughts, emotions, and other present-moment experiences without judging or reacting to them" (APA Dictionary of Psychology, APA Website, 2024).

Mindfulness is also a property of Eastern meditative traditions and of certain Western contemplative traditions and practices. But that gets us into the more religious applications of mindfulness. Like other trainers and teachers in the field, we think it's wise to refrain from bringing the more religious elements of mindfulness into therapy, for perhaps obvious reasons. Christian clients may not relish what they consider Buddhist indoctrination. Nor Jewish clients. Nor, perhaps, many Buddhist clients! To keep our focus on mindfulness and its application in modern Cognitive Behavior Therapy, we employ the psychological properties of mindfulness, as they can be brought to bear on easing the suffering of our clients and on helping them grow in life directions of their choosing.

Let's focus a bit here on the psychological elements of mindfulness practice and how we will teach how to use these elements in therapy. First, we foster the ability to direct awareness and attention, and to hold it, even briefly. This doesn't involve meditation practice, which is a different application of mindfulness. We are in accord with Marsha Linehan, that many clients coming to us for help may be intolerant of the demands required in meditation. Part of Linehan's genius involves her careful translation of Zen and other contemplative traditions into their basic psychological components (Linehan, 2020). Linehan breaks mindfulness down into its key psychological components. She further divides mindfulness skills into three "what" skills and three "how" skills. The "what skills" include observing (noticing or paying attention), describing, and participating (fully engaged in the moment). The "how skills" include being nonjudgmental about experience (this one is quite tricky), being "one mindful", meaning only focused on one thing in the moment, and finally, being effective (i.e. doing what works in the moment).

Linehan is not the only treatment developer in the field to employ mindfulness skills. Acceptance and Commitment Therapy, Mindfulness-Based Cognitive Therapy, and Metacognitive Therapy, all include mindfulness skills as components of their treatments. And all of them rely on the psychological components of mindfulness, rather than the more frankly spiritual components of mindfulness practice. It is those psychological components of mindfulness that we will emphasize in this book.

Common to all mindfulness practices is the ability to pay attention to what's happening in the present moment, and to stay with what one notices or observes in the moment. This can be tricky and challenging, particularly when what one notices is painful or aversive. That can include negatively experienced emotions, memories, body sensations, thoughts, or images. We will show you how to design appropriate interventions that help people pay attention to any form of sensory experience, internal or external. We encourage picking a focus that is most likely to engage the client. For example, let's say a client is deeply fearful of the body states, memories, urges, and images that arise when they pay attention to what's going on inside them: "Great!" we might say. "Okay, how about we just take a moment to pay attention to the colored balloons in the painting on that wall, just noticing. And if any judgments come up, or emotions, or thoughts, can you just notice those, too, and gently bring awareness right back to that colored balloon that caught your attention?"

The entire spectrum of sensory experiences are available to help clients choose an initial focus, for purposes of simply attending to the present moment. Linehan's DBT Skills manual (Linehan, 2015) is filled with examples, and there are many YouTube videos demonstrating them. In Part 2 of the book, when we apply our model to specific cases, we will give more examples of how to do this.

Now, for what purpose do we help access and build the skill of paying attention? It's a bit like lifting weights, in order to build muscle mass. By building the muscle of attention, when that is a treatment target, we foster a skill that allows for a pause to occur. And in that pause, attention can focus on the emotions, urges, thoughts, or action patterns that are implicated in the maintenance of the problems for which the client seeks our help. We foster the ability to do this in a nonjudgmental and nonreactive way. In other words, we aim to slow the machinery of mind and body, just long enough for a pause to occur, a pause in which a greater distance from thoughts, urges, and action patterns occurs. And in that pause, the client becomes freer to determine the helpfulness of those thoughts, urges, or actions that are implicated in their problems.

The therapist may help direct client awareness to specific treatment targets. That might include opening up a space to accept painful memories or events, without fighting or judging either the experiences or oneself. It might include a space in which to look at one's thoughts from a slight distance, with enough curiosity and openness to see if those thoughts are helpful or whether they turn the client towards patterns of functioning that are damaging, either to themselves or others in their lives. It may involve helping a client have a moment to freely choose whether to act on or refrain from acting on an urge. We might employ a mindfulness exercise to help the client focus on the automatic thoughts and images that arise as she sits ruminating about her life. We might direct gentle attention to the body sensations and images of a client who fears having a panic attack if he leaves his house. We might also employ a mindfulness exercise as we map out an imaginal exposure trail for that panic client. The point is that we regard mindfulness as a psychological set of processes that can be brought to bear in a disciplined and creative way, ideographically, meaning as applied to *this* patient, in *this* situation, *now*. Mindfulness exercises can be integrated into other organizing principles in our model, including cognitive and behavioral interventions, emotion regulation, acceptance work, accessing and building self-processes. Again, the limits are only in the creativity, flexibility, and training of the therapist.

CHAPTER SUMMARY

This chapter focused on what we consider the three key domains for intervening in CBT. Those include acceptance, mindfulness, and change processes. We describe what constitutes acceptance, as well as the importance of helping clients foster an accepting posture towards the problems and circumstances they bring to therapy. Paradoxically, acceptance is often a prelude for change, and we demonstrate clinical strategies to foster this step in therapy. We define mindfulness in its psychological components, rather than its spiritual dimensions, and we demonstrated via cases and clinical vignettes how to foster mindful engagement with the present moment. Last, we reviewed briefly the spectrum of change technologies within modern CBT, including cognitive, behavioral, and problem-solving strategies. For interested readers, references are provided for further reading.

REFERENCES

Beck, A., Rush, A., Shaw, B., Emery, G., DeRubeis, R., & Hollon, S. (2024) *Cognitive Therapy of Depression* (2nd edn). New York: Guilford.

Brewin, C. (2006) Understanding Cognitive Behavior Therapy: A Retrieval Competition Account. *Behaviour Research and Therapy*, 44, 765–784.

Burns, D. (1980) *Feeling Good: The New Mood Therapy*. New York: Morrow.

Craske, M., Treanor, M., et al. (2014) Maximizing Exposure Therapy: An Inhibitory Learning Approach. *Behavior Research & Therapy*, July (58), 10–23.

Davis, K. & Panksepp, J. (2018) *The Emotional Foundations of Personality: A Neurobiological and Evolutionary Approach*. New York: W. W. Norton & Company.

Didion, J. (2019) *Joan Didion: The 60's and 70's: The White Album*. New York: Library of America.

Feldman-Barrett, L. (2018a) *How Emotions Are Made: The Secret Life of the Brain*. New York: Mariner Books.

Feldman-Barrett, L. (2018b) *TED Talk: You aren't at the mercy of your emotions—your brain creates them.* https://www.youtube.com/watch?v=0gks6ceq4eQ.

Foa, E., & Kozak, M. (1986) Emotional Processing of Fear: Exposure to Corrective Information. *Psychological Bulletin*, 99, 1, 20–35.

Gilbert, P. & Simos, G. (eds.) (2022) *Compassion Focused Therapy: Clinical Practice and Applications.* New York: Routledge.

Greenberg, L. (2016) *Emotion-Focused Therapy* (Revised edn) Washington, DC: American Psychological Association.

Gustafson, J. (2005) *Very Brief Psychotherapy.* New York: Routledge/Taylor Francis.

Hackmann, A., Bennett-Levy, J., & Holmes, E. (eds.) (2011) *Oxford Guide to Imagery in Cognitive Therapy.* Oxford: Oxford University Press.

Hayes, S. (ed.) (2004) *Rule Governed Behavior: Cognition, Contingencies, and Instructional Control.* Reno: Context Press.

Hayes, S., Barnes-Holmes, D., & Roche, B. (2001) *Relational Frame Theory: A Post-Skinnerian Account of Human Language and Cognition.* New York: Springer.

Hayes, S., Strosahl, K., & Wilson, K. (2016) *Acceptance & Commitment Therapy: The Process and Practice of Mindful Change* (2nd edn). New York: Guilford.

Hofmann, S. (2016) *Emotion in Therapy: From Science to Practice.* New York: Guilford.

Kabat-Zinn, J. (2003) Mindfulness-Based Interventions in Context: Past, Present, and Future. *Clinical Psychology Science and Practice*, 10(2), 144–156.

Kahneman, D. (2011) *Thinking Fast and Slow.* New York: Farrar, Staus and Giroux.

LeDoux, J. (2016) *The Anxious Brain: Using the Brain to Understand and Treat Anxiety.* New York: Penguin.

Linehan, M. (2015) *DBT Skills Training Manual* (2nd edn). New York: Guilford Press.

Linehan, M. (2020) *Building a Life Worth Living: A Memoir.* New York: Random House.

Longmire, R. & Worrell, M. (2007) Do We Need to Challenge Thoughts in Cognitive Behavior Therapy? *Clinical Psychology Review*, 27, 173–187.

May, G. (1982) *Will and Spirit: A Contemplative Psychology.* New York: HarperOne.

Nezu, A., & Maguth Nezu, C. (2019) *Emotion-Centered Problem-Solving Therapy: Treatment Guidelines.* New York: Springer.

Panksepp, J. (2012) *The Archeology of Mind: Neuroevolutionary Origins of Emotions*. New York: W.W. Norton & Company.

Papa, A. & Epstein, E. (2018) Emotions and Emotion Regulation, in *Process-Based CBT: The Science and Core Clinical Competencies of Cognitive-Behavior Therapy*. Reno: Context Press.

Segal, Z., Williams, M., & Teasdale, J. (2012) *Mindfulness-Based Cognitive Therapy* (2nd edn). New York: Guilford.

Teasdale, J. (2022) *What Happens in Mindfulness: Inner Awakening and Embodied Cognition*. New York: Guilford.

CHAPTER 7

Principle #6: Balancing Cognitive and Experiential Interventions in CBT

The purpose of this chapter is twofold. First, to introduce the reader to the perspectives about information processing available in modern CBT. Second, to provide examples of the toolkit of techniques from which the disciplined clinician can draw in daily practice.

COGNITIVE PROCESSES IN BECK'S CBT MODEL

Beck's model of CBT is predicated on the assumption that the human mind is capable of using rationality and logic in the service of self-healing. For Beck, even people struggling with psychosis were presumed to have islands of rationality that could be brought to bear on managing anomalous experiences, such as hallucination. In Beck's model, it is the meaning of events, perhaps more than the events themselves, that determine our reactions (Beck & Dozois, 2011; Beck & Haigh, 2014). The most commonly employed methods in Beck's CBT involve bringing to light those thoughts that are most immediately accessible to awareness, verbalizing them, and then testing them for either their accuracy or their utility.

But meaning is encoded in less verbal modes, as well (Bennett-Levy et al., 2004; Leahy, Holland, & McGinn, 2011; Wills & Sanders, 2013; Wills, 2015; Teasdale, 2022). We "think" in a variety of modes. These include visual imagery, metaphor, sensory experiences, memory. Meaning can be expressed via body sensations, and bodily posture. We need a framework for understanding and accessing all modes of creating meaning. And we need to create interventions that hit a "bullseye", compelling to the rational mind and to our emotions. Without understanding the multiple ways in which meaning is encoded, the therapist can get

DOI: 10.4324/9781003505587-8

caught in the "brain–gut" problem in therapy, in which the therapist focuses on a brief, rationalist approach to cognitive restructuring, only to discover that the client buys it at the level of rationality, yet doesn't buy it on a deep, visceral level. Many a therapist has worked to help a client find a more flexible, accurate, adaptive belief about themselves, only to hear the following: "I know in my head that what we're talking about is true. I'm not literally the biggest loser on the planet. Still, it just feels like it to me."

Beck understood that cognition is layered, in the sense that some forms of cognition are encoded in language, in ways that render them relatively accessible to awareness. Other ways of encoding meaning are deeply embedded, developmentally, in the body sensations, action urges, memory, and images described above. Let's take a look at how cognition and meaning are structured, starting with a Beckian framework. One of Beck's discoveries was the stream of thought that exists on the fringes of awareness, often encoded in words or in visual images. He deemed these "automatic thoughts", because of both their believability to the person and their unbidden nature. They spontaneously arise, seem believable, are a form of private communication, and have a compelling impact on mood and behavior. They go unchallenged, as a rule. Taken at face value, they can exert a powerful impact on daily functioning. Beck developed a cognitive specificity model, in which clusters of automatic thoughts arose in the context of various clinical disorders. Thus, depressed people tended to experience painful appraisals of self, future, and world, what Beck referred to as "The Cognitive Triad" (Beck, Rush, Shaw & Emery, 1979). Anxious people tended to overestimate threats, while diminishing their own ability to manage threats (Beck & Emery, 1985). Automatic thoughts in these clinical conditions gave rise to adaptive impairments, as depressed people tended to withdraw or shut down, and anxious people entered a cycle of avoidance. Capitalizing on the understanding that humans are prone to systematic cognitive biases, Beck adapted his model to a wide range of clinical conditions, noting the cognitive specificity associated with each disorder. In turn, the model then allows for an idiographic approach, tailored to each individual. Beck's model trains clients to notice this stream of private "conversation" and to step back and assess such cognition for either its accuracy or its utility. Clients are trained to observe the systematic cognitive biases they experience, which characterize the clinical conditions for which they seek relief. More accurate and/or flexible beliefs are cultivated in therapy, allowing for more effective adaptive functioning. Another feature of automatic thoughts is their transience. Beck began applying his model in research on *episodic* major depression. Note the emphasis on episodic. Automatic thoughts were seen to arise with depression, and to lift as the episode remitted, either spontaneously or through therapy. The transience of the depression becomes an ally in treatment, because a contrast can be drawn between one's thinking when depressed, and one's thinking when not depressed.

Core Beliefs: Beck recognized that there were also beliefs about self, world, and future that were often developmentally embedded, in the sense that they were more enduring in nature, and capable of being dormant, until activated by the onset of a depressive episode or an anxiety disorder. Core beliefs can be both positive and negative, though it is customarily the negative, painful, core beliefs that we see in therapy. These beliefs frequently cluster around issues of sociotropy (lovability) and autonomy (competence). Core beliefs can develop at later points in life, often in response to events or experiences that are powerful, and out of the ordinary, such as war, or other trauma. These he deemed *core beliefs*. In contrast to automatic thoughts, these beliefs can become a permanent fixture of our sense of self, others, the future, and the world. They often compose a substrate of cognition, or information processing, that characterizes personality disorders (Beck, Davis, & Freeman, 2006). More broadly, core beliefs are called "core", because they are intertwined with one's sense of self. They are part of what Acceptance and Commitment Therapy (ACT) calls "the conceptualized self" (Hayes, Strosahl, & Wilson, 2011), and we'll discuss that in more detail when we deal with self-processes. Core beliefs tend to be quite visceral and durable, often embedded in painful emotions and body sensations. And they can be more resistant to change via the methods that are effective with automatic thoughts, such as the examination of evidence for such beliefs. An example of this difference follows.

Cindy is a 44-year-old woman, with a long history of chronic depression, emotion dysregulation, suicidality, self-injury and substance abuse. She repeatedly claims in therapy that "I'm worthless." As the therapist sought to help Cindy tune in to areas of her life that might show worthwhileness, such as her loyalty to a disabled sister, or her valiant efforts to parent her two children, Cindy rebuffed all such therapeutic efforts. In an effort to understand why and how such enduringly painful appraisals were so compelling to Cindy, the therapist learned that while Cindy was telling herself she was worthless, she imagined her father's voice, and conjured a visual image of him standing over her while she was in her early teens, screaming at her, and telling her that "you are worthless trash." Efforts to dissuade Cindy from this belief fell short, as she was still looking at herself as that young teen, whose worth was completely in the hands of her alcoholic father, deceased years ago, yet still exerting a grip on her deepest sense of herself. Freeing clients from these mental traps often requires other tools and techniques, which we will explore in detail later.

Silent assumptions in Beck's model involve beliefs that often take an "if–then" format, such as "If I become wealthy and famous, then I'll finally be a worthwhile person." These beliefs tend to be inferred after repeated encounters with a client, as patterns emerge in the client's presentation. Silent assumptions can be a very creative mechanism the mind creates, as a way of freeing oneself of the curse of painful core beliefs. Thus, a man who felt he never measured up in the eyes of his powerful, overbearing father, may develop the silent assumption above, with his exit from the curse of "worthlessness" seemingly ensured by the trappings of wealth and fame. Sometimes it works. Sometimes we discover that nothing frees the person from unrelenting painful core beliefs. Silent assumptions may reflect the clever adaptive efforts of the human mind to come to terms with old pain, and to imagine conditions in which one is loved, admired, validated, accepted, and deemed capable and worthwhile. Some core beliefs and some silent assumptions are benign, even salutary. Those, however, are not often seen in our consulting rooms. In cases where there are positive core beliefs and benign silent assumptions, the therapy may well proceed effectively at the level of working with transient depressions and anxiety problems, focusing only on automatic thoughts. The more developmentally embedded, painful, and damaging the core belief, the more unworkable the assumptions, the longer therapy may take.

Rules: Yet another form of cognition involves *rules*. Rules streamline functioning in many ways, guiding action and helping us make sense of the world. In many ways rules are highly useful and serve to create social cohesion and order. Individually, rules help us make sense of the world, promoting internal cohesion when they work, and orienting us towards action. However, the rules in our heads can be arbitrary and ineffective. Rules are ubiquitous, and when problematic, they can be a source of considerable potential mischief in relationships, for example. Imagine a couple coming for therapy. The husband is asked to consider that his wife has needs which he is not meeting. The wife is encouraged to tell her husband what she wants him to do for her, and she says: "He should know what I want without my having to tell him. If I have to tell him, it ruins the favor or the gift." That's quite a trap, for both parties. In this case, one party has a rule that the other party not only doesn't know about, but mustn't be told about it; instead, it must be accurately intuited and followed, or else disappointment follows. Other rules take the form of "musts" and "should", as Ellis noted (Ellis & Joffe-Ellis, 2019). These include rule-driven beliefs such as "I must always be the best at what I do"; "I must be perfect"; "Life must always be fair; People who I think are wrong must be punished." These rules tend to form rigid and inflexible verbal directives, in an attempt to shape one's life and the world according to the dictates of the rule. Humans can become quite punishing of rule violators, including oneself. And often, the rules are hidden from view, even from the one who creates the rule. But rules can often be uncovered in therapy, brought to light and examined for their helpfulness. As with the US Constitution, they can be amended.

A more behavioral account of rule-governed behavior provides important insight into how rules can economically guide behavior towards evolutionarily adaptive ends. Yet when applied inflexibly, rules can impair functioning (Hayes et al., 1986). Lab rats in an operant chamber will go through many trials to learn that when a certain colored light is on it must push the right lever to get food and when a different light is on it must push the left lever to get food. By contrast, humans can quickly learn the rule verbally. "Push right lever when red light is on, and left lever when the green one is on." This economy of learning serves to provide an evolutionary adaptive function for humans. However, and this is an important however, a kind of verbal fly in the ointment of human adaptation: when contingencies change, such as when the lights are reversed, and the rat needs to push the left lever when the red light is on, the rat can rather quickly adjust to the change, and get food! By contrast, humans tend to persist inflexibly, pushing on that left lever, even when it doesn't produce the expected results. This isn't to say that lab rats are smarter than humans, at least not in most tasks. But it does point to a kind of Achilles Heel in our verbal adaptive advantage: applied without sensitivity to consequences, rules can fail us. It isn't uncommon for us to be under the influence of rules that we may never have even verbalized before. For example, a person who is abruptly diagnosed with a life-threatening disease may experience despair. During the therapist's use of Guided Discovery, the client says "I work out. I eat well. I don't drink or smoke. This isn't supposed to be happening." Rules in situations of this sort may reflect an implicit "bargain" that the person has made with life, or with the universe. The rule in this case takes on the form of a silent assumption, also: "If I live well, I should never get sick." Except that the universe doesn't seem to care about the bargains that exist in our own minds. Non-acceptance is often the price of rules that fail to map onto current contingencies. So is ineffective problem solving. In such cases, therapy aims to help humans become as smart as lab rats. When the contingencies of life change, spot the change, and adapt effectively.

The existence and the nature of core beliefs, silent assumptions, and rules has received less empirical support than automatic thoughts, and the more one departs from the more immediately accessible automatic thoughts into the more speculative, the lower the reliability of the case formulations (Kuyken, Padesky, & Dudley, 2009).

IMPLICITLY ENCODED COGNITION

Cognition can be quite implicit also, rather than encoded primarily in words. Our brains send signals to our bodies that encode meaning yet do so in ways that bypass the conscious mind. It's important to remember that our brains evolved not to make us happy, or even to make sense of the world, consciously. They evolved to help us survive and to solve basic problems related to survival, resource acquisition, sex, caretaking, and social cohesion (Gilbert & Simos, 2022; Feldman-Barrett, 2017; LeDoux, 2023). Our work sometimes requires us to help clients unpack what are at times multiple levels of information processing, happening in ways that can be mysterious, frightening, and demoralizing to the client.

First, let's take a benign and perhaps famous example of how memory and sensory experiences can weave their way into consciousness, in ways that may actually bypass verbal modes. Memories can be activated by seemingly random events that may occur outside the awareness of the person experiencing the memory. The "Proust Effect" is a term based on the early 20th century French writer Marcel Proust, who observed that humans were subject to what he called "involuntary memory." In *Remembrance of Things Past*, he wrote about the reverie he experienced tasting a madeleine cake, noting that "just one taste of the sweet, buttery French cake mingled with lime-blossom tea was all it took for childhood memories to come flooding back" (Proust, 2013). Anyone working with PTSD, for example, understands that these "involuntary memories" form a substrate of meaning that is painfully activated in those suffering from the disorder. In this disorder, memory and sensory experience related to trauma can be fragmented and incomprehensible to the client, while also terrifying. Not only are these internal experiences frightening, but they set up a pattern of avoidance of such experiences, in ways that actually deepen client distress (Hayes et al., 2011). Such threatening sensations and memories can be challenging to access and to turn into words.

Threat processing occurs rapidly and in a manner that can bypass conscious awareness (LeDoux, 2023; Feldman-Barrett, 2017). Thus, fear arousal, for example, can occur in ways that are bewildering to the person.

It may arise seemingly out of nowhere and lead the person to construct a story about their fear that doesn't map onto actual threats. This, in turn, can lead to avoidance and other maladaptive behaviors that impair adaptive functioning.

Similarly, Kahneman has proposed two cognitive systems, System 1 and System 2, that operate differently in the human mind (Kahneman, 2011). These proposed systems are hypothetical, and do not necessarily map onto brain processes in a neat and clear manner. Nor are they drivers or "homunculi", little folks in the brain that make us do what we do. Yet System 1 describes the more rapid, automatic forms of information processing, such as threat appraisal. This is a more intuitive system that leads to quick responses to environmental contingencies. It is efficient, yet prone to systematic biases, or errors at times. System 2 is the more deliberative, reflective, and rational mode of information processing, which is slower, effortful, and which may describe how the more rationalistic forms of CBT operate. System 2 needs cultivation and practice, and it may fail when real time contingencies appear to demand a rapid response. It can also fail when faced with emotionally compelling beliefs that are given support by the ecosystems we exist in. To wit: those core beliefs Beck describes, or one's religious or political convictions. Beck's model is particularly designed to capitalize on and build upon System 2 capabilities. That said, interventions need to be created that address both these systems, which we would metaphorically describe as "head" and "heart" interventions.

These findings about human cognition raise a clinically relevant question: is it cognition, behavior, or emotion that is the tail wagging the dog? In our model, it can be all of these. Beck's CBT tended to put primacy on the rationalistic, System 2, forms of intervention. By contrast, Linehan's DBT recognized that dysregulation could swamp the person's capacity for the more deliberative, rational, System 2 processing, and designed a therapy that promoted regulation of emotions, first. We will address this issue of the causal relationship between cognition, emotion, and behavior in Chapter 10, when we show how to create case conceptualizations.

When focusing on cognitive change, and the creation of new experiences of meaning, we have a rich pallet of interventions to choose from. The use of guided imagery, metaphor, and experiential interventions have increasingly become part of the CBT landscape (Gilbert, 2010; Gilbert & Simos, 2022; Stott et al., 2010; Hackmann et al., 2011; Westbrook, Kennerly, & Kirk, 2012; Wills & Sanders, 2013; Hayes et al., 2011; Hayes, S. & Hofmann, 2018; Stoddard & Afari, 2014). Newer elaborations, building on CBT cognitive interventions in an innovative way can be found in the work of Adrian Wells, in the UK (Wells, 2000, 2009; Fisher & Wells, 2009).

We'll explore how these and the more rationalistic interventions can be used to effectively address both the "head" and the "heart" in CBT, creating robust change. To do that, let's briefly look at the following categories of intervention: rationalist Beckian techniques; Beckian-informed behavioral experiments; mindfulness-informed techniques; experiential metaphors; body and postural interventions.

BECKIAN TECHNIQUES

Part of Aaron "Tim" Beck's genius was to turn some of the precepts of psychoanalysis on their head. Psychoanalysis posited that the real core of therapeutic work involved accessing and bringing into awareness long buried, unconscious material. Beck, who was initially a trained psychoanalyst, saw that it was the accessible stream of pre-conscious cognition and imagery that provided a doorway into therapeutic change. He deemed this stream "automatic thoughts", because of the seemingly involuntary automaticity of these thoughts and images. Such cognition functions as a private communication within the patient or client, is experienced as believable, is rarely subjected to rational scrutiny, and exerts a powerful influence on mood and behavior. Beck discovered this stream in a therapy session in which he was meeting with a female patient. When he noticed an uncomfortable shift in her posture, he asked what just went through her mind, to which she responded that she had the thought that she must be the most boring patient in Beck's caseload. This, in turn, provided the opportunity for Beck and the patient to test the accuracy of this belief and to explore its connection to other adaptive difficulties in the patient's life (Weishaar, 1993).

From this encounter, Beck was able to create a clinically derived model of therapy that focused on tended to characterize a variety of disorders. He began with depression, and posited what came to be known as The Cognitive Triad, which involved negative automatic thoughts about oneself ("I'm a loser"), one's expectations of the world ("Nobody in their right mind would love me"), and the future ("Things will never work out for me"). Similarly, anxiety disorders were seen as having a similar "signature", by overestimating threat and underestimating one's ability to navigate potentially threatening circumstances. Each disorder became subject to the development of a clinically derived model and was tested for both the efficacy of the therapy and the accuracy of the theory.

There is no need for us to provide a detailed exploration of Beckian techniques in this volume. There is a rich literature to which the clinician can turn for this (Beck & Beck, 2020; Leahy, Holland, & McGinn, 2011; Padesky & Greenberger, 2020; Kennerley, Kirk, & Westbrook, 2017). Many of the techniques in the Beckian tradition involve the use of Guided Discovery and nothing more than a sheet of paper and pen or pencil. The client is invited to step back from that stream of thought and to examine it with a sense of curiosity: Is this thought truly accurate? Is there evidence for another way of looking at this? Which interpretation appears to be the most accurate? Which way of looking at things feels "right", and which one allows me to more flexibly meet the challenges I face? If some thoughts cannot be proven or disproven, which way of looking at this allows me to live well?

Let's look at two examples, one in which we assess a belief for its accuracy, and one for its effect on the person's life. We'll use the same case for both.

This is a 28-year-old woman, single, living in San Francisco, and working in financial services, specializing in high-net-worth clients. She recently broke up with a partner, with whom she was in a relationship for two years. She has experienced periods of depression in the past, but not, she says, like this. She considered suicide, but recognized, as she said "That's going off the deep end. Too many people would be hurt if I did that." So she sought therapy. Among the emotionally charged, painful beliefs that showed up is this: "There is something wrong with me. I'm radioactive in relationships. I give up."

THERAPIST: Radioactive? That suggests you're like a nuclear blast to anyone near you. Is it like that?

CLIENT: That sounds exaggerated (smiles). And yes, it's like that. I think I chase anyone close to me away.

THERAPIST: Well, we can explore that if you'd like. I don't know. Maybe you do inadvertently find ways to pre-emptively end relationships. If you do, I'm guessing it's to protect yourself from being hurt. May I ask, what tells you that's what happened in this situation (NOTE: one could also ask "What's the evidence?" We tend to advocate a softer approach, one less suited to what might feel like a courtroom interrogation.)

CLIENT: The harder I pushed for him to commit, the more he distanced from me. Finally, I found out he was involved with another woman, a woman he worked with at Goldman Sachs.

THERAPIST: I see. I believe you also said he had a history of this, before he got involved with you, right? Keeping multiple relationships going at the same time?

CLIENT: I thought that would stop. I thought what we had was special for both of us. If I wasn't enough, it's because…(lowers her head and becomes silent)

THERAPIST: Because you're radioactive?

CLIENT: That's what it feels like.

THERAPIST: Would you be willing to consider that feeling it doesn't make it a fact? Actually, may I ask you to consider if there could be any other explanation for his behavior? Let's put it this way. If you had a friend in this spot, what would you tell her?

CLIENT: That he's a jerk, and that maybe you were a little bit of a sucker, or naïve. But not radioactive. At least some of this is on him. Maybe most of it.

THERAPIST: And if it were your friend saying this to you, how would you feel?

CLIENT: (thinking, silent for a moment) I'd feel a little bit lighter. Still in a lot of pain. But lighter.

THERAPIST: Okay. So we have two ways of looking at this situation, at you. Story one? You're radioactive. Defective in some way that chases partners away. Story two? You had some help in the derailment of this relationship. Maybe I don't know all the details, but story two says your ex had a big hand in this. Fair to say?

    (CLIENT NODS)

At this point, we can ask the client to rate the believability of "story 2", the alternate belief we created in therapy. We can also encourage a mindfulness exercise here, in which we ask her to notice in her body and her emotions how each story, or belief, feels. We ask the readers to consider that there are many techniques that can be used in this situation. There are Thought Records, survey techniques, continuum techniques, and techniques that the clinician will make up on the spot. Please take a look at the references provided, above. They make terrific beach reads, and the techniques you will learn will work. If one doesn't do the job, there are literally dozens of others to try.

Now, let's try another angle here. Rather than focus at this point on finding an alternative that is "truer", or more accurate in fitting the facts, let's just see about the usefulness of a belief. Some beliefs aren't easily tested and needn't be. In fact, some beliefs, such as this client's are not only unprovable ("I'm defective"), they become a source of further difficulty, in and of themselves. By labeling oneself as "defective", one is tempted to withdraw or give up. And in the case above, if in fact the patient subtly derails relationships to pre-empt abandonment, then we can validate the logic of protecting herself, while fostering the creation of new skills and a new behavioral repertoire, so that she can have a greater likelihood of creating an enduring, workable intimate relationship. Here's an example, again, using the same client.

THERAPIST: How about we take a look at that thought "There's something wrong with me." Does that thought pull you back into the relationship game, or make you want to retreat?

PATIENT: Retreat.

THERAPIST: Is that what you want, to just hang it up, to give up on intimacy?

CLIENT: Maybe for now. But not forever, I guess.

THERAPIST: Ok. So in a way, it's useful for right now to retreat. But if that belief "I'm defective, I'm radioactive" hangs around, will it help or hinder your wish for closeness?

CLIENT: Hinder. I'll be safe, but I'll be all alone, forever, which is not really what I want.

THERAPIST: So maybe there's a more useful way of looking at this.

CLIENT: That I have bad judgment in relationships?

THERAPIST: Live and learn.

CLIENT: Maybe another way of seeing this is that I'm scared to get burned, and my judgment sometimes is flawed.

THERAPIST: Join the family.

CLIENT: Which one?

THERAPIST: The human family. What if judgment can be improved, and what if creating relationships is a kind of skill to be learned. Clearly, it's not risk free. But from what you said, it sounds like in the long run, you're going to want to take another risk. We can work on that together if you'd like. So, last question about this: we have two ways of looking at this. One, you're defective. Two, sometimes your judgment is flawed, and you get hurt. Which one do you want to take with you into your future?

CLIENT: The second one.

Please note: although the interventions were cognitive, they included a link to a problem for which the client entered therapy, failed relationships, and an invitation to expand not only her thinking, but her behavioral repertoire in order to get closer to what she wants: a relationship that is more enduring and more satisfying. Another way of addressing change in multiple modes of meaning, emotion, and behavior is through the use of Behavioral Experiments, which we turn to next.

BEHAVIORAL EXPERIMENTS

Cognitive Behavior Therapy, since Beck, takes therapy from the consulting room into the client's daily life. The primary focus of behavioral experiments (BE) is to test and revise beliefs and assumptions, based on feedback in the real world, outside of the therapy room. And in doing so, the intention is to create experientially compelling cognitive, emotional, and behavior change. The latter, behavior change, is very important here. Our aim is not just to change how people think about a problem situation. Toward that end, the use of exposure procedures is utilized. Exposure involves having a person place themselves in a situation that has either been avoided altogether, or that is only tolerated with great difficulty, and/or with impaired functioning. Exposure does not involve seeking to immediately extinguish or rid the person of their fears. It seeks to put the person in contact with an avoided situation, while building a new repertoire in the face of the situation that has previously elicited fear or avoidance. Ultimately, it's to help the client have choices about how to engage and behave in those situations. Behavioral experiments have the ability to target both head and heart. We have noted earlier that humans process information using multiple systems or modes (Barnard & Teasdale, 1991; Bennett-Levy, 2003; Bennett-Levy et al., 2004; Kahneman, 2011; Wells, 2000, 2009; Segal, Williams, & Teasdale, 2013). One system is the more intuitive, rapid, emotionally charged, non-verbal. The other is the more rational, verbally mediated, and effortful to sustain. Behavioral experiments derive their power from their unique ability to promote change simultaneously in both systems or modes of meaning, the explicit and the more emotionally encoded implicit system (Chadwick, Birchwood, & Trower, 1996). They are a uniquely powerful method. Let's take a look at the types of behavioral experiments that are available, as well as how to set one up. Then we'll look at a real-life example.

Let's consider what the purpose is of a behavioral experiment. First, it's a test, an experiment, done using some of the same tools that scientists use. Essentially, it's a test of an old way of looking at and experiencing a problem situation. At the same time, if done right, it's a way of opening a door to a new way of seeing, experiencing, and behaving in that problem situation. It takes some bravery on the part of the client, and therapists have to set up the behavioral experiment, so the client fully understands its purpose, and is on board. Most behavioral experiments involve facing a situation that the client has been avoiding in some way. Facing it, fully and completely, involves what DBT calls "Opposite Action", doing the opposite of what the client's emotions and cognitions and behavioral history tell them to do. Most of the time, there is some withdrawal or avoidance happening for the client, in the face of a problem they wish to solve or manage more effectively. There are essentially two broad types of behavioral experiments. First, is hypothesis testing. Second, are observational experiments. The nature of the experiment depends upon a variety of factors: the willingness of the client to engage in an experiment; whether the experiment is an active testing of a hypothesis, usually relating to a client's beliefs; the testing alternative hypothesis (Theory A vs Theory B); observing, for purposes of either gathering information, or as a precursor to the client taking what may feel to them to be a riskier leap. The key is that the experiment creates an opportunity to find new ways of viewing a problem situation and, ideally, behaving in that situation.

In line with what science now increasingly points to, we don't erase or get rid of an older pattern of thinking, feeling, and behaving. Instead, we help the client create new patterns that with practice become increasingly available to the client in relevant situations (Brewin, 2006; Craske et al., 2014). It does take some bravery and some persistence on the part of the client. And the skilled therapist helps the client find a starting point for change, whether it is a very small, relatively risk-free step, or a big leap. A big leap might involve having a client with panic test his belief that if he goes to a public place, alone, he will collapse, and be laughed at by a gathering crowd. A tiny step might involve having a client with a spider phobia just look at pictures of spiders on the therapist's computer, testing whether even that level of exposure will lead to a painful outcome, such as fainting. Another example might be asking the client to gather information about a presumed danger, to help foster a more realistic estimate of threat, and to set the stage for a more behaviorally engaged experiment later. Any step, wholeheartedly undertaken, will help the client meet the challenges they face with greater courage, clarity, and effectiveness.

STEPS IN SETTING UP A BEHAVIORAL EXPERIMENT

a) *Problem identification*: As you will see in Chapter 10, on case conceptualizations and session structure, we create a problem list collaboratively with the client. We specify the problems and select starting points for the therapy. Behavioral experiments are always intended to address a specific problem that is important to the client.

b) Identify a relevant assumption or belief for testing: your process of Guided Discovery will allow you and the client to home in on any beliefs or assumptions that are implicated in maintaining the problem. These can take the form of automatic thoughts, rules, or assumptions. It is useful here to get a rating from the client not only about how much they believe the thought (usually on a 0–100 scale), but also how they feel, bodily and emotionally.

c) Design an experiment that allows for a test of the relevant belief or assumption. Be very specific about how the belief or behavior will be tested. For example, how will the client know what the results are, whether those results confirm the belief in question or disconfirm it. Are there alternatives being tested as well (Theory A vs Theory B), and if so, which theory emerges as most compelling following the BE?

d) *Results and Reflection*: Bennett-Levy et al. (2004) employ a framework in adult learning that encourages reflection after a BE. First, after the BE has been conducted, we encourage the client to assess the results in some detail, and to reflect on what they have learned as a result of the experiment. This is a time when we can revisit those earlier ratings of believability and of the impact on mood and behavior of that belief. This helps to put into words both "head" and "gut" learning from the BE, and to consolidate the learning. From this, the therapist and client discuss ways to take further steps to strengthen learning and to expand the client's behavioral repertoire. Remember, we're not getting rid of an old pattern; we're helping the client build new patterns of thinking and behaving. And those next steps involve helping to systematically build those new patterns in relevant life contexts.

Let's look at a clinical example, to show how this process unfolds in session.

James is 33 years old and comes to therapy because his social anxiety keeps him from speaking up in situations where he wishes he could assert himself. He says he is too timid to send back a meal at a restaurant if it is not properly cooked. He is timid when trying to negotiate prices on cars, appliances, furniture, and so forth. Instead, he remains passive and silent, and later fumes at his perceived incompetence. He sees himself as "sucker bait" every time he has a bad meal in a restaurant or steps onto the lot at a car dealership. His social anxiety also takes a toll on his career advancement and his ability to engage with potential romantic partners of interest to him. His automatic thoughts included: "I'm weak. I'm a sucker. If I try to stand up stand up for myself, they'll ignore me or bowl me over." He cites numerous examples of times when he bought things he didn't want, at prices he could ill afford, and awful restaurant meals about which he remained silent. He feels humiliated by his passivity and timidity.

The client was willing to engage in a BE, once he understood the rationale and saw how it could help him overcome his timidity and his sense that "I'm a sucker in life." Instead, he hoped to be able to stand up for himself in ways that helped him build a sense of effectiveness in the world.

The steps taken to set up the BE included the following.

Setting the objective of the BE: James and the therapist established that this would be a test of James' personal "hypothesis", that he would be bowled over and be shown to be weak and a "sucker".

Designing the BE: An experiment was designed, based on James' willingness to be a little bold. He thought he could handle going to an appliance store, with no intention of buying anything, and asking to be shown various models of the washing machines and dryers. He agreed to ask questions about the operation of the machines, their relative merits, and the bottom-line costs of each. He would then thank the salesperson and leave without purchasing. Instead he would say "you've given me a lot to think about."

Prior to carrying out the BE, the therapist and James role played the conversation, until James said "I'm ready to give it a go." For example, they talked about what might happen in the store that could derail James. Since he really had no intention of buying a washing machine, he was clear that he was unlikely to be swayed into making a purchase. That solved his worst fear: being a "sucker", who committed to buying something against his own better judgment. The therapist and James also discussed the ethics of the BE. James was concerned that he was taking up potentially valuable time of the salespeople, knowing he had no intention of buying. The therapist asked James what percentage of people walking into the store actually bought. James and the therapist got on the office computer, consulted an AI program about this probability estimate, and James learned that it was likely that only a small percentage of people in the store made a big purchase on any given day. With his two main concerns addressed, he was ready to try the BE. He agreed with the therapist that he would make his best effort to put himself fully and with complete engagement into the discussion with the salesperson. He would make eye contact with the salesperson and ask a list of questions that he and the therapist put together to gather information. A central DBT mindfulness skill is Participation, throwing oneself wholly into the moment, rather than relying on avoidance behaviors, sometimes known as safety behaviors, as they create the illusion of safety, while serving avoidance. This includes mumbling, diverting eye gaze, ending a social encounter early, etc. All that was practiced in the role play. That introduced an element of a test of Theory 1 vs Theory 2 about the outcome. James rated the likelihood of each outcome and guessed that Theory 1 would be slightly more likely to occur, though he was willing to be open to another possibility.

Results of the BE and Reflection: James returned the following week, with his results. He said he was scared as he prepared to enter the store, and he noticed the fear welling up in his chest. He approached a salesperson and asked to be shown a variety of washers and dryers. He told the salesperson up front that he was not sure he was quite ready for a purchase but was interested in seeing what was available. He said that as he began talking with the salesperson, his voice quivered a bit, and that his painful thoughts showed up. He turned his attention as much as he could towards the salesperson. And he began to notice that after a while, what felt like a friendly conversation was happening. "I learned a lot," he said. After nearly 20 minutes, after seeing the last of the machines, he thanked the salesperson, took his card, and said "I'll give this a lot of thought." The salesperson ended the conversation saying "anytime you're ready to buy, come on back." They shook hands and he left the store. He rated his fear on a 10-point scale as a 7 when he went in. He felt it was a 2 when he left. He decided that the weight of the evidence from the BE supported Theory Two. He did not find evidence for Theory 1, which had predicted that he would appear as "a sucker" and "weak" to both the salesperson and himself.

In reflecting on the BE, James said that he was persuaded to consider that he hadn't been weak at all in the situation, despite the initial fear. In fact, he found the information interesting, and felt that he had some rapport with the person showing him the washers and dryers. He and the therapist set up another behavioral experiment for the following week, in order to strengthen the learning favoring Theory 2, and to create opportunities to practice new skills, not only in a new view of self, but in dealing with others in daily life.

A more detailed and comprehensive look at Behavioral Experiments is beyond the scope of this book. For that, the reader is well advised to read Bennett-Levy et al. (2004). It is also important to recognize that there are competing models for understanding how and why exposure works. Michelle Craske, a clinical psychologist at UCLA has proposed an inhibitory learning model, which involved setting up exposures to create an "expectancy violation" (Craske et al., 2008; Craske et al., 2014). In line with BEs, Craske's model emphasizes the importance of exposures as a means of helping clients learn that their negative expected outcomes are violated by the actual outcomes of the exposure. However, her work took issue with the use of the Theory 1 vs Theory 2 format, because she believed that too much priming of expectancy change prior to exposures might dampen the very expectancy violation that was essential for successful therapy. This is perhaps a technical way of saying that she believed it was best not to try to change cognitions first, but to let the client draw their own conclusions from a well-conducted exposure trial.

We draw on Craske's work in two ways that we want to emphasize. First, it teaches toleration of fear, rather than the elimination of fear during exposure therapy (Craske et al., 2008). This has to be emphasized in therapy. Many clients come to us hoping and expecting that the therapy will rid them of internal discomfort, as a precondition for changing their behavior in problem situations. That's not how therapy works. We have to teach clients to tolerate, not obliterate their painful conditioning. In line with this, we do not recommend using fear reduction either within or between sessions as a useful measure of improvement. What matters is that the client learns to open up their behavioral repertoire, regardless of whether they experience fear or other painful emotions during BEs, and in their daily lives.

Second, and very much related to our first point, Craske emphasizes the creation of new response patterns that compete with old fear responses. This dovetails with the work of Brewin (2006), whose work we will visit in our next chapter, on self-processes in CBT. Simply put, for now, we are helping clients build more functional and resilient behavioral repertoires (cognitively, emotionally, and behaviorally). These new repertoires compete with, and in time become more accessible to the client than are the older, less adaptive patterns, the one driven by fear, depression, avoidance and rigid patterns of avoidance and withdrawal. That is why it takes time, practice, and persistence to make new patterns of living that are durable and available in new situations.

This literature may seem pretty "inside baseball" at this point. But it's important to know that there is some disagreement in the scientific literature about how to create experiences in therapy that lead to durable change. Which is best? Well, more recently Craske has written that the method she developed, involving prediction error generalization, "may be a stronger driver of exposure therapy effects for some people, whereas reappraisal of feared outcomes may be more relevant for others, such that *different versions of exposure therapy may be tailored for each individual*" (Craske, Sandman, & Stein, 2022, p.418). She notes that "patients may be more engaged in treatment when they are receiving what they need most at the time they need it most" (Craske, Sandman, & Stein, 2022, p.418).

It is important to recognize that we don't have a settled science on the issue of which methods for conducting exposures work best, in an absolute sense. We believe that Behavioral Experiments, when done as we suggest, by de-emphasizing fear removal, and instead emphasizing the creation of new learning, is a sound way to proceed.

We believe the clinician is on solid ground implementing Behavioral Experiments, with the understandings we set forth above: it's not about getting rid of fear as a precondition for change; and we are helping clients build new patterns of functioning that increasingly compete with and are eventually more readily available to the client in situations that previously led to a closing down of effective coping. In the case example above, James will be asked to tolerate some fear, while building a new repertoire of engagement behaviors, essentially akin to building muscle mass in a gym; it requires the ability to tolerate some discomfort in the short term, but it leads to the outcome James seeks: the ability to more comfortably and effectively engage with people in all areas of his life, for pleasure, for intimacy, and for improving his work life.

THE COMPASSION PITFALL

Before moving on to another class of experiential interventions, a word of caution. Gilbert (2021; Gilbert & Simos, 2022) noticed that when he was trying to help clients find alternative beliefs, using Beck's Cognitive Therapy, his clients were sometimes quite harsh with themselves. It was as though another stream of automatic thoughts was operating while the client was learning to address their depressive or anxious appraisals. Such thoughts as "I'm such a fool to even think these things", or "Damnit! Quit thinking that nonsense" kept showing up. The purpose of our efforts is to help free clients from the burden of their self-imposed tyranny, not inadvertently exacerbate it. This doesn't mean that we should refrain from cognitive restructuring techniques, just that we are wise to inquire about whether the clients are learning to create flexible alternative beliefs with a lighthearted curiosity, which frees them, or with the harsh voice of an inner tyrant. If the client is bullying herself into submission, that needs to become an immediate treatment target.

FORM VERSUS FUNCTION: 3RD WAVE EXERCISES FOR STEPPING BACK FROM THE RAINSTORM OF THOUGHTS

In the science of psychology, a new way of viewing and dealing with human cognition emerged through the work of clinical research teams in the US and the UK (Teasdale (2022), Segal et al. (2013), Wells (2000), and Hayes et al. (2011). The newer models of therapy that have emerged within CBT are sometimes controversially referred to by Hayes as "3rd Wave" CBTs (Hayes & Hofmann, 2021). We think the distinction is heuristically useful. Where 1st Wave CBT was early behaviorism, and 2nd Wave CBT is represented by the work of Aaron T. Beck and Albert Ellis, 3rd Wave CBT therapies share a couple of common properties. First, they are based on a different understanding of cognition. Second, they often draw on Eastern contemplative and mindfulness traditions, though they are based in modern psychological science. Where so-called 2nd Wave CBTs tended to focus on rationalist interventions to address problematic cognition, 3rd Wave takes a different route. They don't try to change problematic cognitions through direct, rationalist interventions. Instead, they help people change the way they relate to thoughts and other internal experiences.

Two thoughts here: first, the newer CBT therapies, such as ACT, MBCT, MCT, and DBT are aligned with our own perspective in a very key way: There isn't a delete button on memory, thoughts, emotions, images, or uncomfortable body sensations associated with our learning histories. So instead of focusing on removal of painful or problematic inner experiences, we have to focus on building new ways of relating to them. That approach is fully consistent with how we see emerging trends in the science of psychology, and with our clinical principles. And we recognize that Beckian and other so-called 2nd Wave CBT therapies are not conducted with the intention of ridding the person of "bad" thoughts and replacing them with "good" ones. We do not agree with some in the 3rd Wave community who have expressed concern that Beckian interventions have an iatrogenic effect in treatment and should therefore not be used. If that were true, treatment outcomes for CBT would not be as robust as they often are (Keefe & DeRubeis, 2015). The key is how those and any interventions are delivered. The claim of iatrogenic effects is based on the notion that Beck's interventions involve "disputing" or "challenging" the client, in an effort to expunge "bad thoughts", which may only serve to strengthen client belief in their automatic thoughts. Beck, himself, was always quite clear that we do not challenge clients. As we have described earlier, we use Guided Discovery to more gently foster curiosity and collaboration between therapist and client, as a means of helping clients find another place to stand. Or, to borrow again from Raymond Carver, to find a new path to the waterfall. Let's look at how those newer models of therapy can be used.

The interventions created by Beck and others are effective, and they are also backed by years of outcome studies. They can be delivered in a manner that is fully consistent with our objectives, as we demonstrated in the previous section on Behavioral Experiments. The newer, 3rd Wave therapies also work, and they have evidence behind them. Rather than viewing these approaches as competing with one another for some kind of absolute truth, the evidence suggests we view them as complementary, depending upon how they are used, when they are used, and what will be effective for any given patient.

The disciplined CBT therapist will have a theoretical framework that allows for flexible use of techniques from all "Waves of CBT. The field appears to be moving towards that type of potential integration" (Hofmann, Hayes, & Lorscheid, 2021). What is required is a case conceptualization and a theoretical framework that allows for flexible integration of seemingly divergent models. The central difference as we see it between the 2nd and 3rd CBT "Waves" is that the former tend to address the *content* of thought, targeting the believability of problematic cognition and creating credible, emotionally compelling alternatives. The latter therapies are more focused on helping people step back, observe, and set a course of behavior even in the face of problematic internal experience. They don't focus on cognitive change as a precursor to behavior change. 3rd Wave therapies tend to focus more on the process of cognition and inner experience, and on the function of cognition, not the form of that experience. There is far less emphasis placed on strategies that target the analysis of thought content, or of creating alternative beliefs as a precondition to changing one's behavior. Rather, they help clients understand that thoughts such as "I can't handle it" may function in a way that increases withdrawal as a behavior. And if, instead, the client wishes to engage, then they are encouraged to carry the thought "I can't handle it" with them directly into the action of engagement. Someone with panic disorder, in a 3rd Wave therapy, might be encouraged to view thoughts and emotions as "passengers on the bus", while the client's actions drive them towards the destination of their choice. Here, as in other, earlier CBTs, the goal is not just cognitive change, it is a change of behavior that allows the client to achieve tangible objectives of importance to them.

Form versus Function: Another way to understand the differences in approaches is to consider the difference between form and function. In CBT, one way of understanding and dealing with cognition, or any internal experience, as well as behavior, is to look at its form. So for example, the thought "I'm such an idiot." That thought stings! To address the form of the thought, one might simply try to change the form to something else, such as "I make mistakes, but that doesn't mean I'm an idiot." If that alternative form of thought is credible to the person, it can soften the blow of "I'm an idiot." Change the form, change the impact.

But another way to look at cognition, internal experience, or behavior is to examine its function. In other words, what happens to the person when "I'm an idiot" shows up? For us, especially when it's believed, it

leads to a jolt of emotional pain, and perhaps withdrawing from engagement in life. If "I'm an idiot", why take a risk? But here's the important
thing: the only way to advance one's life, whether in creating and maintaining relationships, working toward a career, moving one's life forward
in any important area, is to take a risk. So if the function of "I'm an idiot"
leads to shrinking away from that which is important to the person, "I'm
an idiot" can destroy a life. But what if we help give it a different function?
What if, instead of viewing the thought as important, compelling, and
worthy of being taken seriously, we help create a new function: humor,
lightheartedness, curiosity, and a helpful distance. Then, if the thought
pops up, which it may very well do, it can be taken less seriously, and it
doesn't have to stop the person in their tracks. One can simultaneously
notice the thought "I'm an idiot", while still pursuing all that matters in
one's life. ACT exercises are well designed to achieve this, for example. So
are other therapies within the CBT tradition that utilize mindfulness and
other strategies for helping people step back and view the thoughts, rather
than be trapped by them. As we have described in Behavioral Experiments,
the goal is not to rid the person of the thought, which we can't do. It's to
help change the impact of the thought, and we think, to allow for the
emergence of a credible alternative.

We are struck by the fact that there is rich evidence that both approaches
are empirically supported. And even though there is some debate about
why each approach works, and which theory best accounts for therapeutic
outcomes, the techniques in all waves of CBT are capable of transforming
the lives of our clients. We agree with Craske that no single approach is
likely to be effective with all clients. She notes that "patients may be more
engaged in treatment when they are receiving what they need most at the
time they need it most" (Craske, Sandman, & Stein, 2022, p. 418). The wise
and disciplined therapist is capable of being flexible, and knowledgeable
enough to select from among those interventions the ones most likely to
help any given patient or client. We therefore need a framework that doesn't
limit the use of one set of interventions, while privileging those from
another "wave" of CBT. We hope we offer that framework in this book.

That brings us to several examples. Acceptance and Commitment
Therapy (ACT) has a rich panoply of interventions that target the function of cognition and internal experience. These consist of physical metaphors, mindfulness exercises, and guided imagery exercises. They are
inventive, oftentimes fun and engaging, and they can serve as a spring-
board for the creativity of each clinician. As with Beckian techniques, the
skilled ACT therapist can create new techniques on the spot, designed to
fit the needs of the client.

One old chestnut in the ACT toolkit is the *Leaves in the Stream* exercise (Hayes et al., 2011). It is a guided imagery exercise, in which one imagines oneself sitting against the trunk of a tree, watching a stream wind past you as leaves drop from the tree onto the water. The client is guided through the exercise to experience their thoughts, dropping onto leaves, onto the surface of the water, and being carried away. This experience can help break the link between the thought and its grip on the person's life. It ceases to exert as controlling an influence on behavior and may cease to be viewed as seriously. It becomes just a leaf drifting along the surface of one's stream of thoughts, nothing to be overly concerned about.

A second example comes from a different, but related therapy. Mindfulness-Based Cognitive Therapy (MBCT) was developed as a group-administered treatment for relapse prevention in major depression (Segal, Williams, & Teasdale, 2013). It has shown results in reducing relapse, particularly for those with more recurrent episodes and histories of depression dating to childhood. Since then, its use has expanded to include treatment of current depressive episodes and other clinical conditions (Tickell et al., 2020a; Tickell et al., 2020b; Strauss, Bibby-Jones, & Jones, 2023). MBCT is based on Beck's model of CBT. But the key intervention does not involve attempting to change the form of cognition, by evidence testing or creating alternative beliefs. Instead, it is based on a novel conceptualization of depression relapse vulnerability: the pairing of sad affect with rumination, in a way that leads to a depressive spiral. By pairing this understanding of rumination with mindfulness practices, the link between sad affect and rumination may be disrupted, reducing relapse potential. Comparable to the Leaves in the Stream Exercise, MBCT's practices involve helping clients achieve a distance from thought, a capacity to notice thoughts with a sense of compassion and curiosity, but without accepting the mind's invitation to spiral into depressive rumination. The therapy protocol contains numerous practices and exercises, one of which is germane here, The Waterfall Exercise. In this exercise, the group is invited to imagine oneself standing on a rock, at the base of a waterfall, experiencing the stream of water coming down on them, and to imagine that the water contains thought. Then, the group is invited to step back from the waterfall and observe the same stream, first of water, then of thoughts, but from a distance. This creates an experiential exercise in which, ideally, people can notice, cognitively, emotionally, and bodily, the difference between being "caught" in the stream versus being an observer of the stream of thought. In turn, this contributes to the ability to watch dispassionately as depressive mental content arises. One is better able to refrain from accepting the mental invitation to ruminate, and to hence spiral into a depression. Here again, there is no effort made to test the truth or the usefulness of that stream of thought. The form of thought is left alone. But the function of thought shifts, from a function that contributes to depression, to one that contributes to greater psychological freedom. Thoughts come and go, and the vice grip that thoughts can exert on mood and behavior is weakened.

Let's end this chapter with an exercise. We'll call this the *Desert Rain Exercise*. It's one we made up, based on the principles that characterize 3rd Wave CBT.

Imagine yourself in a beautiful mountain setting, a high desert area, stretching up into pine and aspen. It's been such a hot day, but as you stand there, in that clearing, you notice clouds rolling gently in, and a spray of rain coming down, first bead by bead, then stronger. It's safe. It's peaceful. And as you stand there, allow yourself to just feel the cooling waters coming down on you...

Now let yourself become aware of any thoughts that arise into your mind. Notice judgments. See if you like or don't like the rain coming down on you. But it's okay either way. Just notice what the mind does, and where it goes as you imagine vividly standing in that clearing in the high desert mountains, with rain coming down. Let the rain, each rain drop, carry a thought or an image, or an emotion down on you. Just notice, paying gentle attention, with curiosity, what comes down on you.

Now, let's take a few steps back under one of those beautiful aspen trees. You are covered by the dappled leaves, gently flashing green and silver as the desert breeze blows through them. The boughs and the leaves protect you from any rain. But as you stand there, under the protective aspen, just watch the rain coming down from the sky, kicking up little flecks of dust and sand as they hit the earth. Let those drops carry the same thoughts and images and emotions with them. Only now, those thoughts coming down are at a distance. You are under that aspen, just noticing them.

Now let's come back to the room you are in. And let's take a moment to reflect. What was it like to be in that stream, with images and thoughts (and water) coming down on you? Was it peaceful or disturbing? And now, what was it like to be an observer, noticing that same stream, but under the protective canopy of tree cover. Did you notice any difference in the two parts of the exercise? Did the function of those thoughts, images, and emotions shift at all? If not, come back and try again another time, or see if another exercise, from ACT or MBCT, might be engaging.

There are frequent caveats about mixing cognitive interventions from 2nd and 3rd Wave CBTs, due to their differing theoretical precepts (Hayes

& Hofmann, 2021). Yet it is also recognized that with a proper under-standing of these differing theories, one can prescriptively select interven-tions to match the needs of any particular case (Hofmann, Hayes, & Lorscheid, 2021). Here is a final example, which uses both Behavioral Experiments and mindfulness-based ACT interventions in a case of psychosis:

Jack is a 45-year-old male, who has persecutory delusions and audi-tory hallucinations. The voice torment led him to contemplate suicide. Over the course of therapy, he was amenable to testing his theory about his voices. Theory 1, Jack's "theory", including the strong conviction that voices from an unknown origin were accusing him of committing child sexual abuse. Such behavior was anathema to Jack, and he was ter-rorized by the idea that anyone would think he could do such a thing. In actuality, he presented as a gentle, compassionate man, whose auditory hallucinations seemed to attack the very foundation of his moral frame-work, as non-psychotic obsessions often do. Theory 2, introduced over time by the therapist, included a psychoeducation model and an explan-atory framework for auditory hallucinations developed by Ralph Hoffman, a Yale psychiatry researcher (Hoffman, 2001). The therapist likened auditory hallucinations to an "electrical storm in the brain", which Jack considered a more benign alternative to Theory 1, if he could accept it. Theory 2 was plausible to Jack; but Theory 1 continued to exert a pull into torment at times. The therapist played a YouTube video in session one day that resonated with Jack. It was a four-minute cartoon of an ACT exercise called The Demons on the Boat. The link is provided here:

https://www.youtube.com/watch?v=z-wyaP6xXwE

The cartoon cleverly demonstrates how a person seeking to take his boat into the shore can be derailed in his journey by voices of demons, screaming at him from the hold of the ship. When one's behavior is con-trolled by the "demons", the ship spins aimlessly at sea. By learning to ignore the demons on the boat, not get rid of them, the client is able to head to shore, despite the noise. Jack found both sets of interventions helpful, though he acknowledged that in times of emotional turmoil from voices, he frequently replayed the video, for relief. The fact that Theory 2 was plausible to Jack, helped undermine the credibility of his delusions, just a tiny bit. If Theory 2 was plausible, he felt it was "safe" to follow the guidance provided in the YouTube cartoon. Was his psychosis cured? No. We can't offer that. But the interventions, which addressed both the form and the function of his voices and delusions, provided relief. And his suicidality diminished.

A FEW WORDS ON METAPHOR

Metaphors in therapy are verbal devices that both carry and transform meaning. Many of the experiential exercises, such as those prominent in ACT, employ metaphor to emotionally transform the functions of language, in a way that helps release the grip of the mental traps we can get caught in. Metaphor also can figure prominently in the so-called 2nd Wave CBTs (Stott, Mansell, Salkovskis, Lavender, & Cartwright-Hatton, 2010). For example, the therapist can point out that there are differences between what the "head" and the "gut", by literally pointing with her finger to her own head and gut (Stott et al., 2010, p. 36). This can help create a metaphor that the client understands, and that can be revisited as frequently as needed in the therapy.

A beautiful example of the transformative power of metaphor comes from neuroscientist Lisa Feldman-Barrett. She talked about the day that her then 12-year-old daughter was testing for her karate black belt. Her sensei, realizing that the girl was scared, likened her fear to butterflies in the stomach. He said: "Get your butterflies flying in formation" (Feldman-Barrett, 2021, p. 79). Turn that fear from the urge to shrink away from a challenge, into something resolute and powerful. The image of butterflies moving from an inchoate mass into a formation, one headed towards an important destination, is, well, potentially transformative. It doesn't mean the fear disappears. Its meaning, though, changes, in a way that helps free a person to pursue what matters, even when scared.

CHAPTER SUMMARY

This chapter explored the broad spectrum of techniques within CBT to address self-limiting, dysfunctional beliefs and cognitive biases. These include mainstream Beckian interventions, aimed at helping clients step back and examine beliefs not only for their "truth", but their function. What sometimes emerges in CBT is a "head" vs "gut" or "heart" dichotomy, in which a client recognizes intellectually that a belief is problematic, yet continues to find the belief emotionally salient and compelling. Such interventions as behavioral experiments are ways of creating emotionally and rationally compelling learning experiences for clients. Similarly in this chapter we explored the use of guided imagery and mindfulness exercises, as well as metaphor, again with an aim of creating compelling and enduring learning experiences in therapy.

REFERENCES

Barnard, P. & Teasdale, J. (1991) Interacting Cognitive Substystems: A Systemic Approach to Cognitive-Affective Interaction and Change. *Cognition and Emotion*, 5, 1, 1–39.

Beck, A., Rush, J., Shaw, B.F., & Emery, G. (1979) *Cognitive Therapy of Depression*. New York: Guilford.

Beck, A. & Emery, G. (1985) *Anxiety Disorders and Phobias: A Cognitive Perspective*. New York: Basic Books.

Beck, A., Davis, D., & Freeman, A. (2006) *Cognitive Therapy of Personality Disorders* (3rd edn). New York: Guilford.

Beck, A., & Dozois, D.J.A. (2011) Cognitive Therapy: Current Status and Future Directions. *Annual Review of Medicine*, 62, 397–409.

Beck, A. & Haigh, E. (2014) Advances in Cognitive Theory and Therapy: The Generic Cognitive Model. *Annual Review of Clinical Psychology*, 10, 1–24.

Beck, J., & Beck, A. (2020) *Cognitive-Behavior Therapy: Basics and Beyond* (3rd edn). New York: Guilford.

Bennett-Levy, J. (2003) Mechanisms of Change in Cognitive Therapy: The Case of Automatic Thought Records and Behavioural Experiments. *Behavioural and Cognitive Psychotherapy*, 31, 261–277.

Bennett-Levy, J., Butler, G., Fennell, M., Hackmann, A., Mueller, M., & Westbrook, D. (2004) *Oxford Guide to Behavioural Experiments in Cognitive Therapy*. Oxford: Oxford University Press.

Brewin, C. (2006) Understanding Cognitive Behavior Therapy: A Retrieval Competition Account. *Behaviour Research and Therapy*, 44: 765–784.

Chadwick, P., Birchwood, M., & Trower, P. (1996) *Cognitive Therapy for Delusions, Voices and Paranoia*. Chichester: Wiley.

Craske, M., Kircanski, K., Zelikowsky, M., Mystkowski, J., Chowdhury, N. & Baker, A. (2008) Optimizing Inhibitory Learning During Exposure Therapy. *Behaviour Research and Therapy*, 46, 3–27.

Craske, M., Treanor, M., Conway, C., Zbozinek, T., & Vervliet, B. (2014) Maximizing Exposure Therapy: An Inhibitory Learning Approach. *Behaviour Research and Therapy*, 58, 10–23.

Craske, M., Sandman, C., & Stein, M. (2022) How Can Neurobiology of Fear Extinction Inform Treatment? *Neuroscience and Biobehavioral Reviews*, 143, 104923.

Ellis, A. & Joffe-Ellis, D. (2019) *Rational Emotive Behavior Therapy* (2nd edn). Washington, DC: American Psychological Association.

Feldman-Barrett, L. (2017) *How Emotions Are Made: The Secret Life of the Brain*. New York: Mariner.

Feldman-Barrett, L. (2021) *Seven and a Half Lessons about the Brain*. New York: Picador.

Gilbert, P. (2010) *Compassion-Focused Therapy*. New York: Routledge.

Gilbert, P. (2021) *Overcoming Depression* (3rd edn). London: Robinson.

Gilbert, P. & Simos, G. (eds.) (2022) *Compassion-Focused Therapy: Clinical Practice and Practical Applications*. New York: Routledge.

Hackmann, A., Bennett-Levy, J., & Holmes, E. (2011) *Oxford Guide to Imagery in Cognitive Therapy*. Oxford: Oxford University Press.

Hayes, S., Brownstein, A., Zettle, R., Rosenfarb, I., & Korn, Z. (1986) Rule Governed Behavior and Sensitivity to Changing Consequences of Responding. *Journal of Experimental Analysis of Behavior*, 45: 237–256.

Hayes, S., Strosahl, K., & Wilson, K. (2011) *Acceptance and Commitment Therapy: The Process and Practice of Mindful Change*. New York: Guilford.

Hayes, S. & Hofmann, S. (2018) *Process-Based CBT: The Science and Core Clinical Competencies of Cognitive-Behavioral Therapy*. Oakland: New Harbinger.

Hayes, S. & Hofmann, S. (2021) "Third-Wave" Cognitive and Behavioral Therapies and the Emergence of a Process-Based Approach to Intervention in Psychotherapy. *World Psychiatry*, Oct., 20, 3, 363–375.

Hoffman, R. (2001) Language Processing And Hallucinated "Voices:" Insights from Transcranial Magnetic Stimulation. *Cognitive Neuropsychiatry*, 6, 1–6.

Hofmann, S., Hayes, S., & Lorscheid, D. (2021) *Learning Process-Based Therapy*. Reno: Context Press.

Kahneman, D. (2011) *Thinking, Fast and Slow*. New York: Farrar, Straus, & Giroux.

Keefe, J. & DeRubeis, R. (2015) A Critique of Theoretical Models of Depression: Commonalities and Distinctive Features, in *Treating Depression, MCT, CBT, and Third-Wave Therapies* (A. Wells & P. Fisher, eds.). London: Wiley.

Kennerley, H., Kirk, J., & Westbrook, D. (2017) *An Introduction to Cognitive Behavior Therapy: Skills and Applications* (3rd edn). London: Sage Publications.

Kuyken, W., Padesky, C., & Dudley, R. (2009) *Collaborative Case Conceptualization: Working Effectively with Clients in Cognitive-Behavioural Therapy*. New York: Guilford.

LeDoux, J. (2023) *The Four Realms of Existence: A New Theory of Being Human*. Boston: Bellknap.

Leahy, R., Holland, S., & McGinn, L. (2011) *Treatment Plans and Interventions for Depression and Anxiety Disorders*. New York: Guilford Press.

Padesky, C., & Greenberger, D. (2020) *The Clinician's Guide to CBT, Using Mind Over Mood* (2nd edn). New York: Guilford.

Proust, M. (2013) *Swann's Way: In Search of Lost Time* (W. Carter, ed.). New Haven: Yale University Press.

Segal, Z., Williams, M., & Teasdale, J. (2013) *Mindfulness-Based Cognitive Therapy for Depression* (2nd edn). New York: Guilford Press.

Stoddard, J. & Afari, N. (2014) *The Big Book of ACT Metaphors*. Oakland, CA: New Harbinger Press.

Stott, R., Mansell, W., Salkovskis, P., Lavender, A., & Cartwright-Hatton, S. (2010) *Oxford Guide to Metaphors in CBT: Building Cognitive Bridges*. Oxford: Oxford University Press.

Strauss, C., Bibby-Jones, A., & Jones, F. (2023) Clinical Effectiveness and Cost-Effectiveness of Supported Mindfulness-Based Cognitive Therapy Self-Help Compared with Supported Cognitive Behavioral Therapy Self-Help for Adults Experiencing Depression: The Low-Intensity Guided Help Through Mindfulness (LIGHTMind) Randomized Clinical Trial. *JAMA Psychiatry*, 2023, 80, 5, 415–424.

Teasdale, J. (2022) *What Happens in Mindfulness: Inner Awakening and Embodied Cognition*. New York: Guilford.

Tickell, A., Ball, S., Bernard, P. et al. (2020a) The Effectiveness of Mindfulness-Based Cognitive Therapy (MBCT) in Real-World Healthcare Services. *Mindfulness*, 11, 279–290.

Tickell, A., Bing, R., Crane, C., et al. (2020b) Recovery from Recurrent Depression with Mindfulness-Based Cognitive Therapy and Antidepressants: A Qualitative Study with Illustrative Case Studies. *BMJ Open*, 10, 2, e033892.

Weishaar, M. (1993) *Aaron T. Beck: Key Figures in Counseling and Psychotherapy*. New York: Sage Publications.

Wells, A. (2000) *Emotional Disorders and Metacognition: Innovations in Cognitive Therapy*. London: John Wiley & Sons.

Wells, A. (2009) *Metacognitive Therapy for Anxiety and Depression*. New York: Guilford Press.

Westbrook, D., Kennerly, H., & Kirk, J. (2012) *An Introduction to Cognitive Behavior Therapy Skills and Applications*. London: Sage.

Wills, F. (2015) *Skills in Cognitive Behaviour Therapy* (2nd edn). London: Sage.

Wills, F. & Sanders, D. (2013) *Cognitive Behaviour Therapy: Foundations for Practice*. London: Sage.

CHAPTER 8

Principle #7: Self Processes

One night in China, 2,400 years ago, a man had a dream. Chuang-Tzu, the Taoist philosopher, dreamt that he was a butterfly, floating dreamily in the air. When he awoke from the dream, he was puzzled. And he asked himself the following questions: "Was I Chuang-Tzu, dreaming I was a butterfly? Or am I a butterfly, now dreaming I am a man?"

Philosophers and spiritual seekers have puzzled over the meaning of this tale ever since. What is a self? Is there a "true self"? Are there many selves, and if so, which one is "me"? For our purposes, the story raises questions about reality and about "the self": who and what is the real "me"? How can I know reality of who and what I am? Philosophers and spiritual seekers have puzzled over the meaning of this tale ever since. What is a self? Is there a "true self"? Are there many selves, and if so, which one is "me"? For our purposes, the story raises questions about reality and about "the self": who and what is the real "me"? How can I know reality of who and what I am? The tale doesn't answer the questions it raises. And we don't pretend that we can solve the conundrum Chuang-Tzu exposed, either. That would be well beyond the purpose of this book. Fortunately, we need not be Taoist adepts or Zen masters, who would admonish us to consider that there is not real or true self. What we *will* attempt to do is to show how an understanding of "self" relates to clinical work in CBT. And we think that there are some very practical answers to at least some of the questions raised in Chuang-Tzu's ancient tale. For our purposes, those practical answers can be found in modern psychology and in CBT.

We will offer what we consider to be a clinically useful definition of the "self" processes we target for therapy. There is a potential problem in talking about "self". First off, "self" isn't a thing, or a homunculus. The idea of a homunculus, or a little man inside the head, that controls our actions,

DOI: 10.4324/9781003505587-9

is a scientific and philosophical "no no" in psychology. It purports to explain behavior but cannot. We consider "self" a set of processes, subject to influence by multiple factors, including context and contingencies, history, narrative, physiology. For our purposes, we want to remain clinically relevant and useful. At heart, we consider the "self" to be a dynamic organizing core of personality. It is that "I" that takes a stand and knows what direction one must take in any given moment. It is also capable of being fragile, transient, and subject to dysregulation in the same way that emotions and urges are subject to dysregulation. Personality theorist Dan McAdams (2018) describes the creation of a "narrative self" as the last stage of personality development. When ACT speaks of values, it is that dynamic organizing core of self that chooses valued directions in life. It can be nurtured and shaped, and is highly subject to cultural and other ecosystemic influences. The ancients nurtured self processes in treatises on character development, which continued through the ages in the work of people like Ralph Waldo Emerson. World spiritual traditions, too, have been a frequent model for the shaping of self processes, and what we often call "character".

So we offer the following provisional definition of "self" as processes. That includes the following:

1. Each of us contains multiple modes or self-processes
2. Some of those processes, or modes, can become entailed with problematic patterns of living
3. We each have the capacity for self-regulation and wisdom, as noted in earlier chapters, and we can tap into those capacities to access and build self-processes and behavioral repertoires that become increasingly available, in place of problematic modes of being
4. Those processes are cognitive in nature, including narratives of self and others, emotionally charged, and bodily experienced
5. Self processes can be tapped into and built through the use of interventions already available in the repertoire of modern Cognitive Behavior Therapy

Let's first explore how we got to the conclusions we reached, and why. Then we'll hopefully demonstrate the clinical utility of our approach.

More than a century ago, William James wrote about various experiential self-states. He described a "material self", a "social self", and a "spiritual self". He concluded that there was also an "I" and a "Me", by which he meant self as the object of experience, and the latter as the subject of experience. He concluded that "thoughts themselves are the thinkers"

(James, 1890). But these experiential self-states that James wrote about aren't just thoughts. They are total experience processes: cognitive, emotional, physiological, behavioral, and interpersonal in their impact.

We know something about the building blocks of these states. One of those building blocks, a big one, is perspective-taking skills. Swiss psychologist Jean Piaget (1972) posited that an infant has only one perspective, his or her own. This is a state of profound egocentricity. The human child learns that others have their own perspectives. This is the capacity to develop known "theory of mind", which involves the ability to recognize that "others have intentions, desires, beliefs, perceptions, and emotions that differ from our own, and that those qualities influence the behavior of others" (APA Dictionary of Psychology, 2007). The ability to discern the perspectives of others helps lead to a sharper distinction between "self" and "others". But it also lends itself to social cooperation and interpersonal problem solving, both of which confer a remarkable survival advantage on our species. The dark side of group perspective taking is the kind of tribalism that leads to intergroup conflict.

The clinical importance of perspective taking skills emerged in an early form of Cognitive Behavior Therapy, one that also incorporated social problem-solving skills (Spivack, Platt, & Shure, 1976). Children with behavior problems were taught to consider alternative perspectives for understanding and solving interpersonal problems. This included understanding the impact of their behavior on the person with whom they were in conflict. Improvements in perspective taking, as well as building problem-solving skills, led in turn to clinical improvements. Social problem solving, including building perspective taking skills, was shown to have significant implications for the development of children's adaptive functioning (Shure & Spivack, 1982; Shure, 1996).

The role of perspective taking skills in self-processes was further developed by Hayes (Hayes, 1984; Hayes, Barnes-Holmes, & Roche, 2001; Hayes, 2016; Hayes, Strosahl, & Wilson, 2012; McHugh & Stewart, 2012; Villate, Villatte, & Hayes, 2012). In fact, we consider Hayes' contributions pivotal in understanding the nature of self processes and to the development of clinically useful strategies and techniques. At heart, perspective taking involves a sense of anchoring in a me-here-now experience, in a process referred to in Relational Frame Theory as deictic framing (Hayes et al., 2001; Törneke, Hayes, Barnes-Holmes, 2010). Framing provides a bridge between language and lived experience. Rather than being only "the thoughts are the thinker", this is an embodied experience of self, derived initially via language and cognition. In fact, to use the term "self" is to recognize the deeply experiential nature of this process. Wilson notes that "self" is a verb, not a noun (Wilson, Bordieri, & Whiteman, 2012), a set of processes anchored in a behavioral repertoire. As a behavioral repertoire, as we will see, it can be expanded through learning and practice. From that "me-here-now" experience, perspective taking leads to innumerable permutations which are the bedrock of relationships, empathy, compassion, and both verbal and experiential learning. In a dyadic relationship, one can shift perspectives from "me-here-now" to "you-there-now" and resonate with the experience of the other. That is essentially what the earlier researchers were doing with young children, teaching them to understanding the difference in perspective between themselves (me-here-now) and another child with whom they were in conflict (you-here-now). There is enormous plasticity and range in our perspective-taking abilities. We can shift perspectives to view self in the future or the past, to imagine beings in the far distant future, in a world altered by time and human evolution, as science fiction writers might do. All of this involves perspective taking. The ability to take perspective forms a bedrock, along with language, for the social cooperation that is a survival key to our species. An absence of perspective taking skills spells adaptive difficulties of all kinds. The capacity for perspective taking allows us to know, or find out, the intentions and self-states of others and to synchronize our behavior with theirs.

ACT initially posited three senses of self: the conceptualized self, a knowing self, and an observing self. ACT is built on a theoretical and empirical foundation of behaviorism, and self states are posited to be behavioral repertoires. As such, they are able to be accessed, strengthened and/or weakened, based on learning. Cognition and language are central to self states in ACT, ranging from the sense of fusion or deeply held beliefs about self in the conceptualized self, to a self that is open to experience and freer from the constraints of language and belief to an observing presence: "seeing that one sees" (Zettle, 2016). The use of mindfulness exercises is employed to help clients increase their psychological flexibility. This flexibility includes becoming freer of the dominance of language, and freer to experience a wider range of self processes, as an individual and as a member of ever-expanding sense of community, ranging into a spiritual dimension, if one so chooses (Hayes, 1984).

Within 2nd Wave CBT, Beck described a theory of "modes" (Beck, 1996; Beck & Haigh, 2014; Beck, Finkel, & Beck, 2020; Neufeld, Correia dos-Anjos, & Pizzarro Rebessi, 2023). Modes are essentially suborganizations within the personality, which become activated in response to specific environmental demands. These modes are composed of an integrated network of cognitive, emotional, motivational, and behavioral components. The theory of modes arose in response to criticisms of the more purely cognitive model that Beck had initially proposed. Modes are essentially the embodied self states we are describing in this chapter. They aren't merely cognitive processes. Modes are embodied self-states that can propel us into action, and they can be activated by changing environmental and internal contingencies. In a sense, when Walt Whitman wrote in Song of Myself, 51, "I am large, I contain multitudes", he was describing modes, or self-states, of which many can exist within a single person.

Historically, and currently, there are many theories and therapies that recognize the notion of multiple selves. Beck was a trained psychoanalyst prior to developing Cognitive Therapy and was familiar with ego analytic therapies. These in turn spawned popular therapies in their time, such as Transactional Analysis (Berne, [1961] 2015) and Gestalt Therapy (Perls, 1992). Internal Family Systems Therapy bears resemblance, as well, though it describes a different historical and theoretical foundation (Schwartz, & Sweezy, 2019).

For our purposes, the problematic self-states we most commonly see in clinical practice involve the kind of dysregulation characteristic of trait neuroticism: emotion dysregulation, changes in cognition, emotion-driven behavior, and self dysregulation. Dread states, fear states, anger and rage states, sadness and grief states, all characterizing various trait neuroticism difficulties, and their attendant unpleasant self states. These states are involuntary in nature, and can be difficult to address solely via more cognitive interventions, which is one reason that Beck created his theory of modes.

In line with what we have presented in previous chapters, and other organizing principles, we don't attempt to eradicate or extinguish problematic self states. Instead, the science of psychology suggests that the correct move is to help access and build potentially competing self states. Brewin (2006) has described how new memory structures are created, by building new cognitive, emotional, and behavioral repertoires, which become increasingly accessible to the person in situations where the older, more automatic, and maladaptive pattern was more likely to have been invoked. Bennett-Levy et al. (2015) have described the use of self-practice and self-reflection methods to build "new ways of being". Gilbert, describes three minds, brain states, or what we would describe as self states, a threat system, an engagement system, and a self-soothing system (Gilbert, & Simos, 2022). He developed Compassionate Mind Therapy, which helps clients employ mindfulness practices, guided imagery, cognitive, and behavioral strategies to invoke the self-soothing system as a way of achieving the objectives Brewin outlines.

In fact, there are many strategies that can be employed in accessing and building such states of being. Dialectical Behavior Therapy (DBT) employs the use of posture and facial expressions to help people experience states of acceptance. One example is the technique called Half-Smile and Willing Hands (Linehan, 2015). This is based on the findings that our facial expressions and body posture impact and alter mood and states of being. This becomes a practice, not a one-time intervention, but a sustained practice intent on building new ways of being in situations that may have previously invoked problematic responses.

One of Marsha Linehan's operating assumptions in DBT is that all people have wisdom. Helping people access that Wise Mind, through guided imagery exercises or mindfulness practices, can help foster the process of change in an intentional direction.

Paradoxically, this is best done not by promoting an internal "fight" between self states in an individual. Instead, by helping to normalize and validate even the most problematic of self states, we can set the stage for a more gentle, deliberate, and persistent building of new ways of being.

The material in this chapter may seem a bit abstract. Let's turn to an example. This is an example of dealing with fear, or more specifically, a medical phobia in the face of a potential health threat. The first author did a lot of work with cancer patients, and this work was rather pivotal in helping him understand embodied self states. In fear states, or anxiety, we have several pathways for intervention. There is a lovely heuristic, developed initially by Salkovskis (1996) and others (Butler, Fennell, & Hackmann, 2008; Wills & Sanders, 2013). As shown below, it states:

$$\text{Anxiety} = \frac{\text{Threat Estimate (likelihood)} \times \text{Perceived awfulness}}{\text{Perceived Ability to Cope} + \text{Perceived Rescue Factors}}$$

First off, we can help our clients assess the actual nature and magnitude of a threat. That is the first element in the numerator, on the left. Commonly, in anxiety conditions, the threat is overestimated. In cancer, however, the threat may indeed by quite large. And the client is not necessarily experiencing cognitive biases or distortions in their reading of the situation. Next, in addition to looking at threat estimates with a client, we can also explore what would be so awful if the threat were true? That is the right side of the numerator. Sometimes, the perceived "awfulness" of a situation is overblown. For example, a socially phobic person might believe that it would be awful if people judged her harshly or negative. But the perceived awfulness could be considerably overblown. In these cases, the therapist might help the client recognize that not everyone has to like us, and that it can be just fine to learn that some people may disapprove or dislike us.

Now let's look at the denominator of the "anxiety equation". On the lower right, we have the perceived rescue factors. For someone who is avoiding facing an anxiety evoking situation, a variety of avoidance maneuvers may be considered "rescue factors". But those aren't the ones we'll focus on here. We want to consider the strengths and resources the person may have access to that can be brought to bear on solving or coping with the problem at hand. That might include people in their social network. It could include a medical team, if the problem is facing a medical challenge. And if you are in the midst of a house fire, what better rescue factor than a team from the fire department, coming in to save the day. You will also note that the processes described in this heuristic mirror those described as maintaining factors for those high in trait Neuroticism: frequent firing of intense, painful emotions in response to real and perceived threats, overestimation of threat probability and/or underestimation of ability to manage threat. People become caught in a vicious cycle of escape and avoidance, even when doing so brings long term harm.

But for purposes of illuminating this chapter, on self states and processes, let's focus in more depth on the final item, on the lower left of the denominator: perceived ability to cope. If that were a thought, it might be "I can handle it", or more likely, if the client were anxious, "I can't handle it." We could use any of the cognitive or experiential interventions we focused on in Chapter 6. For example, we could explore strengths and resources that the client has used in the past, and that can be invoked to help with the current problem. We could help identify a credible alternative belief, such as "I may not like this situation, but I can deal with it." That said, there is another way to help access and build a repertoire of "I can handle this", in a way that comports with what we have explored about modes and states of being. We can help create a lived experience of coping and mastery. Here's an example, a personal one.

The first author (ST), despite working in academic medical centers for much of his career, had a longstanding medical phobia. At age 5, he had a traumatic surgical experience, and the imprint of that remains etched into his brain and body. Deep fear wells up, the heart pounds, the mouth gets dry, and blood pressure spikes when any surgical or diagnostic procedure is required. It can be massively unpleasant. Essentially, that little 5-year-old inside ST is still there and is still scared. And, over many years and many experiences with various medical procedures, there's also, at times, a wise, centered adult self-state within who is present. So here's the example. For this, we'll return to a tale about butterflies, though not the butterfly in the tale of the Taoist master Chuang-Tzu.

ST recently had a CT scan that revealed some potential cardiac problems. He was referred to a cardiologist, for further evaluation. In the parking garage at the university hospital, those butterflies kicked in. The fear state was a full system state: cognition ("This is awful"; "I can't handle this"; "I don't want to go"), body sensations (heart pounding, dry mouth, sweaty palms); behavioral (urges to flee). ST named this self state years ago, as he lay on a gurney, preparing for a minor procedure. Looking up into the single bright light, panic welled, and a memory emerged of a similar light, over the surgical area he lay on as a 5-year-old. He realized that was a self-state, activated by memory. But as an older adult, another mode, or self-state, was also present, and became readily accessible. ST had learned to face fear situations by taking a mindful pause, draw a breath, and settle into a different self state. He learned to imagine and conjur an inner sensei or Zen master. This embodied state had been practiced over the years, tempering fear and urges to run from both uncertainty and from threat. At the cardiology clinic, as in the example of Lisa Feldman-Barrett's story, ST got his butterflies flying in formation, paused, settled, and walked purposefully and resolutely into the cardiology clinic, scared 5-year-old in tow. It was as though that inner sensei reached out, took the hand of that scared little boy and said: "It's okay. I'm here with you now." "I can handle this" can be more than a thought that we repeat to ourselves, in an effort to cope. It can be a lived experience, of a vibrant way of being in the world.

As we've described in this and other chapters, we don't extinguish that 5-year-old self state and its attendant repertoire of thoughts, memory, body sensations, emotions, and action urges. In line with what we know from modern learning theories and neuroscience, we don't completely extinguish that fear. Instead, as we have discussed in previous chapters, what we *can* do is access and build a complex behavioral repertoire, including embodied self states. The more one practices, in an increasing number of relevant contexts, the more readily it is available. As Brewin (2006) notes, with practice these repertoires of behavior become more readily available in competition retrieval with older, less functional repertoires. He writes that "both older and newer variants of CBT appear to be largely consistent with the principles of a retrieval competition approach that suggests negative representations can be deactivated by creating or strengthening more positive alternatives *using either logical or associative reasoning*" (Brewin, 2006, p. 778). In other words, new, more functional patterns can be created and strengthened not only through the rationalist approaches of 2nd Wave CBT, but also by the sorts of experiential interventions that create new self-representation. Those more positive, functional self-states become strengthened with practice, so that they become more readily available in every trip to a medical office.

STRATEGIES FOR ACCESSING AND BUILDING SELF-PROCESSES

There are a variety of perspectives on both "self" and on accessing and building self processes in therapy. Compassion-Focused Therapy (CFT) teaches a tripartite brain system, involving a soothing system, a threat system, and an engagement system (Gilbert, & Simos, 2022). It puts a premium on accessing and building compassionate, wise, soothing self states, to help reduce the engagement of the threat system.

Similarly, ACT teaches strategies for helping clients identify self processes that are caught in the net of language, a conceptualized self, sometimes described as "self as content", meaning identification of self in terms of the content of language ("I am a card carrying XXX"). Self processes in ACT become less wedded to, or fused with, language, and increasingly able to observe and choose, based on values. Self-as-context, and even a "transcendent self" are part of ACT work (Hayes, 2020).

Finally, another self-practice application of CBT, by Bennett-Levy et al., 2015) teaches clinicians to "build new ways of being." They employ a number of techniques that bear resemblance to ACT and CFT in achieving this objective.

These and other therapies share some common clinical strategies, which we will build on: the use of verbally delivered guided imagery exercises, the use of posture, and the use of movement to create not only cognitive change, but experientially derived, embodied self-states, or new ways of being.

Guided Imagery: Guided imagery exercises begin by a basic explanation of their purpose, and an invitation to the client to try an exercise. If the client is skittish, or refuses, we move on to another technique from our toolkit. Most clients are willing, when we provide a rationale. It is also useful to do a very brief check in to make sure which sensory modalities are most vivid for the client to imagine. Most people, but not all, can readily form visual images in the imagination. The following is an example of a guided imagery exercise.

THERAPIST: Sometimes, like the saying a picture is worth a thousand words, an experiential exercise is the quickest way to understand something important. I'm wondering if you'd be willing to give it a go. I'd just ask you to sit back and follow my verbal lead. It's just an imagining exercise, so you don't have to do anything, or say anything. I'll lead, and we can talk about it afterwards. The purpose is to help build a kind of psychological muscle, in this case, let's call it the "noticing" muscle. Sound okay?

CLIENT: Sure. I'm game.

THERAPIST: Okay. Let me ask you to just take a moment to settle into the chair. You can keep your eyes open or closed, as you wish. Just notice. And take a moment to notice the breath. Just settling in, paying attention just to the breath (the client was previously taught box breathing, 4 seconds in, 4 out) (Pause). Really settle in and notice where your body touches the back and the bottom of the chair. Breathing in, notice the weight of your body as gravity pulls at you. Breathing out, notice the contour of your body against the chair. (Pause) Now take a moment to tune in to something. Tune in to the person behind your eyes, the one who is noticing all these sensations. Notice that this person has been here, noticing all the experiences of your life, for a very long time. As you breath, just connect to that person, that "me" who's noticing my voice and the chair, and the gravity.

This is a kind of anchoring device, bringing the client into awareness of an observing "me" inside their skin. And notice that we were beginning also to introduce the temporal stability of that "me" over the course of many experiences that make up a human life. We can go from this to select experiences, some that may highlight client strengths, or courage in the face of prior challenges. We can time travel back to "hot spots" in the person's life, or to cherished and peaceful places, real or imagined. In other words, we can use the kind of perspective taking skills that form building blocks for relevant self and self-other experiences. Such a starting point might be used by the first author, in an effort to help build that observing "me", noticing the scared child in the surgical suite, perhaps extending compassion and understanding to that child, perhaps building the awareness that "I" can handle the challenges I face today, now. The therapist is only limited by client willingness and his or her own imagination and inventiveness. The purpose of the exercises can be honed to target the management or resolution of any problem the client faces.

Guided Imagery for Self-Soothing: Frequently, guided imagery is linked to metaphors that have meaning to a given client. If the treatment target is self-soothing, we can access and/or build that mode of being with the client. For example, a client who takes solace in the outdoors, for example, might benefit from building a safe, comforting space in a shaded glen, adjacent to a rustling mountain forest. The invoking of that imagery, later, in quiet periods of practice, can help establish self-soothing as a doorway into therapeutic problem-solving skills. Again, we are only limited by client willingness and our own creativity.

Guided Imagery for Mastery and Problem Solving: (Introduce as in prior vignette, with a mindful settling into the body and the breath)... Now I'd ask you to look not just at the problems you've come here to resolve, but at the answer to those problems. You, here, now, can look at the "you" who has taken care of what you are here to deal with. Let yourself, if you can, see what your life looks like and feels like when these problems are solved. What are you doing? Who are you with? Take your time, see it. Feel it. And when we are finished, we can describe it, including the actions you'll be taking to live that life every day. Notice that "you" as you live the life you came here to claim. How is she standing? What is her posture? See if you can find and embody that posture right here, now.

The above vignette is highly truncated, for purposes of writerly economy. What we want to emphasize here is the importance of two things. First, instead of remaining focused on removing barriers, such as symptoms, this exercise focuses on living that life the client hopes for. And the exercise fosters imagining that life in rich detail. Out of that detail emerges a potential blueprint for therapy, one that encompasses the cognitive, emotional, behavioral, and interpersonal patterns that will need to be accessed and/or created, to step forward in life. As we will see in Chapter 10, on Case Conceptualizations, we are creating a hopefully welcome alternative to the patterns of living in which the client is currently caught. Second, this exercise can allow the client to experience that self state here and now. That embodied, emotionally rich self state can become a reference point to which the therapy returns again and again as the treatment plan unfolds. It is not a substitute for the more verbal, rationally derived plan of action in therapy. It is a complement and a guide.

Guided Imagery for Acceptance and/or Strength: Now, as you sit there, see if you can create an image of yourself, as a mountain. Find a posture to sit in that reflects the strength and solidity of a mountain. Solid. Strong. Grounded in the earth below and reaching up into the skies above. And see if you can be aware of the rising of the sun and the changes in light and temperature as the days pass into night and back into day. The mountain, through it all, is unchanging. It receives what the earth and the sky give: sunshine, clouds, lashing rains and winds. And all the while, the mountain receives it all. See if you can notice that play of light and temperature, and winds from that place behind your eyes that is always there, always able to be with what comes up. And see if you can just notice, from a place beyond judgments, just noticing what comes up, as though what comes up within is no more solid than the clouds wafting across the mountain top.

Posture and Movement: We showed a brief use of posture in two previous guided imagery exercises. The ability of posture and facial expression to influence emotion is explored in Dialectical Behavior Therapy (DBT) (Linehan, 2015). Linehan drew on the work of James Gross (2015), in her search for understanding processes involved in emotion regulation. Her distress tolerance skills, such as Half Smile and Willing Hands, for example, help reduce emotion dysregulation. It involves sitting with one's hands in the lap, with the hands in an upward, receptive position, while one lifts the corners of the mouth into a half-smile. This posture is intended to foster acceptance and willingness. It is used during times of distress and emotion dysregulation. And it may be used in situations in which one is struggling with non-acceptance of reality. Besides helping to regulate emotions, this skill can also foster the presence of a wise, compassionate self-state, able to manage and navigate inner and outer reality with a bit more equanimity and resoluteness.

Body posture is also a part of a less well-known therapy called Competitive Memory Training (COMET) (Korrelboom, Peeters, Blom, & Huijbrechts, 2014). Korrelboom, Ijdema, Karreman, & van der Gaag (2022) note that fundamental to the practice of COMET is Brewin's (2006) theory of competitive memory retrieval hierarchies. We have drawn on these ideas, as indicated previously, in the sense that by helping to access and build self-states of mastery and competence, for example, the client, through repeated practice, has access to these states, as the older, less functional states see their power and access weakened.

While most traditional CBT procedures focus on the direct challenging, disabling, and modification of maladaptive self-opinions, instead, "COMET on the other hand, employs a more indirect strategy to enhance low self-esteem by enhancing the retrievability of the patient's ('available but hidden') positive self-knowledge" (Korrelboom et al. 2022, p. 534). This may in fact be a mechanism of action for some of DBT's techniques, such as Half-Smile and Willing Hands (Linehan, 2015). With practice, one builds emotion regulation skills, which in turn sets the stage for more effective management of life's challenges.

Paying attention to client posture in session can reveal core beliefs, automatic thoughts, emotion processing, and self states. Role plays asking clients to demonstrate postures of defeat, fear, withdrawal, isolation can be fun and impactful, when done with the proper timing, tact, and respectfulness. Similarly, helping clients embody postures of strength, acceptance, and engagement can also create self states that can be linked to behavior. And the behaviors to which those self states are linked lead to the therapy outcomes that the client has set with the therapist as their target.

CLINICAL EXAMPLE

The client is a 23-year old female, currently living in a women's shelter, and working with her therapist to secure employment. She has been demoralized, and has imagined painful outcomes for any job interview. That fear, and its attendant images, accompany an unwillingness to take a risk. She is caught in a vicious cycle of avoidance, fear, and a self-defeating unwillingness and inability to get a job. A job is a key treatment target for her, as virtually any job at this point will help break the spiral of her life, into a potential upward arc.

THERAPIST: (after introductory guided imagery work) Now let's walk through that door into the interview. In our first pass through, imagine I'm with you, walking with you, just behind you, into the interview. Take a moment to find the posture in your chair that we've practiced together here. How do you place your hands as you sit? Making eye contact. Let yourself imagine that interviewer, in whatever form he or she shows up: friendly, an ogre, it won't matter. You're ready, and the outcome will take care of itself.

Guided imagery exercises of this sort can be used to help cement work done in detailed role plays, or other skill-building procedures, when a behavioral repertoire has been practiced. There is considerable latitude, and again, the imagination and willingness of both the client and the therapist are the only limits.

CHAPTER SUMMARY

This chapter focused on the psychological properties of self states. We began by exploring the history of the notion of "self", including the ways in which this is elaborated within the CBT tradition in the work of Beck,

Hayes, Gilbert, and Linehan. We focused on self as both a cognitive and an embodied set of processes. Clinically, we provided examples of cognitive interventions, experiential interventions, body posture, guided imagery techniques, all as a way of accessing and building therapeutically beneficial self states.

REFERENCES

APA Dictionary of Psychology (2007) Ed. G. VandenBos. American Psychological Association.

Beck, A. (1996) Beyond Belief: A Theory of Modes, Personality, and Ppsychopathology. In P. Salkovskis (ed.) *Frontiers of Cognitive Therapy*. New York: Guilford Press.

Beck, A. & Haigh, E. (2014) Advances in Cognitive Theory and Therapy: The Generic Cognitive Model. *Annual Review of Clinical Psychology*, 10, 1–24.

Beck, A., Finkel, M., & Beck, J. (2020) The Theory of Modes: Applications to Schizophrenia and Other Psychological Conditions. *Cognitive Therapy and Research*, 45, 391–400.

Bennett-Levy, J., Thwaites, R., Haarhoff, B., & Perry, H. (2015) *Experiencing CBT from the Inside Out: A Self-Practice/Self-Reflection Workbook for Therapists*. New York: Guilford Press.

Berne, E. ([1961] 2015) *Transactional Analysis in Psychotherapy: A Systematic Individual and Social Psychiatry*. New York: Martino Books.

Brewin, C. (2006) Understanding Cognitive Behavior Therapy: A Retrieval Competition Account. *Behaviour Research and Therapy*, 44, 765–784.

Butler, G., Fennell, M. & Hackmann, A. (2008) *Cognitive-Behavioral Therapy for Anxiety Disorders: Mastering Clinical Challenges*. New York: Guilford Press.

Gilbert, P. & Simos, G. (2022) *Compassion Focused Therapy: Clinical Practice and Applications*. London: Routledge Press.

Gross, J. (2015) Emotion Regulation: Current Status and Future Prospects. *Psychological Inquiry*, 26, 1, 1–26.

Hayes, S. (1984) Making Sense of Spirituality. *Behaviorism*, 12, 99–110.

Hayes, S. (2016) *Perspective-Taking as Healing*. In *The Self-Acceptance Project: How to Be Kind and Compassionate Toward Yourself in any Situation*, 29–38 (T. Simon, ed.). Boulder, CO: Sounds True.

Hayes, S. (2020) *A Liberated Mind: How to Pivot Toward What Matters*. New York: Avery.

Hayes, S., Barnes-Holmes, D., & Roche, B. (2001) *Relational Frame Theory: A Post-Skinnerian Account of Human Language and Cognition*. New York: Plenum Press.

Hayes, S., Strosahl, K., & Wilson, K. (2012) *Acceptance and Commitment Therapy: The Process and Practice of Mindful Change* (2nd edn). New York: Guilford Press.

James, W. (1890) The Principles of Psychology: The Briefer Course. In *William James Writings*, 1878–1899 (G.E. Myers, ed.) New York: Library of America.

Korrelboom, K., Peeters, S., Blom,, S. & Huijbrechts, I. (2014) Competitive Memory Training (COMET) for Panic and Applied Relaxation (AR) Are Equally Effective in the Treatment of Panic in Panic-Disordered Patients. *Journal of Contemporary Psychotherapy*, 44, 3.

Korrelboom, K., Ijdema, T., Karreman, A., & van der Gaag, M. (2022) The Effectiveness of Transdiagnostic Applications of Competitive Memory Training (COMET) on Low Self-Esteem and Comorbid Depression: A Meta-Analysis of Randomized Trials. *Cognitive Therapy and Research*, 46, 532–543.

Linehan, M. (2015) *DBT Skills Training Manual* (2nd edn). New York: Guilford Press.

McAdams, D. (2018) Narrative Identity: What Is It? What Does It Do? How Do You Measure It? *Imagination, Cognition, Personality: Consciousness in Theory, Research, and Clinical Practice*, 37, 3, 359–372.

McHugh, L. & Stewart, I (eds.) (2012) *The Self and Perspective Taking: Contributions and Applications from Modern Behavioral Science*. Reno: Context Press.

Neufeld, C., Correia dos-Anjos, N., & Pizzarro Rebessi, I. (2023) Beck's Theory of Modes: A Scoping Review. *Revista Brasileira de Therapias Cognitivas*, 19, 2, 244–257.

Perls, F. (1992) *Gestalt Therapy Verbatim* (2nd edn). New York: Gestalt Journal Press.

Piaget, J. (1972) *The Psychology of the Child*. New York: Basic Books.

Salkovskis, P. (1996) The Cognitive Approach to Anxiety: Threat Beliefs, Safety-Seeking Behavior, and the Special Case of Health Anxiety and Obsessions. In *Frontiers of Cognitive Therapy*, 48–74 (P. Salkovskis, ed.) New York: Guilford Press.

Schwartz, R. & Sweezy, M. (2019) *Internal Family Systems Therapy* (2nd edn). New York: Guilford Press.

Shure, M. & Spivack, G. (1982) Interpersonal Problem-Solving in Young Children: A Cognitive Approach to Prevention. *American Journal of Community Psychology*, 10, 341–356.

Shure, M. (1996) *Raising a Thinking Child: Help Your Young Child Learn to Resolve Everyday Conflicts and Get Along With Others*. New York: Pocket Books.

Spivack, G., Platt, J., & Shure, M. (1976) *The Problem-Solving Approach to Adjustment*. San Francisco, CA: Jossey-Bass.

Törneke, N., Hayes, S., & Barnes-Holmes, D. (2010) *Learning RFT: An Introduction to Relational Frame Theory and its Clinical Applications*. Reno, NV: Context Press.

Villate, J., Villatte, M., & Hayes, S. (2012) A Naturalistic Approach to Transcendence: Deictic Framily, Spirituality, and Prosociality. In *The Self and Perspective-Taking: Contributions and Applications from Modern Behavioral Science*, 199–216 (L. McHugh & I. Stewart, eds.), Oakland, CA: New Harbinger Publications.

Wills, F. & Sanders, D. (2013) *Cognitive Behaviour Therapy: Foundations for Practice*. London: Sage.

Wilson, K., Bordieri, M., & Whiteman, K. (2012) The Self and Mindfulness. In *The Self And Perspective Taking: Contributions and Applications from Modern Behavioral Science*, 181–197 (L. McHugh & I. Stewart, eds.). Reno, NV: Context Press.

Zettle, R. (2016) The Self in Acceptance and Commitment Therapy. In *The Self in Understanding and Treating Psychological Disorders* (R. Moulding, G. Doron, S. Bhar, M. Nedeljkovic, & M. Mikulincer, eds.). Cambridge, UK: Cambridge University Press.

CHAPTER 9

Principle #8: A Contextual Account of Human Functioning

Take a moment to consider this question: Do thoughts cause our emotions and our behavior?

If you answer yes, you lean into a mechanistic account of human functioning. A causes B. The human mind seems to seek simple explanations, and mechanistic accounts of human behavior can provide deceptively simple answers to what turn out to be complex and nuanced phenomena. But if you posit that thoughts cause emotions and behavior, don't you also wonder what causes thoughts? Perhaps emotions have a causal relationship, at times, to cognition. Perhaps environmental contingencies have a hand in fostering patterns of thought. For example, in the case example the first author provided, of his medical phobia, it is tempting to conclude that a traumatic childhood surgery caused the phobia. A caused B. But did it? Let's shift from the DSM framework for phobias and consider for a moment a transdiagnostic factor we've explored in chapter 3: temperament, and how it interacts with other psychological and behavioral transdiagnostic factors. What if the author, as a child, was higher on trait Neuroticism, such that many events triggered an autonomic response of fear arousal, well before his surgery? There may have been a prepotent tendency to view the world as threatening and unpredictable, and the self as weak and unable to manage the many threats anticipated. Which came first?

The human mind seeks simple answers, even when those answers might be in error. It's more challenging, but we think more likely accurate, to recognize that simple "A causes B" answers can be helpful, but that they are often incomplete. And indeed, the causal chain of events contributing to an outcome can be so complex as to be impossible to sort out. The further from the event we get in time, the greater the speculation about

DOI: 10.4324/9781003505587-10

the causal relationships. Take a moment to think of all the events for which we impute cause, and how distant they are from the present moment: "My dad's violence at home led me to hate authority"; "If my parents had cared about education, I'd have finished college and gotten a decent job." The simple, mechanistic explanation for our lives gives comfort at times, and allows us to think we can make sense of our lives. And to be sure, at times a mechanistic account can help organize change, powerful change. It is useful. But it is also at times limited.

While there is considerable scientific and technological utility in mechanism, it is not the only account of human functioning. There is also contextualism, which posits that reciprocal relationships exist between elements in a system. That system can include the pattern of thoughts, images, emotions, body sensations, urges, overt behaviors, and environmental consequences, or contingencies. Each element of the system is implicated in the maintenance or disruption of a pattern of functioning. And for clinical purposes, as we will see, each element offers opportunities for intervention. So, for example, if we take another look at our opening question, do thoughts cause emotions and behavior? If so, then changing the thought changes emotion and behavior. Mechanism. However, we can also leave the thought alone and change our *relationship* to the thought. That's the territory of the newer, or 3rd Wave CBTs. Just watch the thought, rather than reacting or acting on the thought. Notice, with some curiosity and compassion, and take a moment to decide whether or to what extent that thought needs to influence emotions and behavior. That's a door into contextualism. There are others, including management of self in relation to the larger ecosystems in which we are embedded in daily life.

The debate between mechanistic versus contextual accounts of causality is thousands of years old. It is also highly salient to our understanding of ecology, biological systems, human functioning, and psychotherapy. In fact, the dialectic between mechanism and contextualism was instrumental in the development of the family therapy movement, where the influence of General Systems Theory (von Bertalanffy, 2015) was substantial. Causality in this model was circular, in the sense that each element in a connected chain had influence over others, in a reciprocal causal manner. For example, feedback loops of this sort explain how a thermostat works. Attempts were made to explain how families engaged in patterns of functioning that exerted causal control via multiple feedback loops.

This debate can become arcane. But it is important for an understanding of modern Cognitive Behavior Therapy. Beck's model of CBT tends towards a more mechanistic model. While recognizing the reciprocal influence of thoughts, emotions, and behaviors, it tends to put primacy on the more causal role of thoughts in the emotional disorders. Change the thought, and the emotions and behaviors change. The Beck Institute for Cognitive Behavior Therapy describes it thusly on their web site: "When people are suffering from a mental health condition like depression or anxiety, they may feel negatively about themselves, others, the world, and the future. This can lead to patterns of unrealistic or unhelpful thoughts in their daily lives. These thoughts, in turn, can lead to unhelpful or maladaptive reactions, creating a feedback loop that can continuously reinforce underlying negative beliefs.

One of the goals of Cognitive Behavior Therapy is to interrupt that feedback loop by helping people evaluate their thoughts and think about the situations in their lives in more helpful ways.

Thought change takes primacy in Beck's 2nd Wave CBT. Newer perspectives began to emerge within the field to explain how and why CBT works. In turn, a new range of perspectives and interventions opened up.

More nuanced perspectives on the relationship between thoughts, emotions, and behaviors began to show up in CBT as the science of psychology evolved, and as newer approaches in the field came online. Within the Beckian tradition, a less linear, more circular case conceptualization emerged, in line with a move from a mechanistic to a more contextual model. Here is an example, employed in the first author's CBT book for work with cancer patients (Temple, 2017).

This heuristic shows how a specific trigger, or activating event, can invoke a cluster of responses, including cognition, emotion, urges and behavior, environmental consequences, and self-processes. All occur in a reciprocally related manner, not one causing all others, but each influencing the other. Here, in Figure 9.1, beliefs are not caused by the activating event, and do not in turn cause the other elements in the vicious cycle. One could just as easily posit that emotions are the first element in the cycle noticed by the client. What matters is that the entire system functions as a contextual whole. And this, in turn, allows us to not only understand a pattern of functioning in question; it allows us to work with the client to identify points of vulnerability in an activating situation, and to design interventions anywhere in the cycle that will serve to help free up the client for another, more freely chosen and adaptive response.

Very often, indeed perhaps most of the time, our clinical work can be completed by focusing primarily, if not solely, on these patterns. That said, a word on the role and importance of clients' life history is in order here. Beck's case conceptualization speculates about more distal factors,

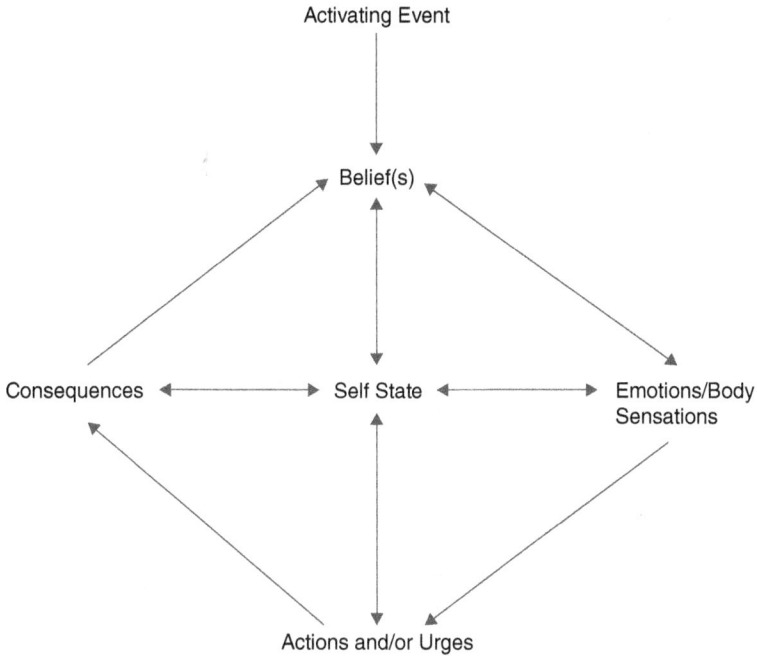

Figure 9.1 Vicious Cycle

Adapted from Wills, 2021

such as early life history, core beliefs, and compensatory strategies. These factors rest atop the vicious cycles in a case conceptualization.

Relevant Life History and Precipitants
Core Beliefs (in current situation)
Intermediate Beliefs (in current situation)
Coping Strategies (in current situation)

Let's take an example. Imagine a 35-year-old man, whose father was an alcoholic, and whom he remembers saying painful things to him. He is left believing he is somehow defective, and he works hard to keep every-one happy in his life today, to the point of feeling like a doormat. He is married, has two young children, and has a very demanding boss. The boss keeps asking more of him, to the point that the client now feels exhausted and humiliated at work. Nothing pleases his boss, and the client is now angry and fearful. His anger and resentment is beginning to spill over into his home life, which his wife is pointing out to him. In fact, her concern sparked the client's entry into therapy. Here's the diagram:

Relevant Life History: "my father was a mean alcoholic. He used to say he was sorry he had me."
Core Beliefs: "There's something seriously wrong with me."
Intermediate Beliefs: "If I please people, they will accept me."
Coping Strategies: "I let people walk all over me, which ends up not pleasing me, or satisfying others."

The vicious cycles that are part of the current clinical picture seem related to the elements above: early history, core beliefs, intermediate beliefs, and coping strategies. These elements can assume considerable importance to the client. And clinicians are advised to be aware of them, with a couple of provisos. First, the more distal the purported causal factors in a conceptualization, the less reliable are the raters (Temple, 2017). Which historical factors are most salient is debatable. The impact of those distal factors are subject to multiple influences over time, many of which are, in fact, unknowable. Part of this unknowability is related to the vagaries of human memory. But much is simply due to the complexity of the long chain of interacting events, creating a causal chain that is vast, and that extends deep into the client's developmental history. Such a causal chain is highly subject to editing. And that editing involves simplification, including the shading provided by one's own information processing biases.

It isn't that history does not matter. What may matter even more, for our purposes, are the stories, if you will, that the client believes about their life. Again, that causal chain is out of reach. The historical facts may or may not be literally true as remembered. What can become important is not only the client's "story" about themselves and their life, but the function that story serves now, today. For example, stories about victimhood can inadvertently reinforce remaining stuck in an unsatisfying life. Marsha Linehan observed that "emotions love themselves". In other words, we can stoke certain emotions by rumination, by urges associated with those emotions, and actions that deepen the emotion. Revenge, grievance, victimhood, helplessness, all can feel compelling, but can contribute inadvertently to staying "stuck". Does this mean that we ignore the many terrible, unfortunate experiences that our clients sometimes share with us? No. Certainly not. Does it mean we adopt a dismissive stance towards the client? Again, certainly not. Therapies within the CBT tradition, whether Beckian, ACT, DBT, or others, all recognize the importance of client life history and its impact. But they handle these factors chiefly in the light of current life situations. And each therapy handles these elements slightly differently. Beck's model lends itself to an exploration of checking the accuracy of one's beliefs, or the functions served by those beliefs, while helping clients create new, more adaptive beliefs about self, world, others. ACT focuses on not only fusion with painful beliefs, but on the ways in which a sense of self, a Conceptualized Self, is created and maintained (Hayes, Strosahl, & Wilson, 2016; Hayes, 2021). The story, or conceptualized self, can actually maintain the problems for which the client seeks help. DBT validation strategies provide a mechanism for validating the person, while gently fostering a fresh look at the function served by staying enmeshed in a painful story of self, world, others.

WORKING WITH HISTORICAL FACTORS IN CBT

There are two conditions in which the clinician is wise to explore and target developmental, or longitudinal, factors in therapy. One, when the client has longstanding adaptive difficulties that appear linked to tightly held painful convictions about self and others. This is especially necessary when an old vicious cycle of avoidance, or of emotion dysregulation seem to block the expression or learning of more flexible, adaptive responses to life. Second, and possibly even more challenging, is when the stories themselves serve a reinforcing function that makes them hard for the client to give up. The latter is in line with Hayes' ideas about a conceptualized self. It may be a problematic conceptualized self, in terms of its function, but clients can resist any effort to change or let go of this set of beliefs, emotions, and behaviors. The harder the clinician pushes, the more the client resists. Why, the therapist might wonder, would anyone want to hang on to grievance, revenge fantasies, or fear-based avoidance, when life could otherwise offer so much promise? The therapist can be left puzzled, defeated, and without a client.

These two sets of conditions require different responses from the therapist. In the first case, let's assume that the client does not derive any kind of hidden benefit from harboring painful beliefs and their attendant emotional and behavioral reinforcers. The most positive interpretation that can be offered, in validating the client, is that given the painful beliefs, it is logical to be worried and self-protective. The beliefs are painful yet have the emotional ring of truth to the client. They might wish to believe otherwise, but as we have discussed in the chapter on cognitive and experiential interventions, they just can't and don't.

In the second case, at some point, after validating both the obvious and the hidden logic of the functions served by painful beliefs, the therapist must offer the client a choice. In situations where letting oneself off the hook for one's sense of grievance, of having been wronged, or of fantasies of revenge or of reconciliation, the client must consider something else. Hayes has asked in such cases, "who else would you be letting off the hook if you were to let go of this belief?" The client, such as the one above, might note that he would feel like a fool for having held himself back, due to these old fears and memories, or that he would be letting his father off the hook for the father's inexcusable transgressions. We might also ask questions commonly linked to DBT: "What is the threat if you were to let go of your sense of grievance and injustice?" And "What stands in the way of radical acceptance of what happened?" All of these questions, and related ones, can tap into the beliefs about letting go of past wrongs and injustices. The most common reaction is the belief that "letting go" or Radical Acceptance means endorsing the injustice. It does not mean this at all. Another reaction is simple grief. Coming to terms with the permanent loss of validation and love one wished for from important others is painful. Linehan has noted that two most painful emotions are grief and shame. And both of these emotions can become entailed in efforts to hold on to old pain. The problem is that by holding on, grief and shame happen anyway. So does sabotage of one's wishes for a better life.

In both conditions, we use Guided Discovery and validation strategies to elicit relevant information, including, longitudinal or developmental factors. And we at the same time listen carefully for what the client makes of that history, their story. We validate the pain of one's history, and at the same time we carefully assess the function served by the story the client maintains. That story becomes evident as we unfold the beliefs, assumptions, rules, emotions, and coping patterns, including especially, those that show up in current problem situations. The point is that we validate the client's behavior in light of historical factors, while not necessarily validating the conclusions they've reached about themselves or the world, or the problem-solving strategies they employ in light of those conclusions or stories. Think for a moment about how one might employ the spectrum of both cognitive and experiential interventions, and how that balance of acceptance and change can be brought to bear, technically, to help clients caught in this painful net of language, emotion, and behavior. We will illustrate how to do this work in greater detail in Part 2 of the book. Some of the most emotionally evocative work in CBT happens in these cases, and some of the most rewarding.

Let's return to the vicious cycle, above. We have seen how the role of mindfulness has entered the field. Notice that in the center of the above figure, we see self processes. We can invoke a mindfulness exercise from that place in the center of the diagram, in which the client can cultivate an observing presence, noticing nonjudgmentally the entire vicious cycle as it is elicited in the therapy session. In turn, and in line with our earlier chapters on balancing mindfulness, cognitive, and experiential interventions, we have a wide range of intervention possibilities. We don't need to posit thought change as a precondition for behavior change. We can focus on letting a thought be as it is, while simply watching it, and recognizing that it is just one element in an overall pattern that we may be caught in, perhaps to our advantage, perhaps to our detriment.

Newer models of therapy, integrating mindfulness into a largely behavioral framework, take us deeper into contextualism, and open new possibilities for case conceptualization and intervention. Acceptance and Commitment Therapy (ACT) is based on a model of contextualism that Hayes calls functional contextualism (Hayes, Hayes, Reese, & Sarbin, 1993; Hayes, 2021). In this account, an entire pattern of functioning, encompassing thoughts, emotions, urges, actions, and environmental contingencies, meld into a system whole. And that pattern is understood in terms of the function served by the maintenance of the pattern. For example, let's take someone who is socially anxious. As we've seen in discussions of neuroticism, action urges associated with social anxiety include avoidance. That might include avoidance of social encounters, particularly loosely structured or unstructured encounters, such as parties. It can include attending parties, but failing to look into the eyes of people, and sitting alone in a corner all evening, or finding one person to hang onto for the entire evening. This in turn can spark a process of rumination, later, in which the person employs their perspective taking skills to imagine the dark thoughts and painful appraisals that others held of their "performance" at the party, which in turn is entailed with a further fear reaction and a wish to withdraw. This pattern, however much as it may create suffering, especially when the person really, truly wants social connection, is purposeful. It serves a function. And that function may be self protection. True, the protection is based on withdrawal in the face of heightened emotion reactivity and imagined social humiliation. But it is functional, even if the fears protected against are imagined, and even if the behaviors of withdrawal contribute to the very social isolation the person fears.

In a functional contextual account, behavior is purposeful. The purpose is determined by the function served by the behavior. So rather than change the thought, ACT seeks to alter functions. And it does so by helping clients think about not only what their problematic pattern does in their life, but what they really want. So for the socially anxious person, making contact with their deep wish for social connection can lead to a new pattern, while mindfully noticing the way that the old pattern invites or pulls the person into withdrawal. In this case, change the behavior, change the pattern. And rather than making cognitive change a precondition for change, thoughts essentially "go along for the ride", mindfully noticed, yet with a weakened power to control behavior.

Another treatment model we've explored, also with deep roots in Behaviorism, is Dialectical Behavior Therapy (DBT). DBT employs a detailed chain analysis, which helps the client understand the detailed sequence of thoughts, emotions, urges, behaviors, and environmental consequences that create a vicious cycle. Rather than viewing thoughts as a primary determinant of behavior, DBT tends to focus on the role of emotion dysregulation. Taking a look at client thoughts in problem situations is useful, in terms of "checking the facts". But interventions may instead target emotion dysregulation as an initial focus, especially when emotion dysregulation is entailed with quick action urges that quell the emotional pain but cause other problems. Cutting, for example, is a quick way to reduce painful emotional intensity. But it's also a way to derail relationships and to end up with ER visits. So does DBT teach that emotions cause behavior?

Like other newer models with roots in Behaviorism, it teaches that our problematic patterns in living are full system responses, involving thoughts, emotions, urges, and behaviors. And those patterns may solve one problem in the short run, while causing others in the long run. As with ACT, DBT fosters the client's awareness of what they really want their lives to be about and directs the therapy towards the accomplishment of those objectives: a life worth living.

Yet another contextual model, deriving from Behaviorism, but taking into account internal experiences such as thoughts and emotions was explored by the second author (Layng, Andronis, Codd, Abdil-Jalil, 2022). This is called a Constructional approach and was initially developed by American psychologist Israel "Izzy" Goldiamond. It bears similarities to both ACT and DBT, in the sense that the hidden logic of problematic behavior patterns are revealed, while the client is encouraged carefully to describe and work towards a newer pattern of behavior, one that leads them to greater fulfillment and reward. This approach doesn't treat problem behaviors as "maladaptive" and in need of removal. Instead, it highlights them, including their potentially useful functions, while fostering new patterns of behavior, more freely chosen by the client. This bears marked similarities to both DBT and ACT, though Goldiamond's work preceded both.

One of the beauties of all these newer approaches is that problem behavior is destigmatized and normalized in the context of client life history. And each model helps clients ask what their lives would be about if they were not caught in problematic patterns of functioning, however logical those patterns may be.

Here's another heuristic diagram, shown in Figure 9.2. This is a "patient roadmap", one the first author and his team used in an inpatient adolescent DBT program. It is broadly applicable and can be used as a tool in modern CBT. Please note that the circle in the upper left includes the entire pattern of functioning involved in a problematic pattern. It utilizes a chain analysis, derived from DBT (Rizvi, 2019; Heard & Swales, 2016), for purposes of mapping out the entire sequence of a problematic pattern: cognition, urges, behaviors, consequences. It contains the "vicious cycle" model, and is focused, targeted, parsimonious, and easily explained to adults and teens. It is absolutely non-stigmatizing and can be conducted using Guided Discovery and Validation strategies. Most importantly, this diagram also highlights the direction the client wants his/her life to go, if not entrapped by the "vicious cycle" of the problem. It therefore sets a course for therapy, and leads to a case conceptualization that builds new repertoires of behavior that can gently take the place of the problematic pattern.

Let's look at an example of how this can be used to both create a case conceptualization and as a tool to guide the therapy. Figure 9.3 involves a case of a 15-year-old girl, who presented for poor adherence to her treatment for Type 1 diabetes. Poor adherence to treatment leads to potentially lethal outcomes for Type 1 diabetes. At the least, problematic adherence can contribute to cognitive, emotional, attentional, and behavioral problems associated with dysregulated blood sugars. At worst, diabetic comas, hospitalizations, and even death can result. At present, there isn't a cure for Type 1 diabetes, but there is a management plan, one that is demanding, and one that nonetheless imposes clearly challenging burdens on the young person.

Figure 9.3 A thumbnail sketch of this 15-year old's problematic pattern is provided in the circle at the upper left. The problems that we put on our problem list include: 1. Management of Type 1 Diabetes, and 2. Conflict between the 15-year old patient and her mother. The sequence, in condensed form, involves conflict with her mother about her diabetes management. The more mom pushes her to follow the treatment regimen, the more the girl rebels, by refusing to check her blood sugars, adjust her insulin, or refrain from eating proscribed foods. The greater the rebellion, the worse the consequences, which you will note include court committed hospitalizations, not feeling well, becoming increasingly ill. The girl is

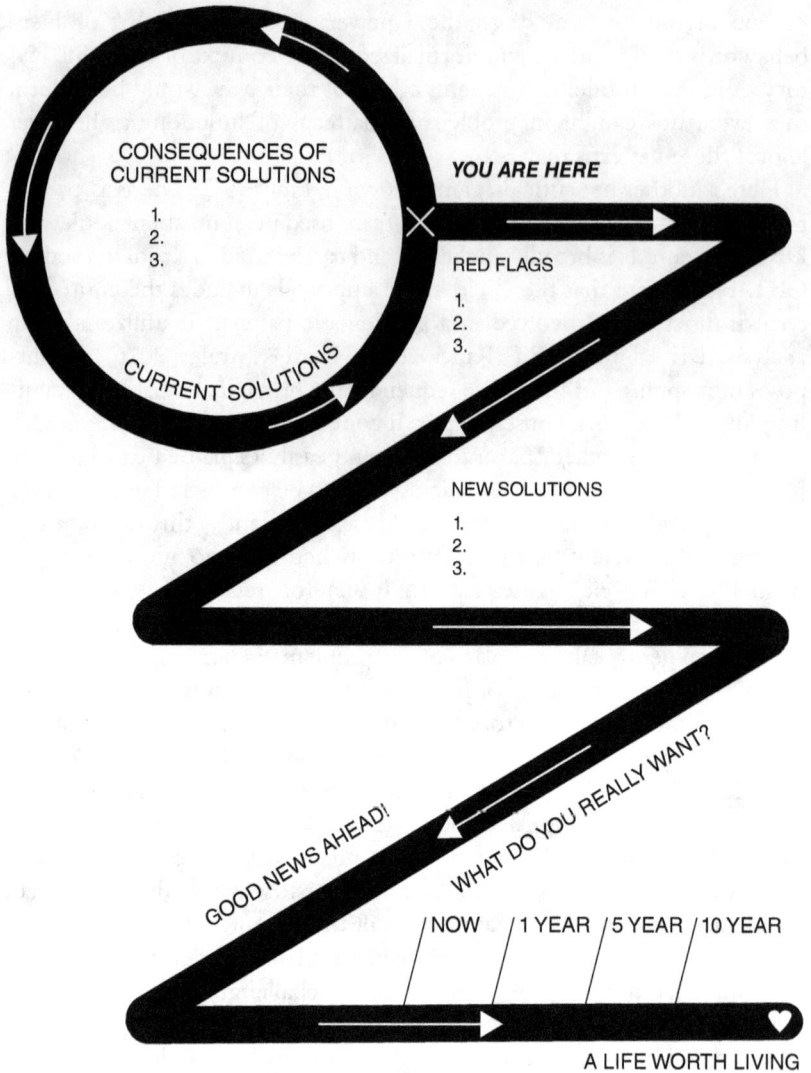

CONSEQUENCES OF
CURRENT SOLUTIONS

1.
2.
3.

YOU ARE HERE

RED FLAGS

1.
2.
3.

CURRENT SOLUTIONS

NEW SOLUTIONS

1.
2.
3.

GOOD NEWS AHEAD!

WHAT DO YOU REALLY WANT?

| NOW | 1 YEAR | 5 YEAR | 10 YEAR

A LIFE WORTH LIVING

Figure 9.2 Patient Roadmap

caught in an interesting bind: the more she adheres to her treatment regimen, the more she fears she is knuckling under to her mother's control. So she rebels, sometimes at her own expense. There are other maintaining factors, as well. Type 1 Diabetes imposes multiple unfair burdens on young people, not only in terms of dietary management, but in terms of the medical management of the illness, and in terms of its social

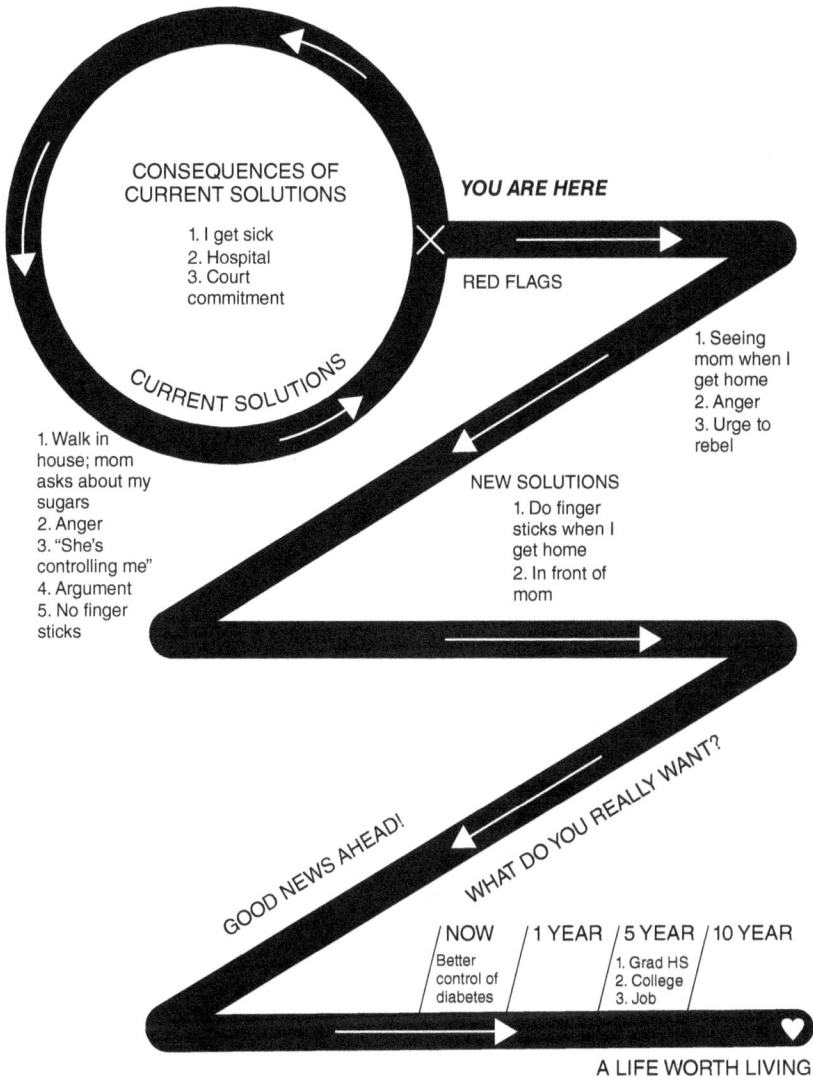

CONSEQUENCES OF
CURRENT SOLUTIONS

1. I get sick
2. Hospital
3. Court
commitment

YOU ARE HERE

RED FLAGS

CURRENT SOLUTIONS

1. Seeing
mom when I
get home
2. Anger
3. Urge to
rebel

1. Walk in
house; mom
asks about my
sugars
2. Anger
3. "She's
controlling me"
4. Argument
5. No finger
sticks

NEW SOLUTIONS

1. Do finger
sticks when I
get home
2. In front of
mom

GOOD NEWS AHEAD!

WHAT DO YOU REALLY WANT?

| NOW | 1 YEAR | 5 YEAR | 10 YEAR |
| Better control of diabetes | | 1. Grad HS 2. College 3. Job | |

A LIFE WORTH LIVING

Figure 9.3 Roadmap for a Teen with Diabetes

consequences. In line with Goldiamond's approach (Layng et al., 2022), we emphasize the functional utility of even this highly dangerous vicious cycle. In Goldiamond's "Constructional approach, no behavior is considered maladaptive. Behavior is considered always to be adaptive, although it can also often be very disturbing or costly (Layng et al., 2022, p. 28)." Costly indeed, for this 15-year old. Yet she resonated with our framing her pattern as understandable, given her wish for freedom and autonomy. She was able to successfully defeat her mom's control efforts and assert her own autonomy, even at the cost of frequent hospitalizations, court commitments, and brushes with severe illness. Fortunately, she recognized the self-defeating nature of this pattern, and its interference with another pattern of functioning that she longed for: finishing high school, going to college, embarking on a career path, and eventually living independently in a new family of her own. That was her idea of a life worth living. Therapy was organized around taking clear, definable, behavioral steps towards that objective, while exploring strategies to deal with derailments by the old vicious cycle. The latter included helping free the client and her mother of the unfortunate pattern in which they were stuck: one of mutual recrimination and a framing of their conflict as a battle for control. In terms of cognitive work, consider the power of altering the framing of this conflict from one of a control battle to one in which mom's efforts were based on a wish to save her daughter from a feared death from diabetes. The daughter was fleetingly able to recognize this as an explanation for her mother's control efforts. In those moments, she was better able to modulate her own rebellious response, in the service of both protecting herself and helping her mother relinquish control.

We want to highlight the following principles, derived from this case example, and generalizable to other case conceptualizations:

1. We begin by identifying the problem(s) for which the client seeks help. A diagnosis may be an entry point; but specific problems, behaviorally defined, form the beginning of our case conceptualization. Together with the client, we set up a problem list.
2. We use Guided Discovery and validation strategies to elicit all relevant information about what may be creating or maintaining the problems the client is facing. That includes the chain of cognitions, images, urges, emotions, behaviors, and consequences that arise in the context of the problem(s). Our interventions depend upon an assessment of where in that chain we can help the client turn towards a new pattern of functioning.
3. We don't inevitably need to speculate about distal causal factors in the client's past, though such speculation may be useful in helping the client create a more functional story of self. There is plenty to work with if we capture the pattern as it exists in the moment the problems they bring to therapy manifest themselves. There is plenty to work with if we capture the pattern as it exists in the moment the problems they bring to therapy manifest themselves. That said, we recognize

that humans are story-telling creatures. We often live inside the stories we tell ourselves and others about distal causes of our life circumstances. For example, a history of frequent moves in a military family can be viewed as causing interpersonal problems in offspring. So can a history of family alcoholism or economic troubles. We do not ignore those historical elements. They are important, certainly to the client. And if nothing else, historical factors help the clinician understand the verbal stories that may contribute to client entrapment. For example, a really tricky story is this one: "If my dad hadn't been a drunk, I'd be married and successful in a career by now." We will demonstrate in detail how to work with distal factors in therapy in Part 2 of the book.

4. We direct our efforts towards understanding the overall function served by this pattern. And we normalize or validate the pattern, not in terms of its ultimate effectiveness, but its short term benefits. In the case we presented, above, this young lady achieved her sense of independence and autonomy in her conflict with her mother. Bravo! That said, this achievement comes with a steep price, one that, upon reflection, she would prefer not to keep paying. Bravo to that, also! We can then create an alternative, one that comports with the client's deeper and heartfelt wishes for a life that works.

5. New patterns in living will often involve helping people navigate their evolved needs to secure necessary resources, both material and interpersonal. The specifics are determined by the client.

6. Now we have a treatment agenda, and we have a means of monitoring when we are on course, and when we veer off. Our efforts will be directed to minimizing the "veer offs" and maximizing the "on course" moments.

7. The entire spectrum of CBT interventions that we reviewed in previous chapters are available to achieve the agreed upon therapeutic objectives.

8. The therapy involves addressing multiple contextual elements. For the case example above, that includes management of the body signals related to illness, as well as the multiple social context of this client's life. All relevant contexts for change need to be addressed.

9. Last, we trust both the client's capacity for wisdom and growth, and the evolutionary needs embedded within us all. Those needs are echoed in Christakis' work on our evolutionary needs (Christakis, 2019). Those include connections, meaning, and securing of resources. In a sense, our therapeutic efforts bend in the direction of the general evolutionary needs of humans, and the specific values and temperamental dictates by which those needs are expressed by the individual.

CASE EXAMPLE

Now let's turn to one more case example, to familiarize the reader with how to set up a case conceptualization, and how that becomes a guide to therapy. In Part 2 of the book, we will show how those case conceptualizations become a guide to the selection of interventions and the completion of a course of therapy.

Ilsa is a 28-year old woman, who comes to therapy for help with depression. She was in a three-year same-sex relationship, which ended when her partner announced abruptly five months ago that she was leaving. No clear reasons were given. And since the breakup, the two have had no contact. Ilsa is able to maintain adequate work performance as an art appraiser, though she is calling in sick more frequently. Her boss, the owner of a gallery where she works, is questioning her ability to continue meeting the demands of this high-pressure position. Ilsa's mood remains deeply sad. She stays at home much of the time, avoiding social gatherings, which she used to enjoy. She says that she spends much of her time at home ruminating about the past, particularly the relationship that ended. She is not suicidal. But she increasingly is coming to believe that there is something wrong with her, and that she will never have the kind of intimate relationship she enjoyed for the three years she was with her former partner. Cannabis is legal where she lives, and she has begun smoking marijuana nightly. She says that cannabis both sparks further rumination and momentarily provides relief from her emotional pain. She would like to preserve her job while finding a footing in life and moving on, which occasioned her contacting the therapist for help.

If we turn to Figure 9.4, we can begin to map out a vicious cycle that is ensnaring Ilsa.

The proximate activating event for her depression is the abrupt termination of her intimate relationship, without explanation, by her partner of three years. Ilsa's history shows brief prior depressive episodes, but none with the intensity or pain of the current one. We might posit that she leans into a more neurotic temperament, predisposing her to a heightened vulnerability to loss. She also displays a number of psychological and behavioral mechanisms that are characteristic of this pattern: emotional pain, which she tries to soothe and flee via substance use; repetitive negative thinking; harsh labeling of self; sense of self as defective and helpless; withdrawal and isolation, ostensibly to avoid the pain of further rejection; bleak assessments of the future. The more she withdraws, ruminates, and uses cannabis, the deeper her depression. Her quest to figure out "what's wrong with me" remains elusive, unproductive, and a part of the problem,

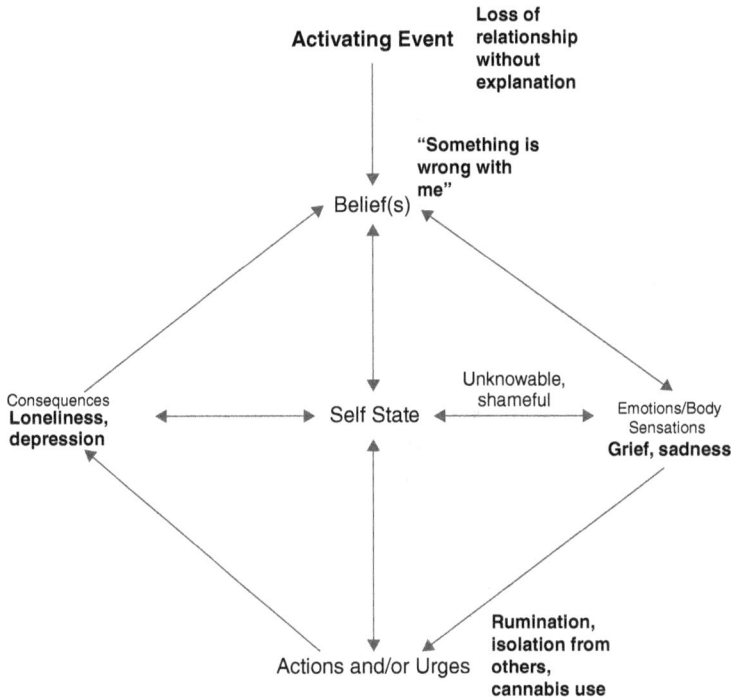

Figure 9.4 Ilsa's Vicious Cycle

Adapted from Wills, 2021

rather than a solution. In addition, the more she remains locked in this pattern, the greater the potential for downstream painful consequences, beginning at work, and spreading throughout her social network.

The therapist would work here to collaboratively set up a problem list, which might begin with "depression". But as we have discussed, "depression" is generic, and says relatively little about how that is playing out in any given client's life. So we want to create a problem list that is idiographic, specific to the person. It would need to include more specific and behaviorally defined problems: 1) managing the intense pain of loss; 2) reduced work attendance, which poses a long-term threat of job loss, and its attendant financial and other difficulties; 3) Acceptance of relationship loss, without necessarily blaming self for what happened; 4) dealing with the pattern of rumination, isolation, and cannabis use. 5) Gradual re-engagement in social relationships, with an eye towards eventually finding another partner.

As part of our efforts at psychoeducation, we would validate the overall logic of the vicious cycle, while helping Ilsa look at the longer-term consequences of it. In the short term, rumination might feel like it's an effort at solving a problem ("What's wrong with me?"; "What did I do wrong that caused the relationship to fail?"). But the actual function served is to prevent feeling the grief and loss of the relationship, for fear, perhaps, that the pain would be overwhelming. In addition, when compounded by nightly cannabis use, the pattern of avoidance and ineffective problem solving is only deepened. In the short run, perhaps, cannabis helps ease the pain, serving as a positive reinforcer, both by avoidance of emotion and by temporary pleasant effects of the drug.

Second, whether or not we use the Patient Roadmap, as a teaching tool in session, we use the ideas in the Roadmap, to help Ilsa consider which set of consequences and which direction serves her best in the long-run. Given her wish to begin by protecting her job, that is the problem we will focus on initially, and that sets the direction for altering the pattern in her vicious cycle.

Ilsa also displays a myriad of strengths that can be brought to bear on dealing with this situation. She has valiantly dealt with previous losses, of different types, including the traumatic death of her father in an automobile accident when she was 17. We might also posit that this loss possibly contributed a vulnerability to subsequent losses in her life. That notion remains in the mind of the therapist, and may or may not be included in the therapy work, depending upon further validation. In addition, Ilsa is highly conscientious in many areas of her life, both at work, in school, and in engagement in civic organizations. She and the therapist elect to start with problem #1: protecting her job, which means practicing behavioral activation, or DBT's "opposite action", by showing up for work and protecting the job she both loves and needs.

In line with the above, a second problem for focus is Ilsa's enmeshment in rumination, which contributes to depressed mood, self reproach, and withdrawal. Both the content and process of rumination are part of the vicious cycle of sadness, grief, non-acceptance, and isolation in which Ilsa is becoming trapped. The therapist posits that with acceptance of the loss might come from an increased experience of painful emotion, in the form of grief. Experiencing this more fully, tolerating the pain of loss, without self-reproach, will be a more distal treatment target. It can be woven into the tapestry of therapy, even if the initial problem focus is on protecting her job. Finally, should Ilsa remain in therapy, involvement in new opportunities for establishing intimate relationships may well be a treatment target, also.

Besides helping Ilsa understand the nature of rumination and the implications of the vicious cycle she is caught in, the therapist's aim will be to help restore the pattern of function she wishes to maintain at work. That is consonant with Behavioral Activation and with DBT's emphasis on the skills of mindfulness and opposite action. Given the generally good adaptive functioning that Ilsa has maintained, she appeared to be a candidate for this approach, which would include helping her spot rumination when it occurs, "unplugging" by coming as fully into the present moment at work as possible, and throwing herself into her work, which she acknowledges to be very engaging. Given the power of rumination for her, the therapist might acknowledge its importance at this time, and encourage scheduling "rumination time" at home, perhaps for 30 minutes in the evening, after work.

In terms of cognitive work, several potential avenues may be fruitful. First, seeing if she can generate potential explanations for the breakup that do not conform to her immediately believable "it's all my fault". She could survey friends to see if they have alternative explanations. She could consider what she, herself, would say to a close friend in a similar spot. Finally, she would be encouraged to tolerate the uncertainty surrounding the breakup. Given the disappearance of her partner, it is quite possible that Ilsa will never know for sure what motivated the partner to end the relationship, and perhaps she might bring some gentle, compassionate curiosity as to why she lands on the harshest possible explanation, in terms of what the breakup says about Ilsa! This amounts to planting seeds, rather than making cognitive change a precondition for tackling the problems on the problem list, as described above.

This case example does not provide a template for how to treat depression in all cases. It is highly idiographic, and is tailored very specifically to the conceptualization of this one case. In addition, the treatment focus is less on removing the elements in the vicious cycle, such as changing thoughts before changing behavior. It is more oriented towards building, or reclaiming, patterns of functioning that serve the purposes of the therapy. We will of course explore techniques in greater detail in Part 2.

CHAPTER SUMMARY

This chapter provides an overview of what we mean by the term contextualism, how it has been elaborated in CBT, and how it leads to a functional analysis. That analysis includes inner contexts, including emotions, cognition, and urges, as well as behavior. The consequences of these patterns of functioning become problematic when clients are caught in what we describe as vicious cycles. These patterns become self-reinforcing, based not only on environmental contingencies of reinforcement, but also the beliefs that become unproductively entrenched. We teach clients to become effective observers, or functional analysts, of the patterns in which they are caught. And we also foster clarity about where clients want their lives to go, once less entrapped by vicious cycles. This dovetails with a focus on client values, so that rather than "removing" an old, entrapping vicious cycle, we are helping the client build new patterns of living, capable of leading to a more meaningful, worthwhile life, as the client defines it.

REFERENCES

Christakis, N. (2019) *Blueprint: The Evolutionary Origins of a Good Society.* New York: Little, Brown, Spark.

Hayes, S. (2021) *A Liberated Mind: How to Pivot Toward What Matters.* New York: Avery.

Hayes, S., Hayes, L., Reese, H., & Sarbin, T. (1993) *Varieties of Scientific Contextualism.* Reno: Context Press.

Hayes, S., Strosahl, K., & Wilson, K. (2016) *Acceptance and Commitment Therapy: The Process and Practice of Mindful Change* (2nd edn). New York: Guilford.

Heard, H. & Swales, M. (2016) *Changing Behavior in DBT: Problem Solving in Action.* New York: Guilford.

Layng, J., Andronis, P., Codd, T., & Abdil-Jalil, A. (2022) *Nonlinear Contingency Analysis.* New York: Routledge.

Rizvi, S. (2019) *Chain Analysis in Dialectical Behavior Therapy.* New York: Guilford.

Temple, S. (2017) *Brief Cognitive Behavior Therapy for Cancer Patients: Re-visioning the CBT Paradigm.* New York: Routledge.

von Bertalanffy, L. (2015) *General Systems Theory* (Revised edn). New York: George Braziller.

Wills, F. (2021) *Skills in Cognitive Behavior Therapy* (2nd edn) London: Sage Press.

Part 2

Case Applications

CHAPTER 10

Introduction and Format of Presentations

The cases in this section were selected to represent the kinds of clinical situations commonly encountered in practice. They do not neatly fall into clearly delineated diagnostic categories. There may be features of several clinical disorders in each case, as well as the life dilemmas with which the client is struggling. We chose these cases because of what we hope will be seen by readers for their "real life" qualities. They are the kinds of cases that show up in clinics that serve broad segments of the community. Remember that as the evidence-based therapy movement developed, treatment protocols and manuals were created to address very specific DSM diagnoses. Beck's model began with recurrent major depressive disorder, and moved on to treat a broad spectrum of mood, anxiety, personality, and psychotic disorders. What was achieved in the lab was accomplished, in part, by setting rigorous criteria for patient inclusion. More complex cases were often excluded. While this helped set the stage for a science-based therapy movement, it sacrificed some of the ecological validity of cases that commonly appear in clinics: those clients who may have multiple co-morbid disorders, or who may not meet criteria for a specific disorder for which protocols have been developed. As we have reviewed in Part 1 of this book, these were among the reasons for the eventual move towards principle-based, rather than protocol-based, treatments.

In each case that follows, any and all of the Eight Organizing Principles can be brought to bear. For the sake of brevity, and for teaching purposes, we will select specific principles that seem most salient, or of interest, to the case in question. The alternative would be a deep dive, involving an exploration of all eight principles in every case. We encourage the reader to consider that in fact all Eight Organizing Principles can, indeed, be

DOI: 10.4324/9781003505587-12

brought to bear on all cases. As we present the cases, we encourage the reader to think through the key principles highlighted in a specific case, while also considering how other principles might also be drawn upon in conceptualizing and intervening. That said, there are some bedrocks that we tend to employ in all cases. We use Guided Discovery and Validation strategies in all cases. We tend to find ways to normalize suffering, using those validation strategies to help clients understand the sometimes hidden, puzzling logic of the vicious cycles in which they are trapped. We routinely search for the strengths, resources, and values that help us set a course for therapy, and that can be mobilized in the service of engaging the client. We routinely begin with the clinical diagnoses that are used in most clinic settings (i.e. DSM diagnoses), but quickly seek to understand the transdiagnostic factors that are implicated in the case presentation. And we are both selective and prescriptive about how we draw upon the organizing factors that contain intervention possibilities. In that sense, we encourage creativity, flexibility, and disciplined strategies for engaging clients in the process of change.

CASE CHAPTER STRUCTURE

Each case will follow a similar structure:

1. A case description
2. A case conceptualization
3. Highlight specific organizing principle(s)
4. Provide intervention options and choice points
5. Create exercises for readers to make choices and give written reasons for intervention choices
6. Demonstrate the options selected by the authors

This format encourages reader involvement. You will note that spaces are provided in the text, so that you, the reader, can write down your ideas about the case and make choices about what you would do as therapist. There is ample research to suggest that writing down your ideas contributes to learning, by fostering reflective practices (Bennett-Levy, McManus, Westling, & Fennell, 2009; Bennett-Levy, 2006; Bennett-Levy & Lee, 2014; Bennett-Levy, Thwaites, Haarhoff, & Perry, 2015). Taking the time to think through and respond to the case material will make you a better CBT therapist. Rather than rely solely on learning from reading or lectures, reflective practices are more active, and involve careful thought and reasoning. The rote learning of ideas, such as those presented in Part 1 is augmented by taking the time to think through and creatively apply ideas in practice. This combines "head" and "heart" learning, which mirrors the kind of cognitive, experiential, and emotionally compelling learning we strive for in psychotherapy.

We don't tie the cases up in a neat bow at the end of each case. We leave the outcomes indeterminate, and instead invite the reader to join us in figuring out what steps we might take, clinically, to help the client move their lives forward. We don't pretend to have all the answers. In fact, "solving" each case is not quite the point. We deliberately picked challenging cases, to spark reflection and learning. Join in by reflecting, writing down your ideas, and seeing how you match up to our own ideas for the case.

CASE CHAPTERS

CASE #1: A DESPERATE MOTHER

Rose is a 54-year old Hispanic woman, the mother of one adult daughter. She is divorced from her daughter's father, whom she described as alcoholic and abusive. For the past ten years, she has maintained a rocky relationship with her daughter, Janine. Rose fears that she overindulged her daughter, out of sadness and protectiveness, given the family's pain. Janine is described as having a substance abuse problem, unstable relationships with men, as well as numerous legal problems, including stealing money and credit cards from Rose. Janine has a daughter, and Rose fears loss of contact with the child, her granddaughter. Rose is burdened by guilt that she is a "bad mother". She blames herself for her daughter's frailties, noting that "I have created a monster" by her indulgence of Janine. She is increasingly depressed and anxious, in the face of her daughter's mounting problems. Rose feels caught between her anger towards her daughter and her wish to protect her fragile relationship with her, and to insure contact with Rose's granddaughter.

CASE #2: THE LONE RANGER

John is a 44-year old attorney, a partner in a large, successful law firm. He is also a former combat officer, an Army Ranger, who served in Afghanistan. He feels inexplicably estranged and alienated from his law firm, and comes to therapy at the urging of his wife, who notes that John is bringing his anger and irritability home from the office. He does not have PTSD, though his combat experiences are intertwined with his disaffection with his law firm. He is becoming more depressed, though without any suicidal ideation.

CASE #3: A CASE OF COKE

Kelly has been struggling with a cocaine addiction for at least 16 years. Now in her mid-thirties, she reports having made many failed attempts to discontinue cocaine use. She's been to residential treatment twice and had many outpatient therapists over the years. She's also participated in NA on and off. She describes her use as sporadic. That is, she can go many weeks without any use, but then go on a binge which lasts "a week or so". She works at a local radio station on the weekends. She says this means she is working when her friends are off and that she is off when her friends are working. This leads her to struggle with loneliness, one of the antecedents to her cocaine use.

CASE #4: PARENTS OF A SELF-INJURING TEEN

Barbara and Tom's 16-year old daughter, Jessica, has been struggling to adjust to the rigors of mid-adolescence. Her struggles are exemplified by difficulties managing her mood, substantial decline in academic performance, and frequent peer conflict. She has also started vaping and smoking cannabis. Perhaps most troubling to Barbara and Tom, she has been cutting herself when she becomes acutely distressed. Because Jessica is either withdrawn or when semi-engaged, arguing with her parents, they feel incredibly anxious because they believe they've lost parental influence with her and because this leaves them wondering what information about her struggles they do not know. It is this distress alongside their feelings of powerlessness regarding their parenting that led them to seek psychological consultation.

CASE #5: THE CASE OF EFRAN: FINDING MEANING

Efran sought services because he felt "nothing really matters". He described his mood as depressed and complained of little motivation. He described his life as one of just "going through the motions". He had been a devoutly religious person until around the age of 30 (he's now 39) when he determined that he no longer believed in God. Efran described losing his faith as the precipitant to his current concerns. His faith had made the world and his place in it meaningful. Though he is not currently suicidal, he is struggling to determine how he can continue his life despite being confronted with the meaninglessness of life.

REFERENCES

Bennett-Levy, J. (2006) Therapist Skills: A Cognitive Model of their Acquisition and Refinement. *Behavioural and Cognitive Psychotherapy*, 34, 57–78.

Bennett-Levy, J. & Lee, N. (2014) Self-Practice and Self-Reflection in Cognitive Behaviour Therapy Training: What Factors Influence Trainees' Engagement and Experience of Benefit? *Behavioural and Cognitive Psychotherapy*, 42, 48–64.

Bennett-Levy, J., McManus, F., Westling, B., & Fennell, M. (2009) Acquiring and Refining CBT Skills and Competencies: Which Training Methods Are Perceived to Be Most Effective? *Behavioural and Cognitive Psychotherapy*, 37, 145–163.

Bennett-Levy, J., Thwaites, R., Haarhoff, B., & Perry, H. (2015) *Experiencing CBT from the Inside Out: A Self-Practice/Self-Reflection Workbook for Therapists*. New York: Guilford Press.

CHAPTER 11

Case #1: A Desperate Mother

Rose is a 54-year old Hispanic woman, the mother of one adult daughter. She is divorced from her daughter's father, whom she described as alcoholic and abusive. For the past ten years, she has maintained a rocky relationship with her daughter, Janine. Rose fears that she overindulged her daughter, out of sadness and protectiveness, given the family's pain. Janine is described as having a substance abuse problem, unstable relationships with men, as well as numerous legal problems, including stealing money and credit cards from Rose. Janine has a daughter, and Rose fears loss of contact with the child, her granddaughter. Rose is burdened by guilt that she is a "bad mother". She blames herself for her daughter's frailties, noting that "I have created a monster" by her indulgence of Janine. She is increasingly depressed and anxious, in the face of her daughter's mounting problems. Rose feels caught between her anger towards her daughter and her wish to protect her fragile relationship with her, and to insure contact with Rose's granddaughter.

Let's turn to an examination of how the Eight Organizing Principles can be used to help Rose. We will go through the use of these principles in a way that encourages you, the reader, to make decisions about how you might intervene.

The Use of Guided Discovery and Validation Strategies. We employ a gentle curiosity in our initial exploration of the problems for which the client seeks therapy. Before intervening to promote change, we must first understand. "Getting" the client means seeing the world through their eyes. This requires us to maintain a nonjudgmental stance; listen carefully at all times; and convey through words, facial expression, and gestures that we are listening. To ensure that we are in tune with the client, we make frequent, brief summaries of what we hear while inviting the client to correct any misunderstandings on our part. The DBT validation strategies of

DOI: 10.4324/9781003505587-13

Listening (Level 1) and Radical Genuineness (Level 6) are present at all times in all sessions. The reader may note that these are bedrock principles of many therapies, and they emanate from the work of people like Carl Rogers. That capacity to be radically genuine will allow the therapist to promote change later on, if and when the client faces some tough decisions and is required to take some brave steps forward.

Here's a sample transcript of how we might use Guided Discovery and Validation with Rose.

THERAPIST (USING A CAPSULE SUMMARY OF WHAT SHE HAS HEARD THUS FAR IN SESSION 1):	So it seems that you feel angry, sad, and also scared right now. Your daughter has been out of control for a long time, and you're blaming yourself for maybe being too indulging and lenient?
ROSE:	Yes. I feel it's my fault that she's had all these problems. I felt so bad for her after her dad and I split up that I just couldn't say no to her. She never learned that word: no. And I was never able to reign in her out-of-control behavior, like drugs and sex. I failed her.
THERAPIST:	OK. Let me file that last thing you said away for a moment, about you failing her. We'll come back to that idea. But for now, that helps make sense of how scared and sad you are, believing you failed as a mother. It also sounds, from what you're saying, that you're scared you'll lose contact with her, and with your granddaughter.
ROSE:	Oh yes. That's so true! If I failed with Janine, and it's too late for her, I at least have to make sure I do what I can for Tyler, my granddaughter. I want to protect her.
THERAPIST:	Well, for what it's worth at this point, I'm hearing that you're actually a pretty loving mom and grandma, who just doesn't know what to do right now in a tough situation. (Therapist provides a tentative counter to Rose's self-punitive image as a mom, a gentle probe.)
ROSE:	Thanks. But I get so angry with Janine, and I think that's a place I get caught. If I lash out, and tell her what I think, she pulls away. If she pulls away now, I lose contact with Tyler. And I lose any possible influence with Janine. It's sort of a lose-lose thing I'm caught in.
THERAPIST:	OK. So let me ask: what would a bit of "win-win" look like?
ROSE:	(silently thinks). That's a good question. Right now I can't even imagine any "win" here.

In this therapy vignette, we begin to identify the binds Rose is in and some painful beliefs about herself that will be grist for the mill in therapy. These include her sense of personal failure as a mother and the management of her own emotions as she relates to her daughter. We will see later that Rose gets angry and judgmental, then retreats into self-recrimination and guilt, after her daughter responds by withdrawing angrily. In addition, the therapist already senses a wish, or a belief in Rose that she "should" be able to control or change her adult daughter's behavior, and that failure to do so makes her a bad mother.

As we are exploring the client's problems, we are listening for those factors that maintain the problems, as well. A knowledge of *transdiagnostic processes* is important here. If we start by considering temperament, for starters, we begin to listen to the client's history not only for potentially critical and formative events, but for clues about temperament. We can also use brief paper-and-pencil measures to help, such as a ten item Big-Five personality test (Gosling, Rentfrow, & Swann, 2003), or more extensive and comprehensive measures that yield information about the five temperamental factors and their aspects. An example of the latter is based on the work of University of Minnesota psychologist Colin DeYoung's work: (https://emilywilloughby.com/research/bfas).

We learn that Rose is highly *Conscientious*, yet prone to *Neuroticism*, in the form of anxiety, worry, depression, and withdrawal. She can also be prone to angry outbursts that are followed by a sense of shame. She is, overall, high in the trait of *Agreeableness*, especially politeness. This combination of Neuroticism, Conscientiousness, and Agreeableness can contribute to the binds Rose finds herself in. Because of her conscientiousness, she is determined to "fix" problems and takes personal responsibility for doing so. When she "fails" she tends to blame herself, brood, become sad and anxious. Meanwhile, her Agreeableness is a double-edged sword. Being Agreeable, including being polite, smooths many social interactions and makes us likable. At the same time, being too polite can allow others to run roughshod over us and eventually lead to the angry outbursts that Rose is prone to. Life requires us to find a balance between being passively agreeable and overly aggressive and impolitic. That, in turn, requires us to understand ourselves a bit better, and learn to act opposite to some of our temperamental factors. In Rose's case, her challenge is to find that balance between taking on too much responsibility for a daughter whose behavior she cannot control and acquiescing self-destructively to her daughter's demands. An added complicating factor is Rose's understandable and admirable wish to protect her 8-year old granddaughter, Tyler.

Among other *transdiagnostic factors are the cognitive and information processing biases* to which she is prone. In the spaces below, take a moment to write down some ideas you can already glean in this case example of the cognitive and attentional processes that might be maintaining Rose's suffering:

_____

_____

_____

_____

_____

You probably noted a variety of potential cognitive processes implicated in the maintenance of Rose's problems. She harshly labels herself a "failure". She has perfectionistic standards for herself and assumes she can be more powerful than is realistic. She is prone to "all or none" thinking about herself. Her attention is biased in the direction of constantly noticing her daughter's frailties (admittedly substantial), while overlooking areas of her daughter's competence. In addition, Rose is prone to minimize her own strengths and to become trapped in treatment interfering pessimism. Behaviorally, she is trapped between silent acquiescence and angry outbursts, potentially making her somewhat unpredictable to her daughter and impairing social problem solving. And finally for now we note that Rose is prone to rumination, replaying interactions with her daughter, and painful events from the past, while also stoking emotions of fear, sadness, and shame. All grist for the therapeutic mill! Which leads to yet another organizing principle: *Normalizing Human Suffering*. Here, we can perhaps begin to help Rose ease up on her harsh self-judgments and blame. She was trapped in a marriage to a violent alcoholic, fearing for her safety, and wanting to provide a stable family structure for her only daughter. She was just 18 when she married, and like most 18-year-olds was pretty clueless about the realities of marriage and about mate selection. Helping her make peace with her own temperament nonjudgmentally and learn to work with the givens of that temperament are valid treatment targets down the road. For now, we simply recognize that we all have personalities – with their strengths and weaknesses – making us full members of the human being club. No judgments. In addition, to have biases in our information processing and attention is part and parcel of the human condition. Those cognitive, attentional, and behavioral processes are seemingly automatic, unwilled, and become self-reinforcing as we inadvertently "practice" unworkable patterns. Those patterns become grist for the mill as we establish a case formulation. Normalizing such patterns can undermine shame and self-blame and open the door not only to taking responsibility for not only our own strengths and frailties, but also to effectively managing the gnarly problems that are inherent to the human condition. This process of helping normalize the client's suffering in light of these transdiagnostic factors is fostered by Guided Discovery and Validation strategies. Yet it must be done in a way that also fosters the client's ability and willingness to take appropriate action, sometimes requiring courage and persistence on the client's part, and strong coaching on the therapist's part.

Let's consider yet another of the Eight Organizing Principles, and how it can be brought to bear on the task of helping Rose spring free of the traps in which she is caught.

A Focus on Client Strengths and Values: Take a moment to consider what you already know about Rose. In the space below, write out what strengths she is displaying – strengths that she may be unaware of, or is minimizing, due to the cognitive and information processing biases she's trapped in. What are some of the strengths and values that can be allies in Rose's case?

_____

_____

_____

_____

_____

We have a partial and tentative list of strengths and values, including Rose's sense of love and duty as a mom and grandmother and her persistence and diligence in looking after her family. She also displayed some steel in her spine by finally standing up to her violent, alcoholic husband, getting both a divorce and a restraining order, which he fortunately honored. Her values begin to show up as well in the importance of being a protector – if not for her daughter at this point, then for her granddaughter. As the therapy unfolds, we will undoubtedly learn more about Rose's strengths and her values, and will incorporate those into the therapy. (More on that when we draw up our case formulation.)

Let's take what we've already done and develop a provisional case formulation. That will include a list of problems to address in therapy, as well as the factors that seem to be maintaining those problems and preventing Rose from solving them on her own. You will note that we've already addressed four of our Eight Organizing Principles. Let's set up our case formulation and then talk about how to use the remaining principles when we discuss our intervention strategies. The material in the "vicious cycle" diagram (see Figure 11.1) is gleaned from the early sessions, in which we used Guided Discovery and Validation as our key interventions.

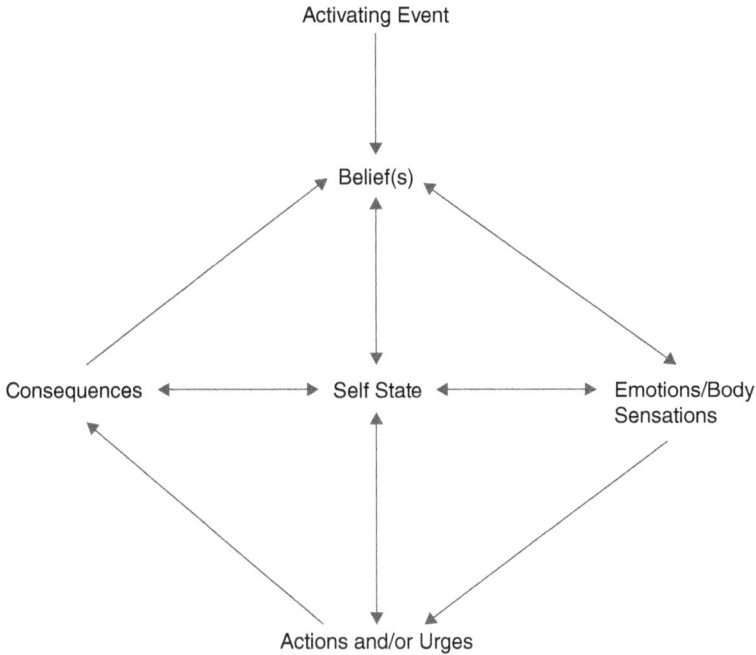

Figure 11.1 Vicious Cycle

Adapted from Wills, 2021

Take a moment to fill in the Vicious Cycle Diagram below. You will note that the cycle takes into account another principle, that of *Contextualism*. We are interested not only in cognition as a driver, but also of the entire inner and outer set of contexts in which the problem in question unfolds. No one factor is "the cause" of the problem, and any and all may be implicated and brought to bear on problem management. So, take a moment to think about what might be the key activating events that Rose experiences here. What thoughts or images arise spontaneously in these situations? What emotions emerge? For behaviors, think from what you already know both about what she both does, and what her urges are when her emotions and thoughts are activated in key problem situations. Write those down below or in the diagram. What are the consequences, to her and/or others (remember context) at this point in the vicious cycle? What do you imagine her sense of self is here, not only in terms of beliefs about self, but also her bodily self? Next, how does this entire pattern relate to the onset of yet another activating event in the future? Finally, think about how you might share this

Activating Event (phone
call from daughter)

Belief(s)
(I'm a bad
mother)

Consequences
(if anger, daughter withdraws:
either way, rumination)

Self State
(shameful
and weak)

Emotions body
Sensations
(shame, sad)

Actions and/or Urges (anger
outburst or withdrawal)

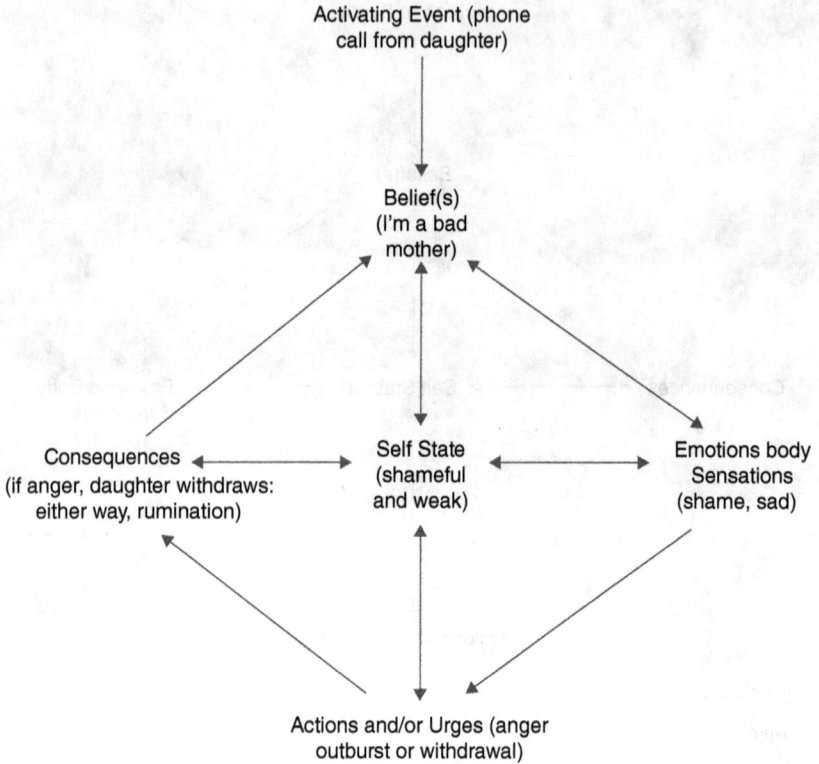

Figure 11.2 Rose's Vicious Cycle

Adapted from Wills, 2021

diagram with Rose, in order to help her understand this pattern and be motivated to work towards change?:

Here's how we filled in this diagram:

First, the activating events can be both internal and external. Rose is a ruminator, so she can become sad, angry, or scared in response to the stream of images and thoughts that roll around in her own mind, even when her daughter is not present. Other activating events can include outside stimuli, such as a phone call from her daughter, or a visit, or another family member calling to convey concern about how the grand-daughter is behaving. It's not that the activating event or any other element in the vicious cycle is a complete "cause" of the problem. The key is that these elements in the diagram flow together, in somewhat of a predictable sequence, and we can select the elements to target for creating change.

How about the thoughts and images in this cycle? Rose quickly concludes "I'm a bad mother", or "I'm a failure", accompanied by emotions of shame, sadness, or fear. Her urges and actions involve acting on those emotions and thoughts, either by avoidance of her daughter, by pleading with her daughter, or by becoming angry and yelling at her. The consequences include the daughter responding angrily, withdrawing, and threatening to prevent Rose from seeing her granddaughter. This can be followed by an agonizing period of silent disappearance. Rose is then left ruminating about her failure as a mom and grandmother, until the next external activating event, when the cycle renews. Note that at the center of this vicious cycle we see a sense of self as frail, vulnerable, shameful, weak, ineffectual, and blameworthy. Rose labeled that self "scared mama", which pointed us in the direction of a preferred sense of self, which she labeled "Mama Bear", for the ferocity and determination a female bear shows, not only in looking out for herself, but for her cubs, whenever they are threatened.

Rose is stuck. Fortunately, we can now put words to the barriers she faces, in terms of her beliefs about herself, her tendency to withdraw or dysregulate, and her limited repertoire of problem-solving strategies in key problem situations. These are all valid treatment targets as we set about building new repertoires/patterns of functioning – work that connects with the client's values as they show up in the Patient Roadmap. One needn't formally provide a written Road Map to all patients but we'd suggest trying it for a patient or two, so you can get the idea of smoothly shifting the focus from "being stuck" to finding a new pattern based on both client wishes and values, as well as what is possible in any given situation. All problems cannot be "solved" or "resolved". Some situations must be tolerated or accepted; in some ways learning how to do that may be the toughest change of all. For now, take a look at a client Roadmap.

Please note that the cycle shown on the upper left is essentially our vicious cycle. It details the sequence of inner and outer events that contribute to the maintenance of the problem, in this case, conflict and distance from Rose's daughter, and Rose's depression, rumination, and anger. Now take a look at the "long and winding road" to the right and lower part of the diagram. Take a moment to write down the following:

1. From what you already know or can imagine, what does Rose really want in this situation, now?
2. What would she want her life in this situation to look like in, let's just say, in one year?

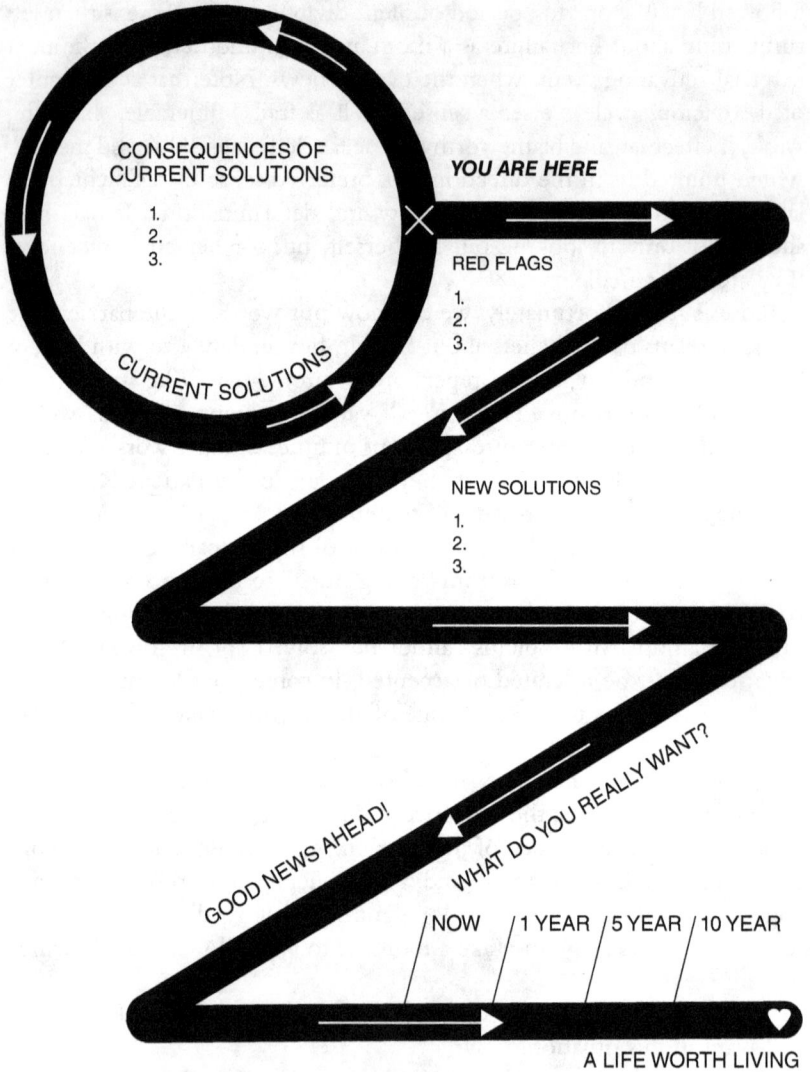

CONSEQUENCES OF
CURRENT SOLUTIONS

1.
2.
3.

YOU ARE HERE

RED FLAGS

1.
2.
3.

CURRENT SOLUTIONS

NEW SOLUTIONS

1.
2.
3.

GOOD NEWS AHEAD!

WHAT DO YOU REALLY WANT?

NOW   1 YEAR   5 YEAR   10 YEAR

A LIFE WORTH LIVING

Figure 11.3 Patient Roadmap

As we help Rose find a way down the road she wants to travel, we will also be on the lookout for two things: First, what actions will she need or want to take towards that outcome? Second, what are the "red flags" – the things that will derail her, steering away from her intended direction, and back into that vicious cycle? Addressing those "red flags" will likely involve using the other *Organizing Principles* to design appropriate interventions to help Rose.

We're guessing that you came up with some of the same ideas that we did. First, what Rose wants is an end to conflict with her daughter, and have steadier access to her granddaughter, with the ability to provide love and guidance to her. However, she is only partially in charge of that outcome. So, what we might do is think about what steps Rose might take to get closer to that outcome in, say, one year. That would give us a chance to identify actual behaviors she wants to practice with her daughter: ways of regulating her emotions, and strategies to manage her own self-punishing cognitions, and managing her tendency to either withdraw in hurt, or unload on her daughter in anger. Recall that Rose's sense of self was of a weak and ineffectual woman, though we see ample evidence to the contrary. That weak self she labeled "scared mama". She chose to label the destination as a sense of self that reflects "Mama Bear." The "red flags" would be all the things she must learn to spot, mindfully – before acting – allowing her to take a moment to pause, reconsider, and behave in a way that fosters moving toward "the road ahead" rather than staying stuck in the old vicious cycle. Finally, for now, we also have to stipulate that Rose's best efforts may not influence her daughter's behavior in the way that Rose wants. Accepting the limits of her motherly influence may be a bitter pill, yet it is the most realistic outcome she can achieve. Fortunately, in the long run, it has the potential to be the most empowering and dignified as well.

So now, we can establish not only a problem list, but a direction for the therapy to go. Problems include:

1. Volatile relationship with daughter
2. Tenuous contact with granddaughter
3. Depression, with rumination and a tendency to withdraw
4. Self-reproach, with shame and guilt
5. Anger outbursts at daughter

Instead of simply trying to "get rid" of the emotions, thoughts, and behaviors that are part of Rose's "vicious cycle", we are helping her find some new ways of dealing with her daughter and of experiencing herself in relation to her daughter. We can't guarantee Rose the outcome she ideally wants. But we can help her make her best effort at changing her relationships, while accepting that the outcome is only partially dependent upon her. And that, by the way, gets us to another of our CBT organizing principles: *Balancing Acceptance, Mindfulness, and Change Processes.* CBT has lots of change strategies: cognitive, behavioral, and those that help regulate emotions. We also foster mindfulness, as for example, in helping Rose develop a strong ability to notice her own thoughts, urges, and emotions, and to choose what to do in a more calm and deliberate manner. That requires some training in how to view one's own experiences from a bit of a distance, with curiosity and with some self-compassion. In that little space we open mindfully, the capacity to choose what to do next emerges. That alone helps a client break free of a vicious cycle – we stop reacting blindly. We become freer to choose what works, rather than what comes automatically. And when our change strategies do not produce all the results we might wish, we can draw on those acceptance practices, to foster the capacity to let go a bit more of outcomes that are not in our control. It may well be that, paradoxically, it is our acceptance strategies that are our most potent forms of change.

Finally, for this case, let's turn our attention to the Organizing Principles that deal with *balancing change and acceptance strategies*, as well as *experiential and cognitive change techniques*.

Let's pick up a few sessions into the therapy with Rose. We've established a problem list together. We've mapped out the vicious cycle she's caught in that seems to prevent a more effective management of the problem(s). And we have a clear road map, pointing towards where Rose would like to be in regard to her daughter. You will note that rather than targeting the removal of depression, we focus primarily on the building of a repertoire of effective coping behaviors, including both change and acceptance strategies.

If we were to employ cognitive interventions, there is an incredibly rich set of techniques to draw upon. Here are some possibilities.

1. Examine evidence supporting the possibility that she is a decent mom. We may not need to focus much on evidence she's a bad mom, since that's what is already salient to Rose.
2. Pursuant to the above, we could do a survey technique, asking her to check with family and/or trusted friends, such as her church group, to see how they view her as a mom. Most likely, she'd get positive comments.

3. We could ask her what she would say to a close friend, in a similar situation. If she had a more compassionate standard for that friend than for herself, we could point out the double standard, an unfair one that she is burdened by.
4. We could do more experiential exercises, including asking her to say "I'm a terrible mom" in a singsong voice, in a goofy pitch. Such exercises need to be done in a spirit of compassion and collaboration, lest they be seen as mocking. But when such interventions work, they can produce quick relief and a moment of freeing distance from the grip of painful beliefs.

Any and all of these intervention strategies are capable of working. Many times, they do at least soften the impact of painful and/or erroneous beliefs about self, others, the world. And as we will demonstrate in subsequent case chapters, cognitive interventions can help improve productive insight and effective adaptation. For Rose, the power and impact of such interventions fade when she faces the emotional impact of conflict situations with her daughter. So rather than assume that we must change her thoughts about herself as a precondition for changing how she deals with her daughter, we might try another, complementary strategy: help Rose recognize her vulnerability to painful self-appraisals, and targeting the impact on her behavior in such moments. Further, this strategy involves helping the client tune in to the function served by painful beliefs, and continue on in their chosen behavioral direction, even in the face of pressures to the contrary. By building new behavioral and interpersonal repertoires, with thoughts as "passengers on the bus", rather than as drivers (Hayes et al., 2016), clients can learn to adopt a more accepting, and less reactive, posture towards internal experience, while "driving the bus" of their life in a way that is more purposeful and effective. In Rose's case, we might focus on helping her remain purposefully in the face of the thought "I'm a bad mom". In time, "bad mom" might fade in its power and in its believability. In line with this, Rose liked the idea of herself as a "Mama Bear" – a mother capable of looking out for her own interest, yet fiercely capable of looking after others.

One of the pleasures and challenges of learning CBT is the development of a big repertoire of techniques. That includes cognitive techniques that help check the truth or accuracy of beliefs; techniques that build resilience and realism in the face of tough situations when the client's feared appraisals turn out to be accurate (such as facing a terrible illness); and techniques to help change the function of beliefs, without necessarily addressing whether the belief is true or false.

In Rose's case, let's stipulate that we've tried a few mainstream, Beckian cognitive and experiential techniques, with mixed results. Let's see what might happen if we instead directly addressed the function of her painful belief, on her behavior, using an experiential exercise derived from Acceptance and Commitment Therapy (ACT). Please note: we do not assume that techniques derived from one type of CBT are inherently better than those of another. We frankly do not know in advance which technique may work for any given patient, in any given moment. As long as we are selecting from among empirically supported therapies, we have a framework for using any technique, as well as making up our own, in the moment. We submit that our Eight Organizing Principles for a modern CBT, coupled with our case conceptualization format, allow for the integration of techniques from a variety of therapies. The key here is that when one technique does not work in a given moment, flexibly choose another.

THERAPIST: So, from what you're saying, it sounds as though when you are pushed by your daughter to give her money, or when you find out she used your credit card without your permission, up comes the thought "I'm a terrible mom", right?

CLIENT: Yeah. And I just sort of shut down.

THERAPIST: If I saw you shut down, what would I see?

CLIENT: Mostly, I'd just get really quiet, and maybe I'd start crying. Then, if she pushed me, I'd start to get angry and eventually maybe even yell at her. After that, after we hung up, I'd be really quiet and sad. And my mind would be telling me I did it again. I was a bad mom, to have a daughter who was so disrespectful and out of control. I mean, I'm trying to keep in mind that she's 32 years old, and I'm not in charge of her. But still…

THERAPIST: But still, it's pretty hard to let go of a really old pattern that you've practiced since she was, what? Seven years old, when you and her dad split? That's sort of like 25 years of practice, so it's kind of automatic, isn't it?

CLIENT: (smiles). I never thought of it quite like that. It wasn't the kind of practice I'd choose now if I could do it over. I'm hoping it's not too late to change now.

THERAPIST: It's not. So how about we take a moment to think through how you would like to handle those moments, when your daughter steals or asks you to bail her out financially, again, and then threatens to never see you again or let you see your granddaughter. I'm guessing that may well happen again, right?

CLIENT: Oh yeah. It'll happen again.

THERAPIST: OK. So, when "I'm a bad mom" comes up, you either get sad and with-drawn and silent, or you kind of explode. We're aiming to find a middle ground here, right? How much, right now, do you believe "I'm a bad mom?"

CLIENT: 50/50. You've helped me a little bit to see another way of looking at this. But in the heat of the moment, it pops up and I shut down or get really angry.

THERAPIST: What do you say we practice how to deal with your daughter in those moments in a way that might work better for you? Even if she doesn't respond to your satisfaction in that moment – how would that "good mom" behave in those moments? In fact, you said you'd like to see yourself more as "Mama Bear". What might that look and feel like?

CLIENT: I'd be clear with her that stealing my card is unacceptable. Ever. And it would mean taking steps to make sure she couldn't access it. I could also talk with her calmly about helping her set up a financial plan. She works, so she does have some income, even if it's not as much as she wants. My fear is always that she would get really mad at me and threaten to not be in touch with me or let me have contact with my granddaughter. "Mama Bear" would stay strong, even if my daughter threatened to disappear again. "Mama Bear" would let her go, knowing that she'll be back, and I'd let her know I'd always keep the door open.

THERAPIST: So, "I'm a bad mom" stops you in your tracks, no matter what anyone tells you or how much people have tried to help you see it another way? That's the "weak mama" you talked about?

CLIENT: Yeah. It's weird. That isn't just a thought. "Weak mama" is wired in with my emotions and my body. I feel sick in those moments and just want to shrink away. Just when I need to actually be strong and engaged with my daughter. No matter what!

THERAPIST: How about we practice those "Mama Bear" actions you want to take. Even if "I'm weak" shows up in your mind, body, and emotions.

CLIENT: Well, that'd make me the mom I want to be, at least more of the time, which is why I'm here.

THERAPIST: OK. Well, suppose we practice some things that you can take with you into your dealings with your daughter. These would be ideas and actions that would just make you the mom you want to be, even if your mind sometimes gives you "bad mom" beliefs. Maybe those "I'm a bad mom" thoughts are just like an old song that keeps playing, even after you're just kind of sick of it.

CLIENT: Like an ear worm, a song that you can't get out of your head, but learn to tune out.

THERAPIST: Oh yeah. Like that.

Helping Rose deal directly and purposefully with her daughter, setting limits, lovingly but firmly, while keeping the door open, and risking ruptures in the relationship, rather than acquiescing to exploitive behavior can also alter Rose's sense of self. That work would likely involve spirited role plays – practicing a rich repertoire of "Mama Bear" behavior, and anticipating possible responses from Janine while remaining as centered, calm, and compassionate as possible and also remaining firm about maintaining her own self-protective stance. Ernest Hemingway's description of courage is apt here: grace under pressure. We see that as a skill to be practiced.

Remember, in the center of that vicious cycle, Rose had a sense of self as frail, vulnerable, shameful, weak, ineffectual, and blameworthy. That sense of self was also embodied. The physical sensations of that hurricane of emotion and cognition led to exhaustion, withdrawal, and fear. We could also include mindfulness exercises, including guided imagery work, to strengthen and build the sense of an embodied self as wise, kind, yet firm and resolute. She labeled that self she was strengthening "Mama Bear". She was able to experience that sense of fierce determination and power in the face of challenges. Her posture altered as she embodied the experience of "Mama Bear." And she noted a sense of lightness afterwards.

As we leave this case, we cannot know the outcome. Despite our inability to predict how Rose's daughter might evolve, we can nonetheless work with Rose to be the self she wishes to be in this tough situation: to keep the door open to her daughter, set proper limits on the daughter's ability to dictate Rose's financial and other support, and do what she can to protect her granddaughter, in hopes that Rose's daughter will eventually improve her own functioning. To the degree that therapy succeeds in this, we also provide Rose some inoculation against her own tendencies towards depressive and anxious states, including emotional volatility and withdrawal. That, in itself, is rather substantial.

REFERENCES

Gosling, S., Rentfrow, P., & Swann, W. (2003) A Very Brief Measure of the Big-Five Personality Domains. *Journal of Research in Personality*, 37, 6, 504–528.

Hayes, S., Strosahl, K., & Wilson, K. (2016) *Acceptance & Commitment Therapy: The Process and Practice of Mindful Change* (2nd edn). New York: Guilford.

Wills, F. (2021) *Skills in Cognitive Behavior Therapy* (2nd edn). London: Sage.

CHAPTER 12

Case #2: The Lone Ranger

John is a 44-year old ex-Army Ranger officer, who did two tours of duty in Afghanistan, during which he was in frequent combat. He is now an attorney, working in a prestigious law firm, in corporate law. He does not have clear symptoms of PTSD. Yet he reports an ongoing sense of estrangement, irritability, and loneliness in his workplace. He says that he does not know who to trust among his partners, and that he does not fit into the culture, despite his intense wish to succeed at the firm. He describes his firm as a bigger "shark tank" than Afghanistan. He comes in for therapy at his wife's urging. And he agrees with her assessment that though the marriage is strong, his irritability with work is spilling over into their home life. He cannot figure out what the problem is. By all accounts, he says, he "should" be happy. But he is not. He has never experienced a depressive episode or sought psychotherapy in the past, but wonders if he might now be depressed.

In the first sessions of therapy, we determined that John was mildly depressed and prone to angry rumination, hence stoking his increasing irritability. He notes that he never felt this way before. We employed a brief temperament scale, which showed moderately high extraversion, Agreeableness, and Conscientiousness. Despite the current episode of mild depression, his Neuroticism was generally low. His temperament appeared consistent with his high levels of achievement and leadership, whether in the military or in his law firm. He provided evidence of generally being well liked, engaging, and one who others rally around for leadership in challenging circumstances. He nonetheless reports an

DOI: 10.4324/9781003505587-14

increased sensitivity to threat, real and perceived. In tracking this in session, his elevated threat sensitivity is a residue of his combat service, though this, along with other features, do not rise to the level of a diagnosis of PTSD. His wife confirms this clinical picture.

John's thinking was peppered with beliefs that he nonetheless did not fit in, was increasingly distrustful, and left with the sense that "nobody has my back". Though not paranoid, a repeated refrain was his sense that "the firm is a shark tank"; "I don't know who to trust." He reports that he recently was asked to lead a team in a new venture for the firm, and that he sensed each member of the team was in it for him or herself, not the team. His depression and angry rumination had increased since taking over the leadership of this team. He noted that he seemed to alternate between barking out orders to the team, and withdrawing angrily, neither of which was effective in his leadership position. He has been called into the managing partner's office, following recent complaints about John's leadership style, and he felt misunderstood and invalidated by his managing partner.

John's strengths are substantial, and among his values are the importance of family, and of honor and duty. He has many friends outside of work. He and his wife have a strong marriage. His wife works as a speech therapist, and the couple have three children, ranging in age from 5 to 12-years of age. John feels caught between his wish to provide for his family by protecting his high income and net worth, while fantasizing an escape from the law firm in which he feels increasingly alone, misunderstood, and alienated.

John's Vicious Cycle: a detailed functional analysis of the most problematic situation at work, John's team meetings, reveals the following:

We treat the team meetings as the key activating event for a cascade of factors. John notices that he becomes tense, to the point of feeling nauseous. He experiences at times a wish to withdraw, while at other times an urge to behave in a controlling and angry fashion, directing his team members and quashing dissent and discussion. In both cases, the consequences include alienation of team members, and the involvement of the managing partner in response to John's leadership style. His beliefs in these situations include "Nobody is on the same page here"; "It's every man and woman for themselves"; "People are out to undermine me"; "I'm failing". His embodied sense of self is that of what he describes as a "scared, angry little kid". John remains caught in an escalating cycle of cynicism, loneliness, fear, anger, and uncharacteristic ineffectuality. The straw that led to the referral was John's rage following being called on the carpet by the senior partner.

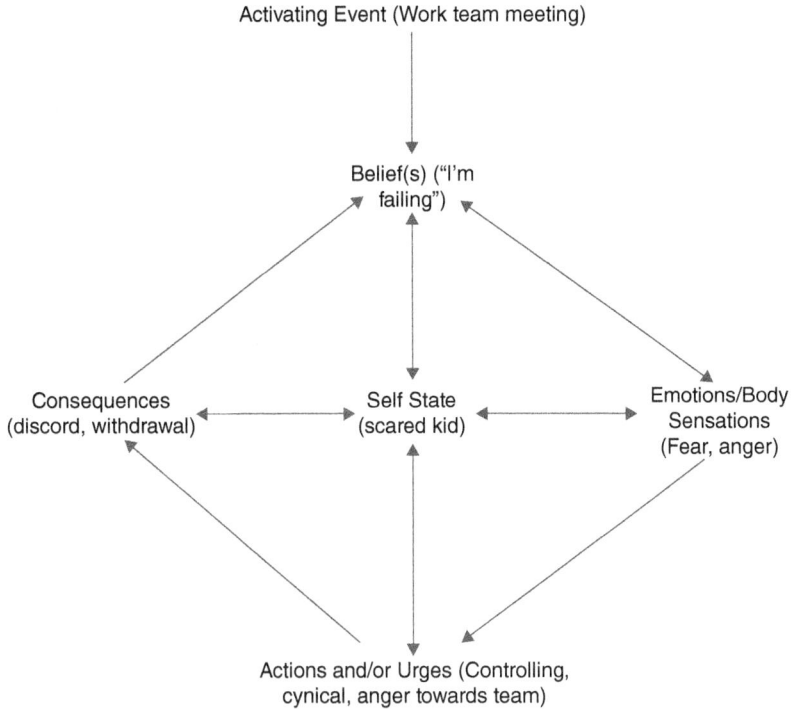

Figure 12.1 John's Vicious Cycle

Adapted from Wills, 2021

Before we move on to consider how to intervene in this vicious cycle, and this rather complex life situation, take a moment to consider how you might normalize John's suffering at this point. Write down ideas about what factors among the Eight Organizing Principles, including possible transdiagnostic factors, might be brought to bear on helping John understand, and in a sense befriend, his predicament:

_____

_____

_____

_____

_____

Our choice is to *normalize* John's pain, in light of one key *transdiagnostic factor*, what we will regard to be an evolutionary mismatch between his war experiences and his experience of his law firm. We will elaborate on this in a moment. We would also tie in John's *strengths*, which include not only those noted above, in terms of strong social ties, but the strengths of his own temperament. It is true that John is displaying numerous cognitive, attentional, and information processing biases. Those are grist for the therapeutic mill. But rather than start by addressing those, we opt to begin with the above focus, to help take the mystery out of his sense of alienation, and to set the stage for a choice about how to proceed in therapy. This strategy can lead to some surprising directions for therapy, closely aligned with the client's values. We posit that his own cognitive and attentional biases, as well as his emotion dysregulation, will make sense to him in light of the factors we choose to address first: helping him make sense of his plight. Please note that the intervention that follows comes after a process of Guided Discovery and Validation, deepening the therapeutic relationship, and setting the stage for a summary. This summary involves not only the material that John provided, but a synthesis that the therapist offers. This synthesis ratifies John's statements, and the vicious cycle in which John is caught. And, it includes an understanding of John's plight that offers a way out. We should also stipulate that part of our inquiry in the early sessions involved an exploration of John's experiences as an Army Ranger. This wasn't idle chit chat, and it wasn't merely to search for indications of potential PTSD, though the latter was of concern to us. What emerged was the realization that John experienced an intense bond with the men and women in the units in which he both served and led in Afghanistan. For a popular volume on the impact of bonding in war, read Sebastian Junger's book *Tribe: On Homecoming and Belonging (2016)*. His work dovetails with emerging findings in evolutionary psychology (Buss, 2024), about the role of the intense and meaningful social bonding that occurred in the environments of our evolutionary history. This type of bonding, for which humans have evolved, is increasingly rare in our modern society, leaving people like John prone to isolation, alienation, and bewilderment. Recognizing that is a first step to finding ways to increase social connectedness.

THERAPIST: So John, first off, let me make sure I have this right. If we look at this little cycle you're feeling caught in (shows John the Vicious Cycle diagram), is this the way it is? Did I miss anything, or fail to record anything accurately?

CLIENT: (John scrutinizes the diagram, and nods). Yep. That's it. That's me. That's the awful team meetings. And that's the outcome: called on the carpet by my boss.

THERAPIST: Okay. Great. I don't mean great that it's happening, but great that you and I are on the same page here. So may I then give a couple of thoughts?

CLIENT: Indeed. That's why I'm here.

THERAPIST: What you experienced in the units you were in was a distilled version of what humans evolved in. I mean to say that science is suggesting that we were meant to live in smaller groups, where we knew each other, and where we knew who had our backs and who did not. When we went into battle, or when we hunted for food, we formed units that either worked, or we died. We either prevailed in our struggles against other tribes, or we starved because we couldn't work together to hunt animals. But we don't live in that world any more. We don't necessarily know who has our backs and who doesn't, because it is so rarely tested. You lived in that reality in Afghanistan, which is why, I suspect, you feel such a deep emotional bond, to this day, with the Rangers in your unit. You had a taste of what I would say is our evolved nature. Deep connection. Deep trust. Shared peril. Honor. Bonding. And you've made it clear, I think, that it isn't war and killing you miss: it's that connection, and that bond of trust. And that connection, if I understand, is what's missing for you at Watson, Anderson, & Meders (law firm).

CLIENT: (Tears up) Yeah. You nailed it. I never quite put that together in the way you just did. I'm so disappointed that the other lawyers in my team are self-serving, disconnected from one another, and so unwilling to work together for the common good, at least as I see it. And I'm the one tasked with herding this group of cats! And I'm failing!

THERAPIST: Well, we can certainly take a look at that thought: "I'm failing." On the other hand, maybe you're just in an environment that became alien to you, especially since you came back from the war experiences you had. A teacher once said [Marsha Linehan, founder of DBT] that if you're a rose in a tulip garden, maybe you need to find a rose garden. Nothing wrong with being a rose. Or a tulip.

CLIENT: (laughs)

THERAPIST: It seems that maybe a choice here is to either find a way to fit in, or find a new garden. What do you think?

Here, the therapist chooses to emphasize the evolutionary mismatch the client is experiencing, rather than immediately tackling the belief "I'm failing". By, in a sense, normalizing the client's distress in the context of this mismatch, the stage is set to help the client experience more compassion for self, and to work with the givens of his life circumstances, either by finding a new job or by finding a new way to deal with the environment he is in. It is important to note that we are not providing the client with an excuse for continued flailing in his environment. We also foster taking responsibility for deciding upon a path, and for acting upon that decision, with the full engagement and support of the therapist, whatever choice the client may make. Let's see how we might do that, by setting a course for the therapy.

CLIENT: What do you think I ought to do? I know you can't tell me that. Here's the bind: to be honest, I make a lot of money. I work my butt off, billing out 40 to 50 hours a week, at over $500 an hour. I've worked hard to become a partner, and I'm proud of the things I can do for my family with that kind of income. Plus, my firm does good work, including pro bono work in the community. I have some sweat equity in the firm, and I just don't feel ready to give it up. Which means, I guess, that I need to figure out how to be that rose in the tulip garden, at least for now.

THERAPIST: (provides a summary and a synthesis of the client's reasoning) So if I understand, it's not just the money, which you say is substantial. This is also about the importance of providing for your family. And about some pride in the firm, which you worked hard to become a partner in, right?

CLIENT: (nods yes)

THERAPIST: So the choice to stay is about some big pluses, not just a knuckling under. Figuring out how to work with the givens of the team you're in, and the firm, serves to protect some values that I sense are vitally important to the husband, the father, the attorney, the citizen you want to be?

CLIENT: Yes. When you put it like that, it's still a tough situation. But I've been in tougher situations in my life. I still have to figure out how to dig my way out of the hole I'm in at the firm right now.

At this point, it's getting clearer how to set up not only a problem list, but how to set a direction for the therapy to take. We can frame the key presenting problem as work-related stress. We can further refine that by helping the client understand that stress, at least in part, as a function of the mismatch between the experiences of bonding, trust, mutual protection, and honor in his combat unit, and the everyone-for-themselves, somewhat cynical environment he experiences in his law firm. We can further posit that John experienced the intense bonding and shared meaning that our evolved natures prepare us for, but in the arena of combat. The absence of that emotional bonding in his current work environment is now felt as particularly acute for him. And as we noted, that creates a choice: to leave or to stay. It isn't the therapist's job to make this decision for the client, since it is the client and not the therapist who bears the consequences of that choice. John chooses to stay, at least for now, for a variety of complex reasons: finances, the wish to protect his family, the wish to preserve his hard-earned status as a partner in a law firm, and perhaps other reasons that may only become evident in a longer therapy. That said, the therapist is in the position of supporting John's choice to stay and to improve his ability to navigate what he calls that "shark tank". Indeed, defining his colleagues as "sharks" is grist for the therapeutic mill. That framing of colleagues immediately places them as sources of danger to him, rather than allowing him to more fully respect the complexity of his fellow attorneys, and to find common ground where that serves his needs and interests. We would seek to build on existing bonds with friends and allies in the firm, and to expand the range of those ties, where both necessary and appropriate. This propensity for overestimation of threat fits with his and his wife's observation that John's combat experiences heightened his sensitivity to threat. This is particularly true in his work environment, rather than at home or in other contexts.

Take a moment to think about how you might proceed in therapy at this point, given John's choice to stay and more effectively deal with his work environment. What among the organizing principles strikes you as a promising avenue for intervention? And what might your interventions include?

_____

_____

_____

_____

_____

The treatment targets now might include the following. The selection of the items would depend upon the scope and duration of the treatment.

1. Practicing acceptance of the givens in his environment, nonjudgmentally
2. Catching himself as he leans towards hostile and defensive interpretations of his co-workers, while also considering other, more benign, and hopefully accurate ways of viewing at least some of those co-workers

3.   Catching himself getting caught in self-blame and self-denigration

4.   Emotion regulation skill building, especially related to anger, both in the workplace and at home

5.   Practicing skills in session, to improve collaboration between himself and his team

6.   Practicing communication skills with his managing partner

7.   Genuinely and wholeheartedly making efforts at building alliances with members of his firm, first with those in whom he has some trust

8.   Framing the therapy as an opportunity to test his and his environment's ability to be a rose in that tulip garden. If the results of the experiment suggest the wisdom of finding a "new garden", that door will open as a new avenue of therapy, and a new life direction. Flexible adaptation, based on client values and life circumstances, is our goal.

9.   Finally, John displays a rich capacity for forming strong emotional bonds with others. His wife and children are a source of solace, pleasure, and affiliation. Therapy might target more systematic ways of enhancing his connections with his wife and children. In addition, we might explore John increasing contact with army "buddies", either through civic projects or informal social contacts. While hopefully improving his sense of place and purpose at work, we might help strengthen his sense of connection in other settings.

To take one item from the above list, let's explore how we might begin to help John not only make sense of his heightened threat sensitivity, but deal with it effectively.

The Sentry on the Castle Wall: This is a psychoeducational exercise described in Temple (2017, p. 137). It involves guided imagery, and can help clients understand and normalize their over-sensitivity to threat. More importantly, it can open the door to other interventions: cognitive, behavioral, mindfulness, and acceptance, which help manage threat sensitivity. Here is an example.

THERAPIST: John, I'd like for us to try a little exercise, one that I think might shed some light and be of help here. Are you willing? It's just a kind of gentle, guided imagery exercise, like we've done before. (Client nods in assent, and settles into chair, closing eyes, hands on lap, receptive.)

THERAPIST: Okay. Let's imagine that we're in a castle, one of those ancient castles one finds throughout Europe. High stone walls with parapets and with runways inside the walls where sentries can observe. There's a moat also protecting the castle. Inside that castle sits the King. And on that castle wall, on the narrow walkway that runs the entire perimeter inside, and at the top of the castle walls, there stands a sentry. The sentry's job is to scan the area outside the castle, for signs of threat. Beyond the moat is a large meadow on all sides, and beyond that, a forest. The trees quiver and shake in the wind. And the sentry? He's a nervous fellow, prone to finding signs of threat. And when he sees a branch shake, he wonders: "Is it our enemies?" And he scans and scans, as his fear is stoked. Finally, he runs down the stone staircase to the King's quarters, knocking furiously. "It's them," he cries. "It's them. Their archers are preparing an assault on us."

The King stops his work and races to the castle parapet, only to discover that the branches in the forest quiver from the wind. There are no archers. No enemies. The King must decide whether to replace his nervous sentry, or provide clearer guidelines for determining when the enemy is present, and when it's just the wind, or an animal. And so some training begins. (End exercise.)

Another, related, metaphor is called *the Radar Screen Metaphor*.

THERAPIST: Imagine that you are in charge of monitoring a radar screen. On the screen you notice movement at times. Some images showing up on the screen are tiny. Some are larger. Sometimes, the screen is quiet. Your job is to tell which images are benign, and which are threats, such as an enemy bomber. If your mind has been trained to be especially vigilant to threat, you might be prone to interpreting all images as bombers. Even if they are a flock of birds. The trick here is to know the difference. We don't want to send our fighter pilots up unless we're dealing with the real thing. What if it's a little like that, John. Your training and your combat experiences have made it a little more likely that you respond to birds as though they are bombers. Perfectly understandable. The key is to read the screen as it is, and respond wisely. If this makes sense, how about we explore how to read that workplace you're in, so you can respond flexibly and in ways that fit the situation a little better?

CLIENT: I'm on board.

This can set the stage for a wide variety of interventions intended to help the client pause, reflect, and decide on a response, rather than impulsively reacting to "birds" on the screen. And this can link with helping John follow his "road map" towards the life he wishes to build. The key is that we aren't trying to remove his threat sensitivity. It is basically an ally. We are trying to temper that threat arousal, in the service of working more effectively with the givens of his daily work situation.

The Roadmap needn't be used with every client. But let's see how it might help us organize our approach to the case of John.

The upper left-hand loop displays a functional analysis of the vicious cycle trapping John. This is the type of analysis commonly used in several types of CBT, particularly DBT. The Vicious Cycle model, while initially developed in the UK, among Beckian CBT therapists is generally consistent with any of the functional analyses used in other CBT models. The winding road on the right displays a set of destinations. For now, as you can see at the bottom, John is committed to staying with his law firm and seeing what he might do to more effectively engage with his current team. The "1 year" sign is useful to indicate that is the time he is giving himself to decide whether to stay or to look for another position. His longer time frame is to live more at peace as an attorney, and to more fully embrace his other important roles in life: husband, father, friend, advocate for veterans, and hobbyist. The "red flags" are there to indicate the moments on his journey in which problematic cognitions, urges, and actions arise, capable of derailing him from moving towards his objectives, and re-ensnaring him in his vicious cycle. We will assume that those "red flag" moments are inevitable. Changing patterns in living requires us to practice new skills and new actions in the very situations that have kept us ensnared. It isn't enough to develop insight into these patterns in the therapy office. Courage, persistence, and practice in "real life" outside the therapy room, are all required.

Last, note that addressing these treatment targets specifically involves *the use of mindfulness, acceptance*, and *change strategies*. It involves *a focus on cognitive and behavioral interventions*. It *builds on client strengths and values*, in fact anchoring the work in those strengths and values. This client has already demonstrated many of the above skills and strategies, though in other contexts. So he and the therapist aren't starting from scratch. Finally, therapy will involve *practicing skills in the contexts* most relevant to the solution of his challenges: work and home. Depending upon how the work of therapy unfolds, the therapist may also consider referring John to an executive coach, as an adjunct, or at some point, perhaps instead of continuing therapy.

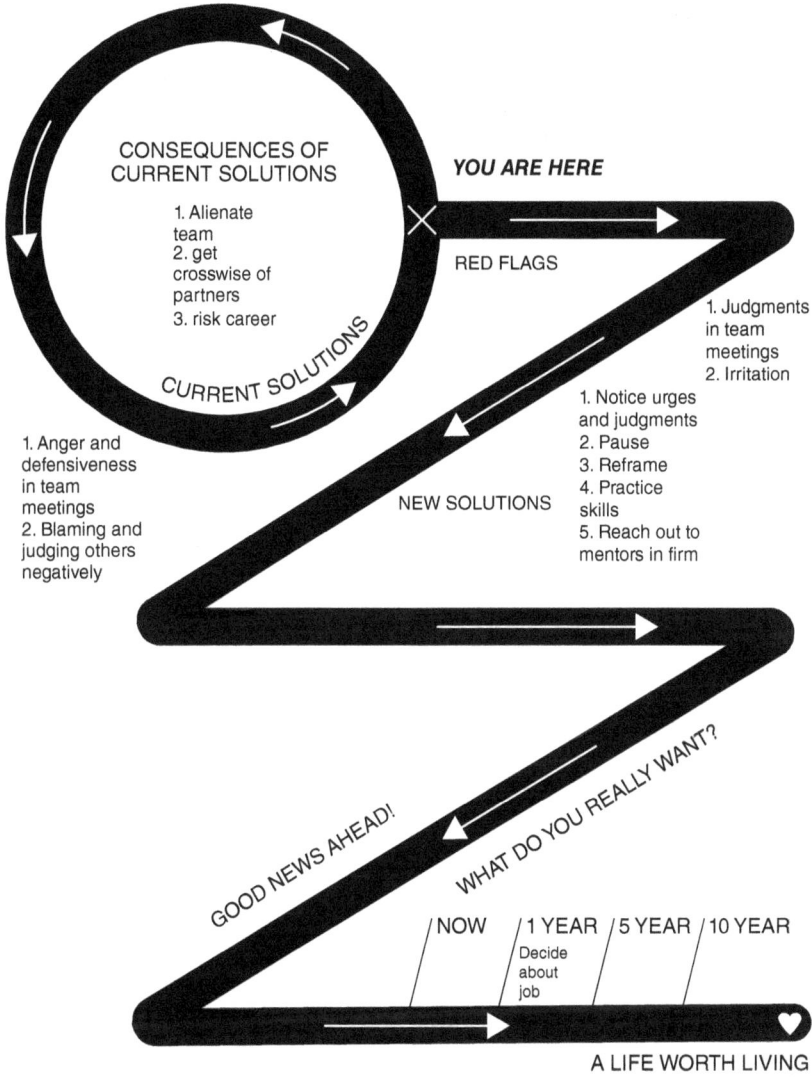

CONSEQUENCES OF
CURRENT SOLUTIONS

1. Alienate team
2. get crosswise of partners
3. risk career

YOU ARE HERE

RED FLAGS

1. Judgments in team meetings
2. Irritation

CURRENT SOLUTIONS

1. Anger and defensiveness in team meetings
2. Blaming and judging others negatively

1. Notice urges and judgments
2. Pause
3. Reframe
4. Practice skills
5. Reach out to mentors in firm

NEW SOLUTIONS

GOOD NEWS AHEAD!

WHAT DO YOU REALLY WANT?

NOW / 1 YEAR / 5 YEAR / 10 YEAR

Decide about job

A LIFE WORTH LIVING

Figure 12.2 John's Roadmap

REFERENCES

Buss, D. (2024) *Evolutionary Psychology: The New Science of the Mind*. New York: Routledge/Taylor Francis.

Junger, S. (2016) *Tribe: On Homecoming and Belonging*. New York: Twelve.

Temple, S. (2017) *Brief Cognitive Behavior Therapy for Cancer Patients: Re-Visioning the CBT Paradigm*. New York: Routledge/Taylor-Francis.

CHAPTER 13

Case #3: A Case of Coke

Kelly has been struggling with cocaine abuse for at least 16 years. She is 34-years old, and reports having made many failed attempts to discontinue cocaine use. She's been to residential treatment twice and had many outpatient therapists over the years. She's also participated in Narcotics Anonymous (NA) on and off. She describes her use as sporadic. That is, she can go many weeks without any use, but then go on a binge which lasts "a week or so". Binges always occur when she spends time with one of her friendship circles, all of whom use drugs in that circle.

Kelly works at a local radio station on the weekends. She says this means she is working when her friends are off and that she is off when her friends are working. This leads her to struggle with loneliness, one of the antecedents to her cocaine use. She socializes with friends who are not working routine day jobs, and who use cocaine. Kelly is angry with herself about her continuing drug use, and says she is "weak". She would like to stop using cocaine, and "have a real life". In exploring the latter with her, that life would consist of completely refraining from cocaine or other substance use, a stable relationship with a man, and a job that puts her in synch with a more "normal" daily and weekly routine. She loves music, and fell into a DJ's position with a local FM radio station. But the work is limited to a weekend show at this point, and provides just enough income to live on. She senses that she is nonetheless working well below her potential, both in terms of career satisfaction and earnings potential. She wants to make a career change.

Kelly was married at age 22, just after finishing college with a degree in business. The marriage lasted two years, and ended, ironically, because of her concerns about her husband's drug and alcohol abuse. She has had

DOI: 10.4324/9781003505587-15

several relationships since then, and has vacillated between men who use drugs and those who do not. At this point, she fears that "any man who I'd want, wouldn't want me". She points to her drug use, and her unconventional work history as reasons for her belief that a "good man" would not want her in his life.

She notes that she has two circles of friends, one of which uses drugs, the other which does not. She is close to one or two drug-using friends, and is reluctant to let go of those ties, not just because of drug access, but because she genuinely values their friendship. The other group of friends are primarily married, work what she calls "normal" jobs, have children, and as, she notes, are "moving on with their lives as grown ups". One of her friends from the latter group has a man she'd like to introduce to Kelly. It turns out her fear and her excitement at this prospect was a key reason for why she seeks another episode of therapy now, with a new therapist.

Kelly's temperamental traits suggest moderately high Neuroticism, particularly emotional volatility. In line with her Neuroticism, cocaine appears to serve two functions for her. One is an appetitive function, in the sense that it brings pleasure. This aligns with her moderately high scores on both Extraversion and Openness to Experience. The other function, however, is an avoidant one, in the sense that Kelly temporarily dampens her emotional pain in the euphoria of cocaine. Depression and anxiety are in the "moderate" range, with no suicidal ideation present. Fortunately, Kelly does not have a history of either suicide attempts or self-injury.

Kelly displays a number of strengths, which can hopefully be brought to bear on the problems she faces: she is gregarious and has a wide range of social contacts and social networks; she is educated and ambitious; she has a strong appetite for life and for new experiences, and by history is capable of the Conscientiousness that shows up on her temperamental traits. Her radio program has a decent-sized audience, and is growing. Listener comments on the radio station web site show enthusiasm for the wide range of new music she brings to the listeners' awareness, for example.

Kelly emphatically stated that she is not interested in trying another drug treatment program. She is open to attending NA, but says it wasn't all that helpful, especially since her sponsor moved to another city. Kelly wants to give another outpatient psychotherapy program a chance, and she heard that the therapist is a first-rate CBT therapist.

In exploring the chain analysis of events that culminate in cocaine use, we see a pattern that occurs across multiple situations. This is displayed in the "vicious cycle", below. Note that the activating events for cocaine abuse can be both internal and external. Internal events include images and memories of prior use, experienced as pleasurable, as well as emotional distress, including boredom, which she can quickly rid herself of by using cocaine. Emotional distress can be linked to external activating events, such as interpersonal disappointments, receiving a large bill in the mail, a negative review of her radio program from an irate listener. Her emotional response includes body sensations of tightening in the chest, accelerated heart rate, queasiness in the stomach, all of which she labels as "fear", and is sufficiently uncomfortable to her that she quickly seeks cocaine to quell the distress. If she doesn't have immediate access to cocaine in her apartment, she contacts her drug-using friends and spends the day or evening with them, having fun and snorting coke. This provides social reinforcement and momentary "relief", then shame and self-disgust at her sense of being "weak". And this, in turn, only stokes her self reproach and depression, and her sense of self as "defective" and "weak". By the time she leaves her friends and returns home, she is bathing in self reproach and shame. And around and around she goes.

In looking at the "roadmap" for Kelly, several things emerged. First off, she stated a wish to exit the vicious cycle she is in: with regard to cocaine use, her job limitations, and her reliance on a social network that supports cocaine abuse. The therapist did a "cost benefit analysis" and employed a commitment technique from Dialectical Behavior Therapy (DBT), involving asking Kelly to make a case for continuing to use drugs, as well as a case for stopping drug use. The DBT commitment strategy of "Devil's Advocate" involved the therapist making an even stronger case for Kelly's drug use, emphasizing the momentary pleasure of a high, and the social connection and fun she experienced with her drug-using, footloose and fancy free friends. Kelly responded with humor and forcefulness, indicating a willingness to commit to a plan that included refraining from cocaine use, while acknowledging that this involves a process, one that includes building new patterns of functioning which are capable of competing with and superseding older patterns that are entailed with drug abuse. She appeared to recognize that if she remains caught in the vicious cycle at the upper left of the roadmap, she will not get where she actually wants to go in life: full time employment in the field she trained in; marketing and public relations; stable intimate relations; a sense of self that is lighthearted, and reflects the joy of embracing life's bounties…unencumbered by ongoing shame, self reproach, and self disgust.

Activating Event (boredom)

Belief(s) ("I need just
one line of coke.
Just this one last time.")

Consequences
(relief, then
shame)

Self State
(rage, weak)

Emotions/Body
Sensations
(churning, queasy)

Actions and/or Urges
(seek drug friends, snort coke)

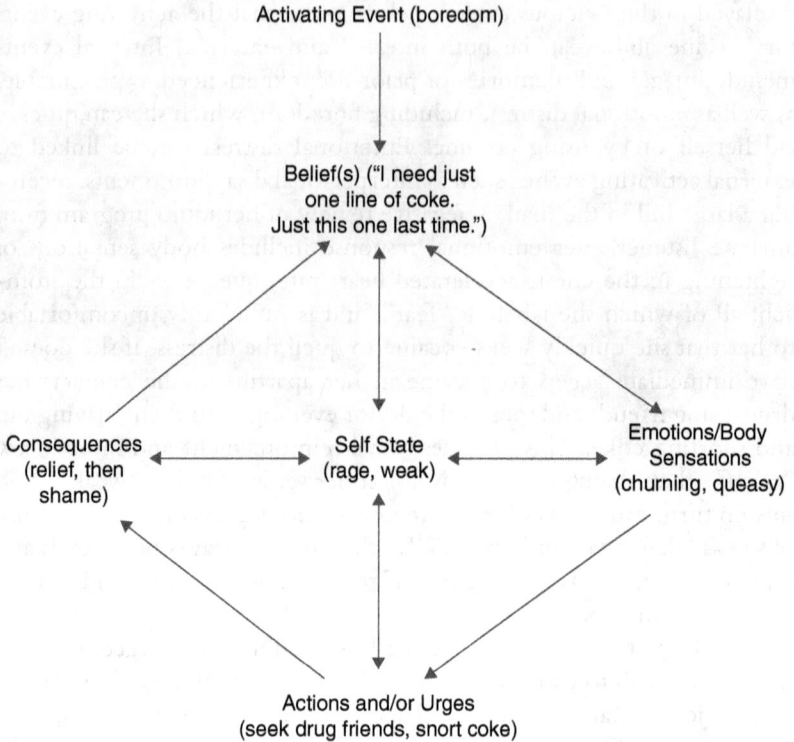

Figure 13.1 Kelly's Vicious Cycle

Adapted from Wills, 2021

We could choose to focus on any and all of the Eight Organizing Principles. Each one can be brought to bear on understanding and intervening in the case of Kelly. However, for purposes of clarity and simplicity, we'll focus on two principles: *building on Kelly's strengths and values*; and intervention strategies that *balance acceptance, mindfulness, and change processes*.

Before focusing on intervention strategies, however, take a moment to consider how you would write up a problem list for Kelly's therapy. And think about how you might collaboratively establish this problem list as a guide for helping Kelly move from the stuckness of her current predicament, toward the roadmap that leads to her desired way of living. In writing problems for the list, think about how to make them concrete, and behaviorally specific, ie capable of being described with clarity and achievability.

PROBLEM LIST

_____

_____

_____

_____

_____

Here's our best effort at creating a shared list of problems to use as a focus for therapy. It includes a focus on not only problems, but potential treatment-interfering behaviors and cognitions that may intrude.

1. Refraining from cocaine use. But while it's tempting to make this an "all or none" choice, we'll be careful to provide detailed, step-by-step processes that will teach skills that support solving this problem.
2. Focus on vulnerabilities that may precede urges, including internal and external cues for drug use.
3. Noticing cognitions that may provide permission to use: "Just this once." "I'll start next week." "I'll hang with my drug using friends without using, myself." "F— it; I just want to feel better, just for tonight."
4. Work and career problems.
5. Inconsistent social contacts that support making changes.
6. Loneliness and a wish for an intimate relationship that works.

We now invite the reader to take a few minutes to write, below, the strengths and values that you think Kelly might bring to bear on solving the problems for which she seeks therapy. Think also about how you might help Kelly become more aware of these strengths and values as she embarks on her therapy journey with you. Think of these as allies that are already in her coping repertoire, and that can compete, if you will, with that sense of self as defective, shameful, and weak. We have provided some ideas in the case description. But let yourself imagine Kelly, as though she were in front of you in the consultation room. Knowing only what you have been told about her in the case description, let yourself imagine any other strengths and values that seem plausible to you and that can help serve as guides, or anchors, for therapy. And take a few moments to imagine how you would find out about her strengths and values, and help her become more aware of how those can be allies in the therapy, and in life.

Here's an example of a therapy vignette, in which the therapist explores Kelly's strengths and values, as well as validates those strengths and values.

THERAPIST: So Kelly, you were telling me about how you select playlists for your radio show. You seem to have a huge breadth of knowledge about music. And an intense curiosity about the arts, and, it seems, about life. You embrace a big life, it seems.

KELLY: (silent for a moment, thinking) Yeah, I'm like that about lots of things. I have lots of interests. And I pursue them with quite a bit of passion. Sometimes too much. I can get scattered. When I explore those interests, it includes reaching out to people who can teach me what I want to know. I've always been that way. I have always had different groups of friends at the same time.

THERAPIST: So that tendency to have more than one group of friends isn't new? And it isn't just showing up with the drug issue?

KELLY: Oh no. It's me.

THERAPIST: So it's sounding as though you have always had a really strong sense of curiosity about life, diligence about learning, and the ability to form social contacts that support that learning.

KELLY: I think so. Yes.

THERAPIST: At the same time, you've said that you want to move on to a new venture.

KELLY: Yes. I've learned so much, and had so much fun learning from some of the other DJs, especially the ones who know a lot about older soul and R&B artists! But I need a more routine day job, one that lets me have a more normal life, to be in a daily routine that coincides with other people, and doesn't leave me so isolated.

THERAPIST: You know, I think that curiosity of yours, that tendency to work really hard and be focused, and your love of people will be allies in helping you get where you want to go. And I'll help every step of the way. A question, if I might: What do you think might be some things that could get in the way here?

Note that here the therapist begins an exploration of potential treatment-interfering cognitions and behaviors, to set the stage for both anticipating and managing those therapy derailing processes. Strengths and values help with the challenges that keep people stuck in vicious cycles. Freeing people from vicious cycles involves helping them keep a focus on the "prize" they seek, while managing all the factors that pull people back into vicious cycles. As therapy unfolds, we focus on building new, more functional repertoires of behavior, ones that help the client get closer to their chosen objectives. In Kelly's case, we can't guarantee that she'll find the partner she ideally wishes for. We can, though, help her behave in ways that shift the odds in that direction. At the same time, the therapist can work with her to pay careful attention to those moments when she is pulled back into the most damaging behavior on her problem list: cocaine abuse, and to have the skills and the determination in those moments to go in another direction.

Let's turn to the second organizing principle we want to highlight in this case: *balancing acceptance, mindfulness, and change strategies.* To do that, let's start by outlining the treatment targets that we might agree to with Kelly. Take a moment to write down what *you* would include among those treatment targets, or treatment goals.

_____

_____

_____

_____

_____

Here's what we might include:

1. Discontinuing all cocaine use, as quickly as possible
2. Reducing or, ideally, stopping contact with friends who use cocaine, while simultaneously increasing contact with people who support a healthier way of living
3. Finding a new job, one that encourages a more "normal" schedule
4. Managing her propensity for negative affect, including volatility, which contributes to a retreat into cocaine
5. Last, after we have addressed #1 on the problem list, help improve skills and ability for an intimate relationship with a partner

Treatment strategies follow from the above. Take a few minutes to think through what techniques you might use, and how you would do so. We're focusing here on the organizing principle of balancing acceptance, mindfulness, and change processes. How might acceptance be a focus of treatment here?

_____

_____

_____

_____

How and why might we employ mindfulness techniques with Kelley?

_____

_____

_____

_____

What change strategies might you advocate? What cognitive techniques, and for what? What behavioral techniques, including social problem-solving techniques?

_____

_____

_____

_____

We'd offer the following ideas about how to balance acceptance, mindfulness, and change strategies in Kelly's treatment.

Acceptance: We would want to help Kelly compassionately accept herself, including her cocaine abuse. In light of her relatively high Neuroticism, which translates into a propensity for the triggering of intense negative affect in the face of life stressors, we would encourage her to consider that there is no moral blame on her. We don't choose our temperaments, including how we emotionally respond to the stimuli that life throws our way. In that light, it is logical that she would seek to quell emotional pain by using a substance that produces momentary euphoria. In addition, her openness to experience suggests that she is a candidate for exploration of altered states of consciousness, among many other things. That, too, is not blameworthy. At the same time, if we were to conduct a cost–benefit analysis, we might guide her to consider that the long-term consequences of cocaine abuse are quite negative, as she already likely understands. The problem is likely that in the heat of the moment, she leans into the short-term consequences, including emotional pain relief and pure euphoria.

Related to the above, we would also work to foster acceptance of her urges, but without necessarily acting on those urges. Urges to use, given the duration of her drug use, will persist. No intervention, and no act of will on her part would erase the urges to use. They will be a part of her emotional landscape for the indefinite future. But in time, and with practice, not only drug use, but the urge to use drugs, diminish. We would encourage her to keep the faith, and we as therapists will keep that faith for her while she is learning.

Here's a sample transcript of how we might foster an accepting posture towards her own urges. Note that this involves a kind of exposure work, involving exposure to the negative emotions that are entailed with her drug abuse.

THERAPIST: Would you be willing to do a little exercise with me? It'd involve imagining and perhaps feeling some of the urges to use. I'd guide you through it, and you can tap out any time, if you feel it's too intense. My bet is that it probably won't be. But it'll be your call. Deal?

KELLY: Sure. I'm game.

THERAPIST: Okay. Let's start with a scenario that's kind of fun, maybe even a little silly. Let's settle into our chairs, back straight against the chair, feet on the floor, hands in lap, eyes open or closed as you choose. (This, you will note, is also incorporating mindful awareness into the exercise; noticing without reacting.) Let me ask you to imagine your favorite dessert of all time, the one that you can't resist whenever it shows up.

KELLY: (smiles, eyes closed). The chocolate eclairs at the French bakery I go to. Divine! My mouth is already watering.

THERAPIST: Yep. Now that you mention it, mine, too. Let yourself imagine that eclair, visualize it, smell it, in all it's French glory. How intense is that urge to take a bite? Scale of 1 to 10, with 10 as irresistible.

KELLY: (laughs) 8.

THERAPIST: Great! Hold that image.

KELLY: My mouth is watering.

THERAPIST: Hold that image, and see what happens.
    (Thirty seconds pass in silence)

KELLY: The urge is dropping. Maybe a 4 now. I'm getting bored.

THERAPIST: Excellent. Very interesting. Let's come back to the room together and talk. Notice that the urge shifts, right? If you hold it, watch it, notice it, then after a while, it drops of its own accord, right?

KELLY: Yeah. Are you suggesting that's what would happen with my urge for coke?

At this point, the therapist could do an imaginal exposure to cue up urges for cocaine, and encourage a mindful, watchful, accepting stance of the urge, while refraining from acting on the urge. This fosters "the muscle of awareness and acceptance", helping to build the capacity to tolerate urges without acting on them. In turn, this can be practiced in vivo, in some of the situations of daily life that may tripwire strong urges to use.

Behavioral Interventions: One behavioral strategy that can figure prominently in this endeavor is *cue removal*. When we learn, through our process of Guided Discovery, all of the key elements in a vicious cycle, we face a choice about how to help people deal with a prompting, or activating, event. One way is to remove it from access, thus denying it the ability to quickly cue or trigger the response. Some cues are either unavoidable, or represent necessary situations for our engagement. For example, if you have a dental phobia, cue removal means never going to the dentist. That strategy works fine until the inevitable happens: a cracked or broken tooth, decay, injury. Better to find ways to put oneself into, in this case, fear evoking situations, because it is wise or necessary or beneficial to do so. However, in some situations, removal of the activating event (or person) is best.

But it isn't sufficient, as a general principle, to create treatment targets based solely on removal of a problem. A prominent behavior analyst from The University of Kansas, the late Ogden Lindsley, described what he called "The Dead Man Test" (Lindsley, 1991), which posits that the therapist ought not ask the client to do something that can better be accomplished by a dead person. "Stop spending time with drug-using friends" can be perfectly accomplished by a dead person. But for Kelly, it's not enough to stop those connections. Her need for social connection, validation, caring, excitement, and support must be honored by accessing or building new connections. This also dovetails with a guiding principle we wrote about in Part 1 of this book, from the work of Israel Goldiamond. We don't focus on removing problems; we focus on building new patterns of living, ones that comport with the client's desired life direction. Our aim isn't to stop drug use; it's to help the Kellys we treat live the lives that matter to them, as fully as possible.

In this situation, with Kelly, we need to work with her to determine the wisdom of removing the cue of her glittery parties and social ties, as a way of ensuring that cocaine use is not cued up. We wouldn't likely encourage Kelly to practice mindfully noticing and accepting her urges while at a party with her drug-using friends. Instead, we want to encourage her, for now, to refrain from putting herself in situations where the cues for drug use are overpowering. And that requires her to use an array of skills, including distress tolerance, emotion regulation skills, mindfulness and acceptance skills, and interpersonal problem-solving skills.

For example, let's say that she truly likes at least some of the people in the social group with whom she uses drugs. We might brainstorm with her ideas about how to not only break away from them, but to find a way to do so that preserves at least the option of remaining friends. Remember, we would only do this if in fact there are people in that social circle she genuinely wants to preserve a relationship with. She might consider talking with some of them directly, informing them of her decision to stop using cocaine, and even enlist their support. That support might involve their expressed understanding of her need to "disappear", and their blessing. If in fact the sole connection to this group is drugs, there would be no need to be socially delicate with them. Simple cue removal, without explanation or a need for validation would suffice. Nobody said this step is easy. When urges are raging, the wish to reconnect will also reassert itself. This makes it especially important to cultivate clear behavioral and interpersonal practices that support remaining drug free. That could include resuming NA attendance, or cultivating a new sponsor, if this seems appropriate and acceptable to Kelly. It could also involve building on existing, though perhaps atrophied social connections, including friendships, mentors, spiritual teachers, or others. It's not enough to stop contact with drug-using associates. Kelly's need for social connection is strong, and building or utilizing others for connection is vital.

Cognitive Interventions: We have already noted that Kelly at times experiences permission-giving thoughts that ease her path into drug use: "Just this one last time", "I'll start in earnest next week" are examples of such thoughts. So too, emotions of shame, anxiety, anger, sadness can prompt urges, and such thoughts as "I just want the pain to stop". Surrendering to such urges becomes easy and well-practiced. Our cognitive interventions might help Kelly understand the functions served by these beliefs, and to learn strategies that support her stated intention of "starting now". Those could involve cognitively reframing, such as reminding herself of what's at stake. It could involve using such moments to reach out for social support, or to employ some DBT Distress Tolerance skills to make it through a tough moment without acting on a self-sabotaging impulse.

There may also be some obvious or slightly hidden cognitions that impede acceptance. For example, we might discover that Kelly believes "I shouldn't have to deal with this." "This should be easier". "This isn't fair that life gave me this burden." "I can't handle this." "This is too overpowering." When we discover that a client is struggling to accept circumstances they find themselves in, it is worth exploring, again via Guided Discovery and Validation, what beliefs, even some hidden from clear view, may be lurking in the background.

Finally, self punishing ideation, such as "I don't deserve a good life" may show up and must be addressed in therapy. A host of potential interventions, experiential and more frankly cognitive, can be employed here. Just as we work with Kelly to notice urges, without reacting, we can employ cognitive and experiential interventions to soften the impact of such beliefs, and in turn, help her "watch" such thoughts and emotions without acting on them. And in turn, we can help Kelly keep her eye on the longer-term consequences she seeks: a life not only free of crippling drug abuse, but filled with the bounties she seeks in its place. And the cognitive and behavioral interventions help bring those bounties into her life now, not just the distant future.

Therapy sessions would include a routine structure involving checking in on weekly progress towards treatment objectives. In turn, the focus would be on steps taken towards the life direction she prefers, while also focusing on the inevitable stumbles back into the vicious cycle. We would use the therapy sessions as opportunities to study what sequence of activating events, emotions, urges, cognition, behaviors, and consequences drew Kelly back into the vicious cycle, and which lead to the road to freedom.

For Kelly, this is a big, multifaceted project, including not just management of urges to use drugs, but career steps, peer group engagement (and disengagement), and creation of validating, intimate relationships. It is important to help Kelly experience that a single step in the direction she wishes to go is already putting her on the path towards her destination. We never fully arrive. We are always traveling towards that life that matters. If there are setbacks, learn from them. Then take that next step back on the path, a little wiser, a little more self-compassionate, and a little more resolute.

THERAPIST: Here's a little story for you, Kelly. Once upon a time, a wise therapist I knew had a drug problem himself. That was before he became a psychologist. When he stopped using, as a young man, for reasons that are not especially relevant here, he needed a job. So he took a job at a fried chicken restaurant. The manager told him he could only pay a few dollars an hour. The young man took the job, and worked 50 hours a week, to make what he needed to make a go of it. Years later, that young man was grown and was working as a psychologist. That job in the fried chicken restaurant was like stepping on an escalator. It was a single step. And it led to all the further growth in his life. One step after another. None with more dignity or worth than the other steps. One day the step was frying chicken. The next it was grad school. The next was a career as a professional. No step was more important than any other. It's the single step that counts. What step will you take? How about today?

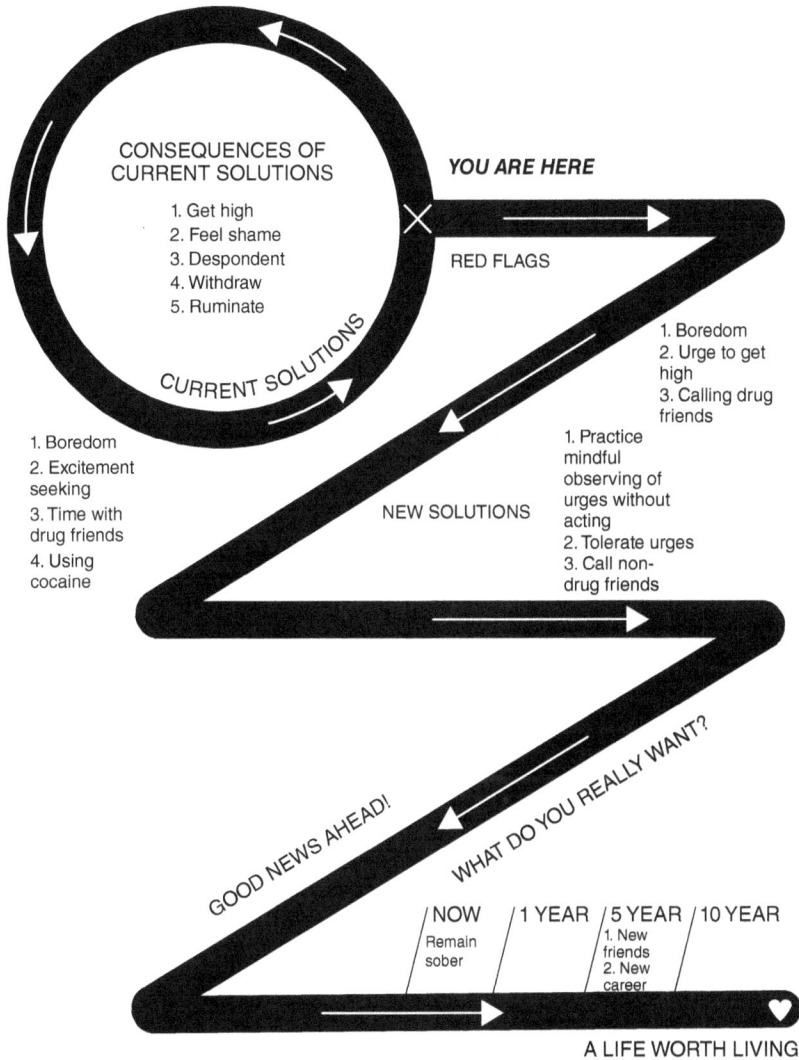

CONSEQUENCES OF CURRENT SOLUTIONS
1. Get high
2. Feel shame
3. Despondent
4. Withdraw
5. Ruminate

YOU ARE HERE

RED FLAGS

CURRENT SOLUTIONS

1. Boredom
2. Excitement seeking
3. Time with drug friends
4. Using cocaine

1. Boredom
2. Urge to get high
3. Calling drug friends

NEW SOLUTIONS

1. Practice mindful observing of urges without acting
2. Tolerate urges
3. Call non-drug friends

GOOD NEWS AHEAD!

WHAT DO YOU REALLY WANT?

NOW	1 YEAR	5 YEAR	10 YEAR
Remain sober		1. New friends 2. New career	

A LIFE WORTH LIVING

Figure 13.2 Kelly's Roadmap

We can't predict what the outcome of the therapy will be with Kelly. We don't want to pretend that all our cases end in success. But these ideas at least point in a direction that we hope offers promise to the Kellys we work with, and the therapists who work with them.

REFERENCE

Lindsley, O. (1991) From Technical Jargon to Plain English for Application. *Journal of Applied Behavior Analysis*, 24, 449–458.

CHAPTER 14

Case #4: Parents of a Self-Injuring Teen

Barbara and Tom's 16-year old daughter, Jessica, has been struggling to adjust to the rigors of mid-adolescence. Her struggles are exemplified by difficulties managing her mood, substantial decline in academic performance, and frequent peer conflict. She has also started vaping and smoking cannabis. Perhaps most troubling to Barbara and Tom, she has been cutting herself when she becomes acutely distressed. Because Jessica is either withdrawn or when semi-engaged, arguing with her parents, they feel incredibly anxious because they believe they've lost parental influence with her and because this leaves them wondering what information about her struggles they do not know. It is this distress alongside their feelings of powerlessness regarding their parenting that led them to seek psychological consultation.

Adding to their distress is that Tom and Barbara are frequently in conflict with one another, often because of disagreements over how to address Jessica's behavior, though not exclusively for this reason. These conflictual interactions become heated quite quickly and frequently involve yelling and cursing, though without physical aggression. After a fight they might not speak to one another for days. They both feel resentful about what they perceive as the silent treatment from the other person during these post-fight periods. In addition, they both complained that they feel lonely and unsupported during these periods of silence, and both say they spend this time ruminating over the contents of the most recent fight. Furthermore, they indicate that Jessica has repeatedly complained that their fights are a significant reason she becomes sad and injures herself. In sum, Barbara and Tom feel a range of upsetting emotions as a direct consequence of their fighting with one another, but also because of the events that occur

DOI: 10.4324/9781003505587-16

because of their conflict. They were, however, unified in saying "we don't know how to stop this", because this is a long-standing pattern and they have been in couples counseling several times before without success. Notably, they denied conflict of any significance prior to the onset of Jessica's problems. This is likely a positive prognostic factor because it suggests healthy couple interaction patterns are available in their repertoire.

Frequently, when Tom and/or Barbara address Jessica's problem behavior, emotions run high, and Jessica's behavior escalates rapidly. There have been three instances in which she escalated to the point of running away from home, which she accomplished by either requesting that a friend or their parent pick her up or by walking to one of their houses even when they were many miles away. On these occasions she'd remain out of the home and out of communication for two to three days. For Barbara, this led to intense worry and sadness. For Tom, the result was anger, though he also admitted to accompanying sadness and worry. Both complained that they "didn't know what to do" because Jessica would always escalate "one step up" and they couldn't think of a reasonable next step. For example, Tom would say, "we could kick her out of the house but then she'd just live with people who will be bad influences for her and her overall situation will get worse. But we can't just let her do whatever she wants while living in our home. I just don't see what options we have."

Complicating matters is Jessica's extensive use of social media. In addition to the sheer number of hours she spends on these platforms to the exclusion of other activities, her emotional problems are exacerbated by social media influences. For example, her posts about her self-injurious thoughts and behavior have recruited positive attention, likely functioning as reinforcement for these difficulties. As another example, she learned novel ways of engaging in self-injury when others shared their methods.

She is tethered to her cell phone, her gateway to social media. An illustrative example involves an occasion in which she was being dropped off at school and realized she had forgotten her cell phone at home. Even though she was planning to be present at school that day up to the point at which she had arrived and was just about to exit the car, immediately upon learning her hand-held device was not present her willingness to attend school ended. She asserted "I can't make it through the day without my phone" and could not be persuaded differently.

We now have enough information to specify an initial list of problems and treatment targets. Before we share our list, take a moment to list below the clinical targets you see.

_____

_____

_____

_____

_____

Our initial list of treatment targets would include the following.

1. Parental emotion regulation skills – It seems parental emotion dys-
    regulation is a problem in its own right, but it also seems that it is an
    antecedent to other problems, though a functional assessment will be
    needed to confirm this hypothesis. For example, by report, their
    addressing Jesscia's problem behavior is largely characterized by
    intense emotion that is occasioning self-injury and other problematic
    behavior, and it is interfering with their ability to be effective as par-
    ents and spouses.
2. Parental cognitions about themselves and their spouse – At least two
    beliefs of importance are known at the present time, though further
    assessment may reveal additional meaningful cognitive targets. Barbara
    and Tom have both endorsed the belief "I'm a failure as a parent".
    This belief is activated when Jessica displays any behavior of concern
    and interferes with their ability to be compassionate toward them-
    selves. In addition, they both have ideas that result in their blaming
    the other for the bulk of Jessica's issues. In Tom's case, he believes that
    Barbara "is too lenient", whereas Barbara believes "he is too heavy
    handed with Jessica". Successfully intervening on these notions
    should increase their compassion for themselves and for one another.
    This in turn should reduce instances of conflict between them and
    should increase their alignment, resulting in a unified front when
    addressing Jessica's behavior.
3. Behavior management skills training – Because they've been ineffec-
    tive in managing Jessica's behavior these skills will help them accom-
    plish at least three things: a) approach Jessica's behavior in a unified
    way, b) discontinue the use of behavior management strategies that
    likely exacerbate the problem behavior they describe, and c) use par-
    enting strategies research has shown to be helpful with these con-
    cerns. In general, this approach entails their learning to shift focus
    from decreasing Jessica's undesirable behaviors to directing their
    attention to the behaviors they want to see happen more often. This
    necessitates their first coming to agreement on what is behaviorally
    important and because the focus is on increasing the frequency of

behavior, they must both make greater use of reinforcement. One reason reinforcement is to be preferred is that it does not come with the "side effects" that come with the use of punishment, such as eliciting unhelpful emotion in the recipient and increasing their tendency to escape or avoid them.

4. Acceptance skills – Though they can learn to be more effective parents there are limits to their influence as research shows peer groups can have greater influence on teens than their parents (Haidt, 2024; Harris, 2011).

5. Environment modification – Because environments powerfully influence behavior, it will likely be helpful to assist Barbara and Tom with guidance on how to rearrange Jessica's environment. Examples of environmental modifications include altering the presence of emotion dysregulation (e.g., by strengthening Barbara and Tom's emotion regulation repertoire); changing the school environment (e.g., changing schools to change the peers she's exposed to); influencing the peer group (e.g., increase communication with other parents and problem-solving these issues with them); disrupting the influence of social media (e.g., placing monitoring software on their phones). We will discuss how this might be accomplished when we discuss the application of the core principles (see below).

We believe it is important to invite Jessica into this conversation because she is more likely to participate in this process if we involve her. Because engaging her may be difficult we will teach the parents engagement strategies. Among the strategies is a discussion of the importance of timing the conversation well because Jessica's openness to participating will likely vary. We will work with Barbara and Tom to identify times this conversation is likely to be successful as well as times such a conversation is best avoided. In addition, and of substantial importance, is teaching Barbara and Tom validation skills, using the same DBT validation skills with each other and Jessica that we employ to strengthen the therapy relationship. The skills translate from the treatment relationship to the clients' daily lives. Next, strategies for inviting her participation will be discussed, including the importance of staying focused on the ask while avoiding bringing up topic areas that will steer the conversation into conflictual waters. It can be helpful to keep the ask small, building on the commitment later. For example, instead of asking her to participate in an entire course of family therapy, they might ask her to merely "treatment sample". This might take the form of "why don't you try meeting with him for 15 minutes or so just to see whether you like him?" This is more likely to produce an agreement to attend a treatment visit at which a skillful therapist can build a rapport and make use of the Guided Discovery and Validation strategies we have used elsewhere in the book. Finally, and crucially, the conversation should be practiced several times via a role-play, titrating the difficulty (e.g., one iteration in which Jessica says yes, one in which she is ambivalent, one in which she refuses), and providing them with immediate feedback.

6. Planful problem-solving skills – These skills are broadly applicable to the range of difficulties they confront. This will also help them work with their emotions more effectively during their problem-solving efforts and improve their sense of hopelessness regarding these difficulties. Training sequence is important, however. Problem-solving skills are likely to be more successfully trained once validation and distress tolerance skills and emotional regulation is improved.

Barbara and Tom's Vicious Cycle: a functional assessment of a severe and representative interaction between Barbara and Tom, and Jessica revealed how they were caught in a vicious cycle with their daughter, and with one another.

Jessica's school refusal was identified as a prototypical activating event. School/work week mornings are typically "frantic" for Barbara and Tom as they try to balance getting themselves ready for their day and ensuring the kids (Jessica has a sibling) get ready for school in time so that Barbara can take them to school on their way to work. Both report feeling tired and agitated during the morning "getting ready" period, which they dread. When they notice Jessica hasn't come to the kitchen to eat breakfast, they worry she has not yet gotten out of bed. Barbara or Tom will then try to call or text her to ensure she is awake. Frequently, there is no response. When they are unable to reach her this way one of them will go to her room and discover she is still sleeping. When they attempt to wake her, Jessica will provide a reason she cannot attend school that day. Typical reasons are "I need a mental health day" and "I'm dealing with a lot right now". Hearing these excuses, Tom will often think "she needs to toughen up. It's something every day". Most often he will feel frustrated and angry, but will also feel sad at times because he thinks the situation is "hopeless". In response he commonly says "you have to learn to do things even when you don't feel like it" and "don't come crying to me when you have to repeat the school year". Jessica responds to these comments with anger accompanied by crying, with the interaction between the two of them escalating in unhelpful ways from there. Ultimately, Tom abandons his

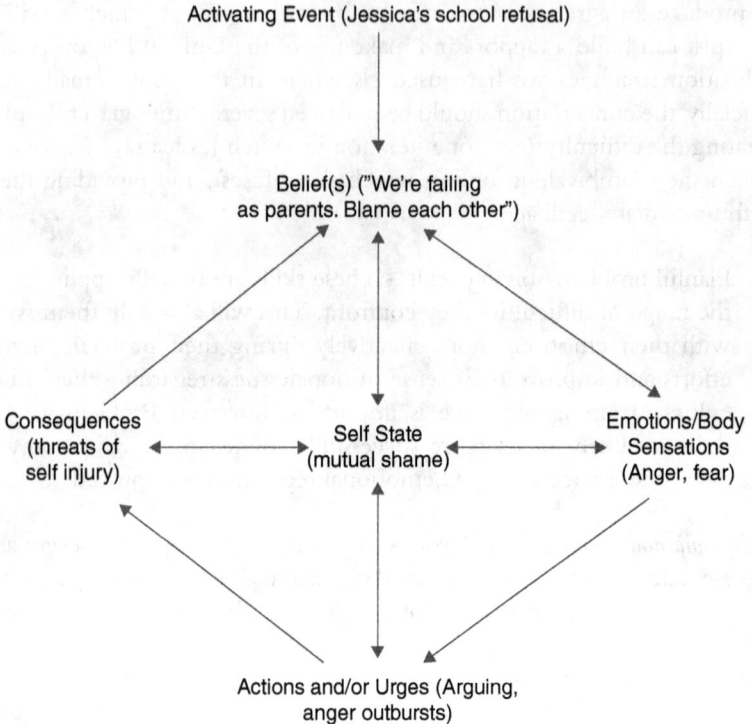

Figure 14.1 Barbara and Tom's Vicious Cycle

Adapted from Wills, 2021

attempt to coax her to go to school after which Barbara expresses anger towards Tom because she believes he came on too strong with Jessica and shut her down. A fight between the two of them ensues.

The situation worsens because Jessica, overhearing their fight, becomes more distressed and yells "can't you two ever stop fighting!" They both report urges to continue trying to get their points across, eventually withdrawing from one another. It is during these periods that Jessica frequently self-injures. Consequently, in addition to ruminating about their anger with one another, Barbara and Tom feel anxious and worried that Jessica will hurt herself.

There may be "residual" fighting in the immediate aftermath during which Barabara tells Tom "Jessica is just immature. You need to loosen up and be less critical." Tom then thinks "Barbara doesn't understand how serious this is. It's more than immaturity" and "she can't even align with me in parenting our daughter." Consequently, he blames much of this on

Barbara. Barbara similarly experiences distressing cognition. She thinks "he just expects too much from her" and "he comes at her much too strongly", leading her to blame Tom for much of Jessica's predicament. Ultimately, they fully withdraw and don't talk for several days and sometimes longer.

Often, a wise treatment strategy involves arranging treatment targets in a hierarchy. Sometimes this leads to an economy of treatment whereas at other times resolving some targets is a prerequisite to successfully addressing other targets. This is not to imply that in such cases treatment can always proceed linearly. Indeed, the reality of treatment is that it is often necessary to cycle through a hierarchy of treatment priorities multiple times. We believe that specifying a hierarchy of targets would be useful in this case. Before we share our prioritization, what is your sense of how to arrange a priority of targets? And why? Please write your thoughts here.

Here is our hierarchy of targets:

1. Parental alignment. We will consider them aligned when they are in agreement about the behaviors that are important to address as well as how to address them, and when they effectively manage their emotion dysregulation so their ability to collaborate with one another is optimized.
2. Engaging Jessica.
3. Parental engagement with other parents and Jessica's friends.

Rationale: If the parents are aligned there should be fewer episodes of dysregulation, and thus occasions for self-injury. They will also be more effective in implementing parenting strategies. In addition, alignment is an important ingredient in engaging Jessica. For example, when they fight they are aversive to Jessica. Humans are "wired" to avoid/escape aversives in their environments. Thus, if they are aligned they are not in conflict, and thus they are less aversive to Jessica. Finally, if Jessica is engaged the parents will be in a better position to engage systems outside the family and Jessica is more likely to participate and respond to such engagement in a positive way.

If the parents are aligned we move to target number two. However, if they fall out of alignment we move back to target number one and do not return to our second priority until we've restored alignment. Treatment will involve dynamic movement of this kind across the hierarchy or priorities we've specified.

Before we discuss our approach to this vicious cycle, take a moment to consider how you might approach it. Which principles might you make use of? Write them down here.

_____

_____

_____

_____

_____

As with every case, all Eight Principles can be applied. With this case we choose to illustrate these three principles: *normalizing human suffering, balancing change and acceptance strategies,* and *a more contextual model of human functioning.*

Let's begin with our first principle, *normalizing human suffering.* We would allow them to "tell their story", while actively listening, providing appropriate validation. At a strategic time point, we'd ask permission to provide them with some information that we think might be helpful to them. This fits with the principle of using Guided Discovery and Validation, via making a capsule summary of what was heard, checking with them to ensure we "get it," only then proceeding to offer ideas. If they are agreeable, we would make them aware of two findings in psychology. The first is the degree of influence peers have relative to parents. Surprising to many parents the ratio favors peers. We might recommend the book *The Nurture Assumption* by Judith Rich Harris (2011), which details this research in a lay friendly way. Second, we would discuss how Jessica's generation is facing a unique set of challenges that Tom and Barbara's generation did not confront (see Haidt, 2024). So it makes sense that they and Jessica would have difficulty negotiating many challenges because they are new and we do not yet have a reasonable roadmap for traversing these problems. It may be useful to follow this up with a good question(s) such as "What's your sense of how this research relates to your (Barbara and Tom) responsibility for these influences?" "What about Jessica's?" These and similar questions may help them discover that these are powerful factors that neither they nor Jessica are responsible for.

Now let's look at our second principle, *balancing change and acceptance procedures.* Before we discuss how we might implement this principle, please take a moment to consider what your approach would be. Which change procedures might you use? Please write them down here.

_____

_____

_____

_____

_____

_____

Our choice is to begin with planful problem-solving training (Nezu & Nezu, 2019). There are many component repertoires that can be trained as part of this approach. We will first address their emotion regulation difficulties as it interferes with their effective implementation of problem solving strategies. This is a common difficulty and is reflected by the most recent iteration of problem-solving therapy now including emotion regulation strategies. It has even been renamed "*emotion-centered* problem-solving therapy". Both changes reflect the significance of emotion in problem-solving activity.

A wide range of emotion regulation strategies are applicable here. We will suggest a few, recommended by Nezu and Nezu (2019). What's nice about these is they are not difficult to learn or to begin implementing quickly. The first one is Fake Yawning. This is advantageous because it has a range of positive effects, including relaxation (Newberg & Waldman, 2010). Ideally, a client would do this several times in a row to optimize its effects. Other strategies include diaphragmatic breathing, mindfulness meditation and various forms of counting. We think it's important to not just teach these strategies once but instead pull for the client to use them many times in session. For example, they can be used every time it seems one or both of them begin to dysregulate. Not only does this give them lots of flight time, it strongly signals the importance of these tools. These aren't mere suggestions. They are crucial to their success. At first, the therapist might observe out loud that they seem to be getting emotional followed by a prompt to use one of these strategies. Then, after several instances the therapist can ask the clients to try and "catch" their emotions before they do and to initiate the skill. In this way, the therapist gradually fades the responsibility over to the client(s).

Next, we illustrate how we would address one rational problem-solving deficit area, generating alternative solutions, in the dialogue below.

THERAPIST:	I like for us to try an exercise. (Walking up to a white board and uncapping a dry erase marker) What are all the creative uses you can think of for a cardboard box? I want you to tell me everything that comes to mind, no matter how silly it seems.
BARBARA AND TOM:	Well, you can put things in it.
THERAPIST:	Good (writes this on the white board). What else?
BARBARA AND TOM:	You can draw on it. You can hold a door open with it.
THERAPIST:	(Recording these on the board) Good. What else?

BARBARA AND TOM:	Hmm. (After a few minutes) maybe you could wrap it up so it looks like a gift, like in a store display. But that's all we can think of.
THERAPIST:	(After putting this idea on the board) Good. I have a question. Is this like you two? By that I mean when you try to find solutions to problems do you find that you can only generate a few ideas?
BARBARA AND TOM:	We suppose so. We hadn't thought about that previously but, as we think about it now, yes.
THERAPIST:	In some ways that's good news. Here's what I mean. We might have just found one reason you've been stuck. It turns out that we are more effective at solving problems if we can generate a large number of ideas. In general, the more ideas the more likely we are to identify a solution. This is something that we can work on together. I can teach you some strategies for being more effective at generating many ideas.
BARBARA AND TOM:	That makes sense. If you think that would help we'd be interested in learning how to do that.
THERAPIST:	I suspect it would be helpful. I also notice that the solutions you gave were similar in the sense they made use of the standard configuration of a box. Another thing that relates to our ability to solve problems is the variability of ideas. By that I mean the more variable your alternatives are the more likely you are to identify an effective solution. For example, in addition to the types of solutions you generated during this exercise, if you produced ideas involving a collapsed box, a box combined with another box, or a single box cut into pieces you would have generated a variety of solution types. I can teach you strategies for doing this too. Would that be of interest to you?

Assuming they are interested, the dialogue, and likely subsequent sessions, would involve teaching them brainstorming strategies. Generally, this is first taught in relation to things that are not their primary problem (e.g., creative uses for a box) before assisting them in applying the techniques to their presenting problems. We would work with them to apply this to identifying additional solutions for rearranging Jessica's environment and for addressing the problem of school refusal. Furthermore, if we were successful in inviting Jessica into family treatment, it would be useful to involve her in this process after strengthening the parental relationship. Her inclusion would bring a range of benefits. She may identify useful solutions that Barbara and Tom are unable to generate. Also, she is more likely to "buy in" to strategies she helped produce. And finally, the activity is an opportunity for them to work in unison with a problem they share, them against the problem, rather than working against one another.

Another set of change procedures we would implement pertains to behavior management skills. Like planful problem-solving strategies, there are many component skills that are likely to be useful, more than we can illustrate here. The essential skills involve shifting focus from the problem behavior to desirable behavior and providing positive reinforcement when the desirable behavior occurs, or initially, at least approximations of it.

Consider the average household (whatever that is!) in which two young siblings have been playing together cooperatively for an hour. How much attention do you think they receive? Our sense is that it's typically little to none. Now assume one of them takes the other one's toy. Now what happens? That's right, it's very likely there's now a lot of attention. This can be a problem because attention, even "negative" attention, can function as a reinforcer. This means that the parents, unintentionally of course, are reinforcing the problem behavior and placing the desirable behavior (cooperative play in this example) on extinction (i.e., they withhold reinforcement). To put this simply, the contingency is backwards. Teaching parents to ignore problem behavior (unless it's severe or someone will get hurt) and to reinforce the desirable behavior (e.g., "mommy loves to see the two of you sharing and playing nice") is an effective approach. This will increase the occurrence of the desired behavior. To extend this to Barbara and Tom, they would generally want to ignore Jessica's problem behavior (again, unless it's serious like her self-injurious behavior) and provide reinforcement for the behavior that is more functional for her. For example, on the occasions she shows up to breakfast on time they might say "Jessica, we're really happy to see you ready for breakfast. We can see you are working hard to get to school today." They might even, at times, follow it up with something like "because you are working so hard we'd like to take you for ice cream later" (Jessica loves ice cream). This is important because a behavior does not become more probable unless it's contacting reinforcement.

In addition to reinforcing the right behaviors, this shift in attention from problem to desirable behavior reduces the number of situations in which they lock horns. It also increases the parent's "reinforcing value" because they have likely become associated with aversiveness. This, in turn, improves their relationship.

Jessica's inclusion in the problem-solving process, as mentioned above, can also facilitate changing the nature of their relationship from one with highly aversive qualities to one with greater reinforcing properties. It provides a venue for Jessica to negotiate for change, providing her with some sense of control and likely paying off at times, and it allows her to request an alteration in reinforcers. There are other considerations and, as previously noted, many other relevant parenting skills that would be helpful to them.

Finally, as noted earlier, many parents have difficulty implementing these procedures because their emotions get in the way. Barbara and Tom are no different. For example, they feel angry when Jessica's behavior is not to their liking and are quick to address it with punishment. This occurs because their anger restricts the alternatives they see in the moment and because it has likely paid off for them in the past, at least in the short-term. Because the immediate consequences of behavior are the most reinforcing, their short-term success with this approach has likely reinforced their use of punishment. Consequently, it will be important to teach them to regulate their anger and other difficult emotions so that they become more successful in negotiating this barrier to effective action. A useful way to do this is to work with them to identify "high risk" circumstances in which they would benefit from using emotion regulation skills. Once noted we would discuss an emotion regulation plan followed by in session practice. The following is an example of what that practice might look like.

THERAPIST:	One of the difficult situations you identified is when Jessica asks you for something that you feel you must say no to. Can you think of an example that is likely to occur in the next week or so?
BARBARA AND TOM:	Lately she has really been pushing to drop out of school, which she needs our permission to do. We can just about guarantee she brings that up multiple times this week and once she starts with this she's like a dog with a bone.
THERAPIST:	I have a sense of how you might answer this question but I'd like to check out my perception with you. When she gets going with this, do you become emotional? (*In addition to clarifying for ourselves, we are modeling the importance of checking the validity of our assumptions.*)
BARBARA AND TOM:	Yes! We're just so sick and tired of it. Why does she always have to be so unreasonable? It makes us so angry!
THERAPIST:	It makes sense to me that you'd feel like you are at your wit's end. You care deeply about her and this seems like another thing that would worsen the course of her life. What impact does your anger have during these conversations? (*Here we provide Level 5 Validation and ask a question that will help them connect the dots between their emotions and this problem situation.*)

BARBARA AND	
TOM:	It makes it worse. These conversations just go off the rails.
THERAPIST:	This sounds like a good situation for us to practice then.

(Note: We've now identified a specific example of a hot button issue that is likely to recur, and we've confirmed that dysregulation is likely to be present and an important contributor to an undesired outcome. Having identified a meaningful target we can now work with them on an emotion regulation plan.)

THERAPIST:	Do these conversations occur out of the blue? Or do you have a sense of when she might bring up the topic?
BARBARA AND	
TOM:	Sometimes they seem to occur without warning but most of the time we know it's coming. When we pick her up from school, for example, I can just about guarantee one of the first things she says when she gets in the car is that she wants to drop out.
THERAPIST:	We can talk about what to do when you are surprised by the conversation but since you are mostly able to predict when she'll bring this up let's focus on that for now. Do you recall any of the emotion regulation skills we previously discussed? Any sense of what might be useful here?
BARBARA AND	
TOM:	We remember that one of them was to yawn. But if she sees us yawn that will probably send her over the edge.
THERAPIST:	I think you are exactly right. Yawning multiple times in her presence wouldn't be the best idea. But what about yawning before she gets in the car? Since you have the advantage of knowing that after school pick up is a high risk situation, you can start using the yawning skill at the very beginning of the situation and before she can see you do this.
BARBARA AND	
TOM:	We hadn't thought about that. Yes, I guess we can do that.
THERAPIST:	Great. Let's practice this. If you are open to it, can you close your eyes? I'll guide you through some practice imaginally.
BARBARA AND	
TOM:	Sure (closing their eyes).
THERAPIST:	Imagine as intensely as you can that you are in your car, in the car line and school has just been dismissed. See everything there is to see. Hear everything that is there to hear. Experience the situation as best you can as if you are there right now. Now, while you continue to imagine the situation as intensely as you can, yawn several times.

BARBARA AND	
TOM:	(Yawning)
THERAPIST:	Continue yawning as you drive further up the car line and until she enters the car. Let me know when she's in the car by gently raising your finger.
BARBARA AND	
TOM:	(they raise their fingers)
THERAPIST:	Okay, you can open your eyes now.

Next, we would debrief the exercise with them. And, importantly, we would work with them to plan to practice this several more times, including before they leave home to pick Jessica up from school.

We would also work with the parents to connect Jessica with a Dialectical Behavior Therapy program (i.e., comprehensive DBT). It is important to note that many practitioners suggest they offer DBT, when what they are actually offering is "DBT-informed" treatment. That's different. Also, they might not have been intensively trained. It would be important to educate parents about this distinction and assisting them with identifying an intensively trained, adherent, comprehensive DBT program.

The final principle we want to illustrate is a *more contextual model*. Here's where we would collaborate with Barbara and Tom to really drill down on the specific environmental circumstances that encourage Jessica's behavior, and to make modifications to the degree possible. It's important to recognize that multiple ecosystems and levels of analysis must be knitted together seamlessly in this case. For example, there's Jessica (individual level) whom we have to help the parents "reach". Then there's Barbara and Tom whom we have to work with as a dyad, while also working to understand each individually. There's also the entire family, who are working together towards a shared aim. Finally, we have the larger ecosystem, involving the peer network, their use of smartphones, and the parents of those kids. Complex cases often require thinking through multiple contextual factors and drawing on CBT for formulations at each level of analysis.

What's nice here is we can make use of some of the previously taught skills and recruit them for use in this context. For example, in collaboration with Barbara and Tom, and ideally Jessica, we might determine Jessica's friend group is deeply, negatively influential. We might then formulate a problem to be solved, the essence of which is "how to reduce their influence on her self-injurious behavior". They can now apply their brainstorming skills to this problem. Ideas generated during brainstorming need not be limited to the original ideas of clients. They might ask themselves: "Where can we get ideas for solving this problem?" and/or

"Can we identify individuals with subject matter expertise who might have recommended solutions?" Fortunately for Barbara, Tom and Jessica, Jonathan Haidt (2024) made several recommendations in his book *The Anxious Generation: How the Great Rewiring of Childhood Is Causing an Epidemic of Mental Illness* and they would be wise to consult this resource. For instance, he suggests the families of adolescents in the same friendship network meet to discuss how to collaborate around their shared problem of social media's impact on their children. We might offer to facilitate such a multiple family group meeting. This is a bold strategy, but their adolescent's well-being is at stake afterall.

In this case illustration, we looked at how to implement three of our principles. However, it is important for the reader to understand that the execution of these principles could be applied more deeply than what was articulated here. Our goal was merely illustration and not to describe a complete course of care.

REFERENCES

Haidt, J. (2024) *The Anxious Generation: How the Great Rewiring of Childhood Is Causing an Epidemic of Mental Illness*. New York: Random House.

Harris, J.R. (2011) *The Nurture Assumption: Why Children Turn Out the Way They Do*. New York: Simon and Schuster.

Newberg, A. & Waldman, M.R. (2010) *How God Changes Your Brain: Breakthrough Findings from a Leading Neuroscientist*. Ballantine Books.

Nezu, A.M. & Nezu, C.M. (2019) *Emotion-Centered Problem-Solving Therapy: Treatment Guidelines*. Springer Publishing Company.

CHAPTER 15

Case #5: The Case of Efran— Finding Meaning

Efran sought services because he felt "nothing really matters". He described his mood as depressed and complained of little motivation. He described his life as one of just "going through the motions". He met DSM5 criteria for Persistent Depressive Disorder, a chronic, low-grade state of depression that never dipped into severe depression or suicidal ideation.

Efran was the only child of parents who immigrated from the former Soviet Union in 1989, when Efran was four years old. His parents were professional people, who were and remain devoutly Russian Orthodox, though steeped in a wish for freedom from the repression and economic hardships of life in Soviet Russia. Efran had a difficult time adjusting to life in his new culture. He looked back on his early years in America with a sense of self as "different". Despite quickly learning English, he was aware of his speaking with an accent, and he struggled to find friends and a place where he fit in. He had been a devoutly religious person until around the age of 22 (he's now 39) when he finished college, took a job in the computer technology sector and finally found like minded friends. He married an American woman, whose life and values were vastly different from those of his family of origin. Efran and his wife moved to California, for work, and were now far from each set of parents, all of whom lived in New York City. The couple both work full time, she from home, he in Silicon Valley. They have a young daughter, age 3, and are considering having a second child. They have a wide social network, mainly through their workplaces and social connections in their tech fields. Efran's new-found freedom had considerable benefits, financially and socially. But he notes that it may have come at a cost. He drifted further from his religious

DOI: 10.4324/9781003505587-17

beliefs and practices, until he determined that he no longer believed in God. Efran described losing his faith as the precipitant to his current concerns. His faith had made the world and his place in it meaningful. His wife is nominally from a Protestant family. She is sympathetic to Efran's sense of loss, but has no interest in religion, herself.

In exploring Efran's sense of meaninglessness, the therapist was able to learn that Efran showed longstanding Neuroticism and a tendency towards Introversion. Neither of these temperamental traits were in an extreme range of functioning. He was highly Conscientious and Agreeable, both of which contributed to generally quite successful functioning in his marriage, social life, and work. His neuroticism had manifested in a tendency towards withdrawal, rather than emotion dysregulation. And he remained prone to gloomy rumination, with his mind focused on finding the source of his personal flaws and limitations and, more recently, those of the world that he now found increasingly devoid of sustaining meaning. At no time has Efran been suicidal. Nor has he resorted to drugs or alcohol to dampen his sense of gloom, meaningless, and sadness.

Efran's conscientiousness at work, and his commitment to his family, kept him engaged in his job at a Silicon Valley tech firm. We mapped out two areas of functioning that seemed especially implicated in times of depression. Those times were identified by having him keep a mood log for two weeks. Times when he was particularly vulnerable to gloomy rumination were found, and we focused on helping Efran understand the nature and function of rumination (Watkins, 2018). In essence, Efran learned that his tendency to ruminate represented a highly practiced, but unproductive, effort to "solve" his life problems, in two ways: first, he became focused on finding out "what's wrong with me", as though there were a productive answer to this; and second, he would become trapped in an endless loop, going over many of the real and perceived "failures" and disappointments in his life, further stoking his sense that "something is wrong with me, and I need to find out what it is". Finally, he was prone in those vulnerable times he identified, usually when alone, to focusing on what he felt was the stark contrast between the solace he once felt in church, and the "emptiness" he felt now. The latter connected with his sense that "my life has no meaning"; "the world is an empty place". His sense of isolation and loneliness was increased when he attempted to recruit his wife into his gloomy perspective on life. She not only disagreed, but she tried to point out to him the many blessings she saw in their family, and for Efran. The more she pointed out blessings, the more Efran pushed back. He had tried other therapies in the past, but thought it was worth seeking out a CBT practitioner this time.

Let's consider the cycle that Efran is caught in. Activating events for depressive rumination are both internal and external. And they are many. This is common in repetitive negative thinking, in this case depressive rumination, as there tends to be a spread of stimuli and cues that can quickly, and often outside of awareness, spark rumination: for Efran, certain sad music, breaks in the flow of his attention at work, events in daily life that once cued a sense of beauty, late night quiet. Efran also spends time reading news from a variety of sources, focusing on the "dark side" of humanity, for which he finds abundant evidence. This, too, sparks his sense that humanity, and he, himself, may not be "redeemable". Once activated, the rumination often focused on such thoughts as "What's wrong with me?" or "What's wrong with this world?" He also experiences a stream of visual images, as though imagining painful scenarios of future situations, always with a dismal outcome. He often replays painful events from his past, while imagining how he might have handled it differently, to produce a positive outcome. While ruminating, he feels what he describes as a "hole" in his stomach, and a deep sadness alternating with states of fear and dread and entrapment. His sense of self is that of one who is damaged, or even "I'm among the damned", which further sparks despair. He asks himself "Why? What's wrong with me" in a recursive loop that leads to withdrawal and isolation, even while at home, with his wife and daughter. The consequence of this pattern is a further sense of loneliness, meaningless, and entrapment.

We also take note of Efran's experience as the child of immigrants, and as an immigrant, himself. He grew up straddling two worlds. His depression is likely amplified by the adaptive challenges of finding a place and a sense of meaning, given his history of navigating two highly divergent cultures and interpersonal contexts. He grew up in a home that maintained a tightly organized worldview, steeped in the Orthodox Church and the community of like minded Russian immigrants. Role expectations, gender norms, expectations for educational and career attainment, family boundaries, religious belief and participation, all were clear. But the other world he navigates is the secular society of his Millennial peers (Twenge, 2023), one in which norms and boundaries are often confusing and ill defined. In effect he has one foot in each of two very different cultures. One gave him a sense of belonging and meaning, until those connections were finally broken by his engagement with the secular, and somewhat fragmented society of his adulthood. He finds his current environment materially satisfying, but empty. And he both mourns and is repelled by the culture he was born into. One consequence of the above is that when Efran ceased to believe in the God posited by his Orthodox Church upbringing, he felt estranged from his entire cultural, religious, and family heritage. This, in turn, represented an enormous sense of loss, contributing to his depression.

We ask the reader to take a moment to reflect. Based just on what we've presented, which Organizing Principles might you want to bring to bear on Efran's case? And how might you set up a problem list? From that problem list, we can establish a hierarchy in collaboration with the client, and then select intervention strategies to address those problems.

_____

_____

_____

_____

_____

Remember, these Organizing Principles are interrelated. One can draw on any or all in each case.

For purposes of illustration, we decided to focus on: *Guided Discovery and Validation* and on *Balancing Acceptance, Mindfulness, and Change Processes.* Helping Efran understand and essentially normalize his confusion will also be a target of Guided Discovery and Validation strategies. Interventions will focus on helping address the central problems we collaboratively identify.

Our problem list is truncated, for purposes of illustration and focus. We think the central problems include:

1. A temperamental vulnerability to Neuroticism, now manifesting as depression, withdrawal, and rumination.
2. Depressive cognitive biases: these include a tendency to overgeneralize, catastrophize, discount positives, dichotomous thinking, and biased memory for negative over positive experiences.

We offer the following vignette, to illustrate how Guided Discovery and Validation Strategies might help Efran make sense of his difficulties, and set the stage for change. After carefully and empathically listening to Efran (Levels 1 and 2 Validation), and using a gentle questioning style to elicit key beliefs, images, emotions, and actions, the therapist provides a kind of capsule summary. This summary, you will note, is provisional, and invites the client to modify, to insure that the therapist truly understands the client's life.

THERAPIST: So Efran, it seems from what you've said that you may be feeling a kind of grief for the loss of your old way of living [Level 3 Validation in DBT, making an educated guess about what the client may think or feel, but that hasn't been articulated yet]. When you talked about the feelings you had when you went to church as a kid, there was a kind of grandeur and calmness you must have felt. Am I getting that right?

EFRAN: (smiles) Yeah. That's about right. I felt at home. My accent was no different from everyone else's. Most people could speak Russian. I understood them. And I have great memories of the services, too. So yes, I think you could say I feel a kind of grief for that. But that doesn't change the fact that I can't go back. I'm no longer among the believers, and I'm finding a way in the world my wife and I live in now.

THERAPIST: I like the way you put that. It's like you're in some ways caught between two worlds: the one you grew up in, and the one you're in now. It makes sense that there's a disconnect, though, doesn't it? One world provided comfort and security. Things made sense. Life had a kind of order that was comforting. Life now is very, very different, and in some ways not so comforting.

EFRAN: Maybe not so comforting. But it's more realistic. And I'm in the world where my wife and I will live and work. No matter how much money we make, and right now we're doing pretty well, I feel we're just on a kind of treadmill. It feels meaningless, except for getting the bills paid.

THERAPIST: It makes sense to me that you'd feel that way. After all, no matter how your religious beliefs may have changed, there was an orderly world before, and now there isn't, at least not in the same way. Like I said, doesn't it make sense that you might feel caught between those two worlds, and feel a sense of loss for one, even though you don't feel you can re-enter it? (Level 4 Validation)

EFRAN: I suppose it does. But what do I do with that now? I can't go back.

THERAPIST: Great question, Efran. For just a moment, if you would, I'd ask that we just sit with that. Let that question percolate. It's a great question. (Silence.) Before we tackle that, I had another thought, if I might. (Efran nods.) We've talked about your having a tendency towards some depression. No fault of yours, or anyone's. We all have temperaments we don't choose, but can learn to work with. That includes your therapist! [The therapist adds another transdiagnostic factor in Efran's clinical picture, and normalizes it in the context of temperament.] (Efran smiles.) Does it make sense to consider that a man with a tendency towards some gloomy rumination and depression might enter a tailspin when he feels caught like that between the world he grew up in and the one he's in now? And on top of that, your faith in God has been shattered, as you put it. If so, then yes, that's something we can figure out what to do with that. I have some ideas.

EFRAN: Now you've piqued my curiosity.

The early moves in CBT involve developing an understanding of the client's inner world and overall patterns of thinking, feeling, and behaving, in the contexts of the client's life. That's how we cultivate the knowledge needed to create a formulation. Then, and in tandem with this, we socialize the client to a model of therapy. That often begins by creating a shared understanding of the problems the client brings to therapy. Then, we intervene.

Now take a moment to consider how you might intervene with Efran. He recognizes that he has a propensity for depressive rumination and withdrawal, and that his current functioning is colored by the fact that he has never come to terms with having a sense of belonging and of self. His loss of his religious convictions has left him feeling adrift. There are a number of potential intervention strategies you might consider. Take a moment in the space below to write down what you might choose:

_____

_____

_____

_____

Here's where we decided to intervene.

Given that withdrawal, depressed mood (negative affectivity), and rumination were prominent, we tried to think of an intervention that might target all three. There is research literature suggesting that early treatment gains deepen the therapeutic relationship (Feeley, DeRubeis, & Gelfand, 1999). We consider it important to make a beginning move that has the potential to create a discernible gain, even a small one, as it can help set the stage for deeper engagement. In addition, we believe that a focus on core problems can spark change in other areas of a client's life, later.

Remember that Efran initially framed his difficulties in terms of a loss of religious faith, the end of his belief in the God of his upbringing. Quoting Pascal, Haidt notes that "there is a God-shaped hole in every human heart" (Haidt, 2024, p. 215). The challenge for therapists is to take that seriously, while refraining from pointing the client in any specifically religious direction. Fortunately, a way to introduce a more frankly spiritual dimension into CBT has been paved by people like Hayes (Hayes et al., 2012) and Linehan (2021). Hayes has emphasized the importance of present moment experience, or mindfulness, and connecting to self states that promote connection with deeper client values. Linehan, in particular, provides a technology of mindfulness that is rooted in her Buddhist and Christian contemplative and meditative life. She has translated those practices into secular terms, in the form of DBT Mindfulness skills (Linehan, 2014). It also turns out that entering the present moment, via mindfulness practice, is an antidote to repetitive negative thinking. It can also help impact the tendency to wallow in negative affectivity and to withdraw. Mindfulness, in the form of throwing oneself wholeheartedly into the present moment, can be a prelude to engagement in meaningful activities.

With Efran, this might take the form of providing mindfulness training, not meditation. That would include practicing in session the "whats" of mindfulness: observing, describing, and participating in the moment; and the "hows" of mindfulness: one-mindfully, nonjudgmentally, and effectively. While these core skills of DBT are customarily taught in DBT skills groups, over the course of months, it is possible for practitioners to learn to implement them in individual therapy. For Efran, we might practice simple present moment experiences, placing full awareness on the back of the hand as sunlight comes in through a window. We could build the capacity to return awareness to that sensory experience, any time Efran notices the mind wandering, including into rumination. This can begin to break up the belief that one is helpless in the face of rumination. In addition, the flexible deployment of attention into a sensory experience can also help restore a sense of calm. For Efran, throwing himself wholeheartedly into the moment, via the skill of participation, also opens a door to a possible practice between sessions, i.e., a homework assignment. The following is an example of how this might be done.

THERAPIST: Efran, I'm thinking of some ways you might practice what we did here, these mindfulness skills, between now and the next time we meet. You could practice taking a few moments each day, just sitting and paying attention to a sensory experience, like we've done today. Or, we could try for something a little more bold, if you're game.

EFRAN: What do you mean by bold?

THERAPIST: I was thinking about something you said, about how much you love reading to your little girl, right? (Efran nods, smiling slightly.) What if you could jump into the moment with Ilana, just pick a moment when she's playing, and just sit with her, noticing, maybe even just describing her activities, and entering into her world with her. And if you notice the mind wandering, come back to her. Just back to this moment, with her.

Efran agreed, and the therapist spent time helping Efran learn how to practice mindfully being present with Ilana as she played quietly. The following week, when Efran returned, the therapist spent some time exploring how the homework assignment went.

EFRAN: (his eyes tear up) I just had such a lovely little moment with Ilana. We just sat there. She played, and she kept looking up at me, handing me some blocks. And we just built a little tower together. She took the lead. I followed.
THERAPIST: How long did that happen?
EFRAN: Maybe ten or fifteen minutes.
THERAPIST: Where was depression? Where was meaninglessness during those ten or fifteen minutes?
EFRAN: (eyes deflect, as he thinks) You know, they weren't there. It was just me with my little girl. I just felt filled up to the brim with…with lightness, and love for her.
THERAPIST: Would you say that moment was in any way meaningful?
EFRAN: I'll say.

In Beck's CBT for depression, behavioral activation often revolves around engaging in activities that are either pleasurable or that spark a sense of mastery. In Efran's case, his sense of both mastery and pleasure coalesced in this experience around a sense of meaning. And in mindfulness and other contemplative practices, without reference to any specific religion, meaning is often found in the present moment, each moment of one's life. An experiential practice such as the above can help set the stage for not only behavioral activation, but for re-engagement in a meaningful life, as defined by the client.

Therapy at this point can focus on three key areas: 1)reducing time spent in rumination; 2) countering tendencies to withdraw via behavioral activation; and 3) addressing cognitive biases and other beliefs implicated in maintaining his sense that life is "meaningless" if he doesn't believe in the God of his family's church.

The first, countering rumination, would include helping Efran become more cognizant of when he is ruminating, and helping him "unplug" from the recursive loop of repetitive negative thinking, by engaging in a competing activity. Competing activities could include activities that are capable of bringing pleasure, mastery, and meaning. Finally, cognitive and experiential work, to address ways of finding meaning in his life. These could involve more behavioral experiments, such as with his daughter, and cognitive and experiential interventions, to help him in an experientially compelling way identify meaning in his life, whether or not he reconnects with his original religious beliefs (Frankl, 1992, 2019).

Whether Efran chooses to find ways later to explore his spiritual needs in a more formal manner is, of course, up to him. For Efran, turning towards moments in daily life, at work, with his wife, with his daughter, may eventually lead to greater engagement in community life, with or without his former belief in God. Therapy will ideally help him recognize that balance of givens in his personality and practices to help him tilt the balance towards engagement and greater freedom from Neuroticism, including a tendency to withdraw into rumination and gloom. An added sense of meaning, so important to Efran, can be a further protective benefit of therapy.

REFERENCES

Feeley, M., DeRubeis, R.J., & Gelfand, L.A. (1999) The Temporal Relation of Adherence and Alliance to Symptom Change in Cognitive Therapy For Depression. *Journal of Consulting and Clinical Psychology*, 67, 4, 578–582. doi: 10.1037//0022-006x.67.4.578.

Frankl, V. (1992) *Man's Search for Meaning*. New York: Beacon Press.

Frankl, V. (2019) *Yes to Life in Spite of Everything*. New York: Beacon Press.

Haidt, J. (2024) *The Anxious Generation*. New York: Penguin Press.

Hayes, S., Strosahl, K., & Wilson, K. (2012) *Acceptance and Commitment Therapy: The Process and Practice of Mindful Change* (2nd edn). New York: Guilford.

Linehan, M. (2014) *DBT Skills Training Manual*. New York: Guilford.

Linehan, M. (2021) *Building a Life Worth Living: A Memoir*. New York: Random House.

Twenge, J. (2023) *Generations: The Real Differences Between Gen Z, Millennials, Gen X, Boomers, and Silents——and What They Mean for America's Future*. New York: Atria.

Watkins, E. (2018) *Rumination-Focused Cognitive-Behavioral Therapy for Depression*. New York: Guilford Press.

Index

Note: For figure citations, page numbers appear in *italics*.

For Product Safety Concerns and Information please contact our EU
representative GPSR@taylorandfrancis.com
Taylor & Francis Verlag GmbH, Kaufingerstraße 24, 80331 München, Germany